D1130951

True Women and Westward Expansion

NUMBER TWENTY-FOUR
*Elma Dill Russell Spencer Series
in the West and Southwest*
Andrés Tijerina, General Editor

SERIES BOARD
Alwyn Barr
James Crisp
Rebecca Sharpless
Eric Van Young

True Women & Westward Expansion

Adrienne Caughfield

TEXAS A&M UNIVERSITY PRESS   COLLEGE STATION

The paper used in this book
meets the minimum requirements
of the American National Standard for Permanence
of Paper for Printed Library Materials, Z39.48-1984.
Binding materials have been chosen for durability.

LIBRARY OF CONGRESS CATALOGING-IN-PUBLICATION DATA

Caughfield, Adrienne, 1971–
    True women and westward expansion / Adrienne Caughfield.
        p. cm.—(Elma Dill Russell Spencer series in the West and
    Southwest ; no. 24)
    Includes bibliographical references and index.
    ISBN 1-58544-409-X (cloth : alk. paper)
    1. Women pioneers—Texas—History—19th century.
2. Frontier and pioneer life—Texas.   3. Women—Texas—
Attitudes—History—19th century.   4. United States—Territorial
expansion—Public opinion.   5. Public opinion—Texas—
History—19th century.   6. Women—Texas—Social conditions—
19th century.   7. Sex role—Texas—History—19th century.
8. Texas—History—19th century.   9. Texas—Social conditions—
19th century.   I. Title.   II. Series.
F390.C385   2005
976.4'05—dc22   2004019731

Contents

Preface

Manifest destiny, the belief that Americans had the God-given right to expand into new territory, especially to the west, played a prominent role in early-nineteenth-century history. To date historians have paid little attention to women's perceptions of this phenomenon or their participation in it. Typical studies focus on more obvious manifestations of expansionism, namely, events such as the acquisition of Texas and the Mexican War. Such a perspective limits scholars' understanding of manifest destiny as well as American expansionists in general, only revealing half of a crucial concept. Although men did play the more prominent role because of their nearly exclusive hold on politics and war, our picture of the social environment surrounding expansionism remains incomplete.

Many scholars have attempted to explain manifest destiny. The best work remains Albert K. Weinberg's *Manifest Destiny: A Study of Nationalist Expansion in American History*. Weinberg interprets his subject broadly, covering the entire nineteenth century. All motives have a turn in the spotlight: political, sociocultural, even agricultural. For this reason alone *Manifest Destiny* is the seminal work on nineteenth-century expansionism, but Weinberg's work also provides numerous primary resources that today can be difficult to find. (Often footnotes in other books begin with "Quoted in Weinberg.") Later works offer variations on Weinberg's theme. For example, Frederick Merk's *Manifest Destiny and Mission in American History: A Reinterpretation* suggests that manifest destiny was only one of two themes running through the American narrative. In *Manifest Design: Anxious Aggrandizement in Late Jacksonian America,* Thomas R. Hietala strips manifest destiny of its seemingly accidental appearance, insisting instead that the concept was merely a pragmatic rationalization of an active pursuit of national gain. On yet another note, Reginald Horsman's *Race and Manifest Destiny: The Origins of American Racial Anglo-Saxonism* focuses exclusively on the implications of race on expansionism, tracing sentiments of Anglo-Saxon superiority from England across the Atlantic. This is far from a complete list of relevant books, but it serves to indicate the depth of attention historians have paid to expansionism in its various forms.[1]

To combat—or perhaps more accurately to complement—this view, this work examines women over a forty-year period prior to the Civil War to determine not only how they felt regarding manifest destiny's ideals, but also how it affected their lives. A variety of factors made up this gendered understanding of expansionism, and the support and contributions of women helped lead to manifest destiny's successes in the period. For the sake of research, my study is limited to women in Texas primarily because Texas bore much of the continent's focus where manifest destiny was concerned. In a large part these women's contributions emerged through the conceit now known as the cult of true womanhood. They helped not only by maintaining their homes, in keeping with contemporary ideas of true womanhood, but by encouraging the progress of civilization in the region by doing so. Their views concerning new neighbors of all races matched those of their men and helped rationalize for manifest destiny in many respects.

Yet women did not always support expansion in this way. For instance, women actively promoted the Texas Revolution and contributed supplies and even labor during various other crises. These examples challenge the idea of women as solely passive: the defended rather than the defenders. The chief difference lay in nineteenth-century views of gender. Although men and women had different responsibilities, their goals were the same. Men may have dominated politics, but room still existed for women to interact with contemporary issues. Very little that women did was actually passive when dealing with expansionism, regardless of the roles they had been assigned by society.

Women described their ideals freely in letters, diaries, or memoirs that captured for future readers the dreams the authors had of a new life and the means by which to achieve it. Such information has rested on library shelves or in archives for decades without receiving attention, but that does not make it any less crucial. All this indicates is a scholarly lack of interest. What has helped this work remain untouched or unstudied is the context in which their authors wrote. Because women rarely had a political arena from which to speak (although a select few did have that opportunity), nor a way to participate fully in the public sphere, their expressions of approval or agreement regarding expansion were more subdued. Still they remained, waiting to be found, hidden behind veils of domesticity and "women's work" that many historians simply determined to be of lesser importance. As a result the bigger picture also remained undisclosed because not all perspectives had yet emerged.[2]

Part of the reason these diamonds remained hidden for so long was because of a narrow, gendered interpretation of expansionism. Usually when scholars refer to expansion they are thinking primarily of the rationalization of distinctly political actions—the annexation of Texas, for instance, or the absorption of the Mexican Cession after the U.S.–Mexican War. Indeed, that is the context in which the expansionist term "manifest destiny" first emerged. In July, 1845, the *United States Magazine and Democratic Review* published an article on the annexation of Texas that enlisted the benevolent intentions of a higher power to endorse taking the maverick republic. Those limiting American expansion, the article declared, limited also "the fulfillment of our manifest destiny to overspread the continent allotted by Providence for the free development of our yearly multiplying millions." Suddenly it became the responsibility of the government, if not the American public as a whole, to realize the goal that Providence had set before the young nation, at least in the eyes of the *Democratic Review* and other enthusiasts who nodded vigorously in agreement. From that perspective, it makes sense for Americans to have considered expansion as the duty of men of vision to attain and complete and not necessarily their women.[3]

Although I desire this work to be inclusive—Texas, after all, has been multicultural for centuries—I must still acknowledge the various parts women found themselves playing when acting out the drama of manifest destiny. This work will therefore present the perspective of white emigrants—Anglo and, to a lesser extent, German—who carried with them the cultural standards of expansionism and "civilization." Part of the reason for this focus is that other groups—Native American, Hispanic, and black—simply did not leave behind nearly as much information as did whites, and much of what exists comes from secondhand sources. Such women also typically found themselves on the receiving end of manifest destiny rather than being actively involved. This includes being the target of suspicions fueled by racial differences. As a result, these pages will generally reflect the views of white women toward them and not the other way around.

Acknowledgments

Many people deserve credit and gratitude for their help in completing this book. The librarians at the various institutions I used for research provided tremendous assistance. I wish to thank the staffs of the Center for American History at the University of Texas at Austin, the DeGolyer Library at Southern Methodist University, and the Texas State Library. In particular I would like to thank Jean Carefoot for patiently helping me decipher the system the TSL has in place.

Thanks go also to my dissertation committee at Texas Christian University: Mark Gilderhus, Gene Smith, and Steven Woodworth. Their advice helped my efforts substantially, both to finish my degree and to turn my work into something publishable. In particular I want to thank Ken Stevens for his revisions and encouragement. I spent more time in his office discussing the graduate experience than he probably had available, but it was invaluable to me, and I greatly appreciate it.

I was fortunate in having good friends and family providing encouragement as I completed my work. First of all, thanks go to Mary Lenn Dixon and Jennifer Ann Hutt of Texas A&M University Press, along with my anonymous reviewers, for their efforts in completing this project. Edward Countryman, David Cullen, Kathleen Wellman, and Kyle Wilkison provided tremendous professional assistance and encouragement as well as a sounding board for my ideas. Caroline Castillo Crimm, Arnoldo DeLeón, Nora Rios McMillan, Kendra Trachta, and David Weber all kindly took part in my quest for Tejana sources. Andrea Boardman and Vicki Tongate offered several suggestions as I burrowed into the material. Thanks also go to Doyle Maynard and Jenny Parum, who are not historians, but they let me gripe endlessly about the process and kept me sane. Many thanks go to my parents, Charles and Barbara Rigsby, who raised me to love reading and sent me down the path upon which I now find myself.

My own family has been tremendous help. Although she is preverbal, my daughter, Megan, has provided perspective on the life of nineteenth-century women. At the least, I have come to understand more clearly why many women lacked time to write anything down. But most of all I would like to thank my husband, Lance. This experience has been as hard on him as it has been on me, and he deserves credit for much of my work. He has always been a tremendous encouragement and help, kicking me in the pants when I needed it and being my editor, audience, and best friend. Words and actions cannot begin to demonstrate my love and gratitude for all he has done. Thank you.

True Women
and Westward
Expansion

1

Domesticity and Expansionism

The San Felipe de Austin *Telegraph and Texas Register,* like many newspapers of its day, saved important news for the second or third pages. The front page contained advertisements, jokes, recipes for the ladies, and the occasional blurb of inspirational poetry. The January 27, 1837, edition was no different. On its face the *Telegraph* proudly displayed a poem entitled "The Mother of the West." A paean to western femininity, the work lauded the efforts of those brave women who moved into the wilderness to raise strong, dutiful families. Their sacrifices were enough to bring a tear to the roughest settler's eye as he considered his own good mother and all she had done for him. Although these women lived and died in relative anonymity, the poem concluded,

their graves shall yet be found,
And their monuments dot here and there
"The Dark and Bloody Ground."

Whether this statement would prove true or not remained to be seen. Nevertheless, while these ardent pioneers might have no monument of stone to their name, they could be certain that the thankless labors they endured would bear living fruit in the lives of their grateful progeny.

Usually newspapers ran poetry and anecdotes with little comment. In the case of "The Mother of the West," in contrast, the editors thought it necessary to wax poetic on the subject. (Apparently they also had mothers of whom they were fond.) They added their praise of "a spirit so resolute, yet so adventurous—so unambitious, yet so exalted—a spirit so highly calculated to awake a love of the pure and noble, yet so uncommon." Never before, they wrote, had any woman had such a glorious effect on her environment. For the men at the *Telegraph*, women could achieve no greater end in life than that of mother, and that noble role only grew in honor in a rude country such as Texas. The *United States Magazine and Democratic Review* agreed. In an article discussing a new volume of poetry, the editors added to the discussion of the importance of such women. "'The Mothers of the West,'" they said, "performed so important a part in the history of emigration, that they are entitled to a more especial commemoration, than as simply incidental to the accounts given of their hardy husbands and sons."[1]

The poem proved particularly appropriate for the *Telegraph's* readers given its date of publication. Texas had won its independence from Mexico less than a year before. For almost twenty years, Texians worked to establish a home on that nation's northern frontier, founding it on their own sweat and blood. Those who lived there were not just settlers. They were warriors for the cause, men and women alike. Everyone's contribution, regardless of its size or nature, would prove invaluable. Although women did not fight in battle, they waged war elsewhere, protecting the symbols of civilization: home and family. Such battles may not have merited statues and celebrations, but they were no less important than those more obvious, according to the editors of the *Telegraph* and the *Democratic Review*.

But how much of this poetry was rhetoric and how much was based in reality? As is usually the case, both myth and truth played a role. The early nineteenth century birthed a flurry of sentimental poetry, essays, and other literature placing women on a prominent but narrow pedestal. Within certain prescribed boundaries, women did, in fact, rule the world—or at least the hearts of those surrounding them. Woman was, as one person wrote, "the comforter of man, and main supporter of his life." Such thoughts saturated the collective American subconscious.[2]

This idealistic view of women did not always consider the hard truth of life in this era, frontier life in particular. However, the poem noted it, acknowledging the challenge of the taxing move west that so many Americans were taking. The "Dark and Bloody Ground" bore the remains of those who broke themselves upon the wheel of progress. Yet evidence remains that, despite the challenge of living in Texas, women did apply the ideal, at least insofar as they could. Women applied the image to their own lives, transforming both themselves and their society according to its precepts.

Given the predicament emigrant women frequently found themselves in, such adaptability worked to their benefit. The United States felt a call to pursue the horizon, capturing it for personal gain and then, eventually, for the nation as a whole. After all, it appeared to be a land unoccupied by any recognizable or capable government. It only made sense that God (or Providence) had predestined it for Anglo American use. Orators, observing this westward trend, declared this national goal one of destiny made manifest—more familiarly, manifest destiny.

Texas provides an excellent study for manifest destiny. Mexico had recently opened its northern province to settlement by Stephen F. Austin and other entrepreneurs to supplement the thin Tejano population already there. As more people arrived, news spread regarding the wonders of this new territory, encouraging even more willing pioneers. At the least, the region sparked a push for territorial aggrandizement that ended in the absorption of much of northern Mexico into the United States. But Texas also typifies the expansionist experience in other ways. From its beginnings as a target for enthusiastic emigrants, the American desire to obtain Texas grew alongside the push for continental conquest. The republic, when it became a state, reached the pinnacle of expansionist fervor as it contributed to the war between the United States and Mexico. Finally, as expansionism became less a national and more a sectional, Southern issue, Texas revealed its Southern heart and continued to endorse expansion until the Civil War and its aftermath brought all such dreams to an end.[3]

Although Texas history paralleled that of the United States, it also served as a microcosm of the nation's populace. Emigrants arrived from all regions of the country, carrying with them regional mindsets that would play out in miniature what Americans did at large across the continent. Add to that the arrival of trans-Atlantic immigrants, let alone the presence of Native Americans and Hispanics who had lived there for generations, and the discourse grew increasingly convoluted. What place did expansion have in America's future? Texans discussed the question as eagerly as did anyone else; however, because Texas was in a sense the heir of past expansionist endeavors, the argument tended to be skewed. Nevertheless, Texas opinion was by no means unified. When sectionalism crept into the discussion, slavery tucked firmly under its wing, Texans debated the political and social ramifications of both. Then as emigrants arrived each year from other places, they refreshed the conversation with new ideas and new energy.[4]

The fever for manifest destiny spread quickly across the country and eventually across the continent. Countless Americans looked to Texas for new opportunities and land and gathered up family to travel there. Typically men made this decision as the heads of households, but their choices affected all those around them. As a result, wives, mothers, and daughters also journeyed past the United States into barely charted territory, often leaving behind friends, family, and everything with which they were familiar.[5]

Or did they? While women could not transplant houses, gardens, relatives, or sometimes even their own belongings, that did not mean they traveled without cultural baggage. In particular, they carried the framework that historian Barbara Welter calls the "cult of true womanhood," or the "cult of domesticity." This concept emerged from the United States' rapidly changing social structure in the early nineteenth century. Prior to this period, gender roles were as they had largely been for centuries, part of a preindustrial, agricultural culture. However, a shift in work patterns occurred with the rise of the new republic. By the 1830s, the United States already had a basic social hierarchy within which citizens worked, played, and lived, and this framework remained largely uncontested or unmolested. Each person had a particular niche in which he or she moved. It was in this period that the middle class began to emerge as a powerful influence in the young nation. This influence covered not only economic issues, but also matters of gender; the middle class was the chief architect of true womanhood.[6]

According to this concept, men and women operated in separate "spheres" of movement. As American society shifted from a preindustrial to a commercial structure, business and home became separate both physically and figuratively. Men worked in business, politics, and other public arenas. Meanwhile, women remained at home to exercise influence more subtly. Each gender had its role to make life function smoothly. Men cared for public matters; women, private ones. Because home life was now exclusively feminine territory, proponents of separate spheres emphasized the inestimable value of a woman's touch upon her family. To tend to the needs of her children and spouse was a woman's responsibility above all else. "The Mother of the West" captures the trope of true womanhood clearly. In fact, in a sense the poem plays to it. No higher place was available to westering women than the throne of domestic life, raising moral children in a rugged new world.[7]

Welter considers true womanhood to be an inferior position for women, cutting them off from the political and economic machinations of their husbands and brothers and forcing them to care for home and family. However, other scholars disagree with such a limiting perspective. Even some women of the period argued that domesticity offered women a position beyond what they might otherwise have. Catharine Beecher, for instance, argued that the home could be in a sense the base of operations from which women could extend their influence in their community, their nation, and ultimately the world. For Beecher, domesticity was more than staying home with the children. It was a position of power.[8]

As this position indicates, the argument of "true womanhood" as Welter defines it frequently overlooks less tangible tasks which early-nineteenth-century women were capable of doing, even within their "separate spheres." Many Americans who lauded domesticity as the greatest of all virtues ignored the public role it allowed female citizens to play. Separate spheres of influence for men and women did exist, but they did not hold anyone back with iron fetters. The boundaries set for each gender proved more fluid than some have assumed. Women were able to function publicly, although in a limited fashion in accordance with the dictates of true womanhood. The emergence of women's benevolent societies, which will be discussed in more detail later, is a case in point. Because voluntary associations remained low-profile, largely apart from center stage, they could engage society in ways that might otherwise be prohibited. In this way, they provided an added dimension to public behavior; men dealt with issues through politics while women worked through benevolent societies and other organizations—or, more simply, at home—to combat the same issues from a different vantage point. This demonstrates merely a gendered participation in events, not a total segregation of activity.[9]

Women's activism was in a sense the second side to the coin of domesticity. This aspect stemmed from the concept of republican motherhood. In the fledgling United States, women had the duty of preparing the next generation to be good citizens. From their homes, they could teach their children republican virtues and prepare them for roles as nation builders. Because of this, many women took their responsibility a step beyond into society at large. The home was no longer the only arena in which they moved; the community needed the feminine touch as much, if not more so, than just one household. If labor at home was important, many reasoned, how much greater was work done beyond it? In voluntary associations, then, women found a way to utilize their domestic roles for a greater number and make their contributions more meaningful.[10]

Domesticity became even more important in a region such as Texas. As families joined Austin's Colony and other settlements in their first hesitant steps, they faced difficult circumstances. Technically the area was still part of Mexico. This meant that not only was it an underpopulated wilderness (assuming that the colonists recognized that local tribes or Hispanic residents populated the area, which at the time proved rarely the case), but one under the control of a people whose level of civilization they considered questionable. The colonists needed everything possible to make themselves more comfortable and give the land the feeling of home. It is at this point that women's role—whether as bastions of virtue at home or an influential force elsewhere—became crucial and where the call to bring civilization to the wilderness grew louder.[11]

Although their roles were distinct, women still had vital responsibilities impacting more than their own households. The poem in the *Telegraph* sets women if not on a higher plane—and many contemporaries would have argued this—at least on an equal footing with men. Both genders had a duty to help construct civilization in the wilderness, each with a distinct set of responsibilities. Although men moving in political circles or writing for periodicals functioned as the chief promoters of American expansion, women also heard the call to move across a God-given continent and use their unique station to ready it for further settlement.[12]

And women answered that call. They were no less players in the drama of manifest destiny than were men. Certainly women approached expansionism differently than did men, despite some similarities due to its political and ideological framework. Manifest destiny affected western women in one of two ways: as its beneficiaries or its victims. Whites found themselves in the former camp; Indians, Hispanics, and blacks, almost always in the latter. White women's roles in supporting and endorsing manifest destiny range from active participation in pro-expansionist activities to holding views indicative of an expansionist mindset, with the largest number somewhere in between. Since the arrival of filibusters in Texas in 1820, women helped to further American interests. Their own desires were often admittedly personal—the protection of themselves and their families—but their vision was broad enough that self-interest encompassed the interests of the colony, the republic, and eventually the state and nation. Although war remained the traditional business of men, women nevertheless volunteered their assistance within accepted boundaries. If a situation became more severe, women in turn offered more help. Such help came in several forms: money, clothes, ammunition, information, and in some circumstances even themselves. In fact, during the various filibustering endeavors of the 1850s, some women worked to promote aggressively expansionist endeavors. One woman even attempted political machinations at home and abroad to this end, although her actions tested the limits of domesticity beyond reasonable boundaries for many.[13]

Nevertheless, such a stretch makes sense, given the flexibility of true womanhood in other areas. What proved equally important was the emergence of the expansionist movement in the same period. An entire continent lay to the west of the United States practically begging for absorption. A highly developed ideology emerged to support the claims of expansionists. This ideology provided the structure necessary to bolster and justify the movement's political ramifications. At its heart, expansionist philosophy closely paralleled domesticity so that adherents to the latter tended to accept the former. The true woman, then, would tend to agree with the rationale behind territorial aggrandizement and, within her separate sphere, work toward it.

Of course, not all Americans who embraced expansionism did so out of ideological impulse. Many simply saw available land and moved west to claim it. In doing so they maintained a pattern that had existed since the first Europeans set foot on the continent. Nevertheless, by the 1820s and 1830s such ideas had become part of the nation's structure, and pioneer farmers often agreed tacitly with them, regardless of whether or not they articulated them. This is not to say that some did not try. One traveler in Texas endlessly praised the land's fecundity, inviting his readers to enjoy the available territory. *DeBow's Review,* a Southern journal devoted to commerce, agriculture, and the mechanical arts, lauded Texas as "the true springs of national greatness and individual prosperity." Such a place promised wealth and a fresh start for those wishing to do well for themselves.[14]

However, Americans tended to take land hunger and redefine it with loftier descriptions. *DeBow's* had already done so by alluding to possible "national greatness." The greatest example emerged as the desire to re-create Eden, the "Garden of the World," on American soil. As God had given man the opportunity to bring the earth under submission, so farmers had a calling to complete this work with the plow. Cultivation was an integral part of civilization. Only savages allowed the earth to lie fallow as they grubbed about for roots or berries; modern people used their intelligence to delve into agriculture and do more with the land for the sake of the nation. After all, was this not Jefferson's agrarian republic, destined for population by the hero of the land, the yeoman farmer? As such, it became the near-patriotic duty of Americans to plant crops or domesticate animals. Communities developed, broke the soil and transformed their surroundings into something beautiful: mile after mile of fields.[15]

Such attitudes adapted easily to Texas due to its natural "beauty and loveliness." Some observers hoped it would take less work to reshape the landscape as a result. In their *New Guide to Texas,* published in 1845, Richard S. Hunt and Jesse Randel exalted in the "sunny plains of the southwestern garden," where they hoped other Americans would make their home. Of course, the land still required work. Texas may have been the land of milk and honey, said *DeBow's,* but "*first milk the cows* and *gather the honey.*" "The earth belongs to the race that will till it," the journal added sagely. Without the shaping of human hands, what could be a garden would merely be a beautiful wilderness, and such a waste of potential was a violation of the basic tenets of the nation.[16]

As an active part of the agricultural household economy, women moving to Texas could easily endorse the appropriation of available farmland. This mentality was less a facet of domesticity than of mere survival. Emigrants came to Texas for the land above all. However, once they arrived, women found the need for established communities—for civilization—just as great as that for fertile soil. Here the civilizing aspects of domesticity came to bear. Similarly, as part of the household economy, women remained tied to the home and all it had come to symbolize. Their husbands would tame the land with the plow; they would tame it with the spinning wheel.[17]

Americans' ties to the earth ran deep for men and women alike. Land was not just land; it was a physical manifestation of pride in country. The freedom to till the soil paralleled other freedoms nineteenth-century Americans held dear. As far as the *Democratic Review* was concerned, the United States bestowed three blessings on its citizens: liberty, equality, and free land. The three worked together to create a perfect union. No other country had accomplished what the United States had: the creation of a new nation based on a radical concept of government. More shocking, the experiment had so far worked. The republic held together and persevered without reliance upon soldiers on every street corner or a political system gone corrupt. Citizens were free to live as they pleased without fear of reprisal or harassment by government officials.[18]

Such freedom had two effects on westward movement. First, Americans could move west to pursue their futures in a new location with little, if any, official supervision. (Although soldiers were present, they were stationed in the West for the protection, rather than hindrance, of potential settlers.) Second, the ability to spread out created a bond between emigrants and their seventeenth-century forebears. Upon arrival in the New World, Puritan John Winthrop compared his people's mission to being a "city upon a hill," emitting a shining example to all those who followed. Their journey carried a greater purpose than simple survival. The Puritans intended to reshape the world by their lifestyle, and their example carried down through the centuries.[19]

Expansionists intended to do the same, one way or another. Americans not only wanted to use freedom for themselves but also to transmit it to others. The republic's freedoms and the culture it had developed as a result served as examples for the entire world. As the *American Quarterly Review* put it, the United States was "the beacon, the example, the patriarch of the struggling nations of the world." For the editors of the *American Quarterly,* their nation would only be the first in a long series of republics worldwide; as other countries saw the glories of democracy that the United States offered, they would follow suit.[20]

Nineteenth-century women inherited the responsibility to instill in their children the knowledge and proper understanding of that freedom. The republican mother of the late eighteenth century provided their example. Mothers were in a prime position to elevate national consciousness and perpetuate patriotic feeling. *Blackwood's Magazine* recognized the hidden yet necessary duties women had to perform. A woman's dignified task was "[n]ot to make laws, not to lead armies, not to govern empires, but to form those by whom the laws are made, and armies led, and empires governed." If not for the "frail and yet spotless creature whose moral, no less than physical being, must be derived from her," women would for many have little higher purpose. As with "The Mother of the West," the women glorified in *Blackwood's* could measure their worth through the good deeds and virtue of their offspring. The fate of the future American empire lay in their gentle hands.[21]

Such responsibility followed women even to the rough terrain of Texas. Their work took on an added urgency there. Good citizens would help to erect virtuous institutions in their new communities. Following the pattern of American virtue would make all this possible. If, however, women failed in their role as moral instructors, the foundation of all their sons' efforts would be nothing more than sand, and, when the storms of adversity assailed it, its destruction would be great. Clearly such work was not for the weak or half-hearted, and its repercussions extended beyond the borders of the United States or Texas to where the rest of the world stood by, watching and waiting to observe its ultimate success or failure.

Many Americans believed it better to take such benefits abroad themselves. Destiny called for absorption into the one great republic of the world, and nothing else would do. "New territories *will* be planted, declare their independence, and be annexed!" exulted *DeBow's*. "We have New Mexico and California! We *will* have Old Mexico and Cuba! The isthmus cannot arrest—nor even the Saint Lawrence!! Time has all of this in her womb. *A hundred States* will grow up where now exists but thirty." For this journal, manifest destiny called not only across what would become the contiguous forty-eight states, but Mexico, the Caribbean, and even Canada, all to the glory of liberty. Some took this concept even further, as did expansionist Anna Ella Carroll. "We, then, my countrymen," insisted Carroll, "have a mission to perform, out of our country; we have to throw our weight, in behalf of equality and justice, over the countries of the world, and to guard with a vigilant eye the principles of Protestantism and Americanism, that our own strength shall increase, our own resources expand, and an additional impetus be given to our moral, commercial, and political greatness." This statement revealed expansionist philosophy in its truest form. For those such as Carroll, it was not enough to spread the light of freedom abroad. The cause of the United States was also the cause of righteousness.[22]

As such statements indicate, expansion did not have the endorsement of the Founding Fathers alone. It also contained the divine sanction of Providence, as the *Democratic Review's* "Annexation" claimed boldly in 1845. The first stirrings of manifest destiny came in an era when Protestantism had experienced a resurgence, thanks to the second Great Awakening. As more Americans converted to evangelicalism, they began to apply it to their own situations. Christianity became the foundation upon which the United States was built; like the Puritans, evangelicals saw their land as the new Israel. As dedicated children of God, their duty was to spread the gospel beyond its current boundaries, except by this point politics and religion intertwined so tightly in the thoughts of many that the resultant mass became a civil gospel. As one man wrote:

Let thy noble motto be
GOD,—the COUNTRY,—LIBERTY,—
Planted on religion's rock,
Thou shalt stand in every shock.

To embrace Christ meant more than the rejection of sin; it meant accepting the God-approved, Western, civilized lifestyle. Ultimately, all this would result in the increased "moral greatness" of the United States.[23]

As a result, Americans went after new territories not only with patriotic fervor, but with missionary zeal. In fact, they supported the work of such itinerant preachers as if it went hand in hand with the civilization process; the two melded in a burst of Christian republican enthusiasm. For fur traders such as Gabriel Franchère, missionaries instilled their charges in the Pacific Northwest with not only "the faith of Christianity," but also with "a living germ of civilization" that would bring the natives into the American fold. Oregon settler Alexander Ross agreed that evangelism was important but stressed that Indians primarily needed "time to dispel that thick and heavy cloud of ignorance and barbarism" that kept them from understanding true religion. Missionaries had the resources to accomplish that feat easily, Ross believed. *DeBow's* agreed, noting that "Christianity will not spread where ignorance and superstition prevail." Because the journal believed that all commerce had been designed to civilize and Christianize, not to indulge selfish desires, religion and civilization were inseparable. By spreading out into new territory and rescuing pagan barbarians, Americans could serve both God and man while benefiting themselves.[24]

Missionary fervor translated easily to domesticity. Not only did women have the high patriotic calling of republican motherhood, they were also called to a life of piety. Americans perceived women as being more attuned to spiritual matters. This bond to holiness gave them the right to teach and encourage others to live godly, decent lives. Part of the reason women appeared morally superior was because of the sanctifying atmosphere of the home. The marketplace tainted the souls of men who gave themselves to its service, thinking solely of earthly matters; women had no such difficulties. Instead, they had the time to organize such events as a ladies' fair in Houston where proceeds would go to charity. Which charity would receive the profits made little difference to the journalist reporting the sale, whether feeding poverty-stricken orphans or rescuing savages halfway around the globe. In this way, women could help bring civilization not only to their own community, but to the world at large, aiding in the extension of republicanism to pagan lands.[25]

One reason Americans equated paganism with savagery was due to their firm belief in a global racial hierarchy. Ever since the English had developed a sense of superiority over the Spanish during the Reformation, colonists and, later, Americans championed the Anglo-Saxon as supreme. Two centuries of bloody encounters with the natives had cemented this idea in place, as had interaction between slaveholders and their African captives. Both to maintain nationalistic pride and to justify further subjugation of Indian and black alike, racialism became a necessity. Such chauvinism multiplied when combined with the belief that the United States had created a government far greater than any other in the world; this compounded the call of manifest destiny over citizens. Not only did the nation have a responsibility to share its republican ways with its neighbors, but, because Americans were superior, they had every right to do so.[26]

This view carpeted the United States in the nineteenth century. "Great is the destiny which leads on the vanguard of the master race of the human family," Thomas Hart Benton declared in a speech extolling the "American Empire." "Barbarians conquer to destroy; civilized men to improve and exalt," the Missouri senator continued; "the Anglo-Saxon will carry his civilization wherever he goes." Benton's speech emphasized two points. First, men could identify civilization by its improvement of its surroundings. The civilized man would make a garden of any new environment, ultimately making everything more beautiful rather than destroying all with his presence. The senator's second point was more subtle. Not only did he declare Anglo-Saxons—meaning here Americans, not Englishmen—the eternal bearers of civilization, but he encouraged expansion of that civilization into areas bereft of such benefits. Similarly, the *Texas State Gazette* declared Anglo-Saxons "ahead of every civilized race of the world," masters of superior law, religion, and government. The editors implied the need for Americans to take advantage of this position. In time, they would establish "an empire which is felt, respected and feared, in every quarter of the globe," while inferior specimens would disappear. The *American Whig Review* believed this would not take long, as Anglo-Saxons possessed an "energy and vigor" in territorial conquest that other races apparently lacked.[27]

True womanhood also carried with it some racial overtones. It was, after all, the product of the white American middle class. Therefore the cult of domesticity naturally carried the implication that those who did not—or could not—heed its principles were inferior or immoral. Poorer women, particularly women of color, who had to work outside the home found themselves in the dubious position of appearing to be less than civilized and, in a sense, not true women. Another way to interpret the situation is to say that, as white Americans, many women who followed their husbands west held as many racialist ideas as their men. Perhaps race trumps gender in this case. But regardless of the reasons, emigrant women's writings often bear a tinge of racism, including an implication of a strict ethnic hierarchy.[28]

So manifest destiny played out not only political visions of a unified continent, but also dreams of a cultivated wilderness, tamed by good government and a good God, controlled by those at the apogee of humanity. The various aspects worked together to present a powerful and persuasive argument for expansion. Even better for expansionists, these criteria did not necessarily require a political voice in order to work. All they needed was someone who believed them and was willing to follow through by moving west, wordlessly carrying the banner of manifest destiny alongside their wagons. By their presence, emigrants demonstrated their faith in the American claim to the continent, and by their actions once they settled, they put manifest destiny to work and made it work.

American women implemented expansionism this way as did others. In some ways, they surpassed masculine endeavors in this regard. Although they had no public platform from which to declare their enthusiasm, they did so from their homes or elsewhere. They helped to cultivate a verdant wilderness and bring it under the plow as they worked beside their families in the fields (unlike other professions, agriculture remained available to both genders, as it always had). As good, dedicated Christians and mothers, they passed on moral and patriotic values to their children and fulfilled them as best as they could in their own lives. They held to race as a rationalization for their endeavors, as extant writings will indicate in later chapters. Western women might never have used the phrase itself, but manifest destiny in all its forms nevertheless played an active role in their lives.[29]

The women whose stories form the basis of this study contributed in their own way to the flow of ideas. Early colonists had little except their accrued experience to sustain them and answer the questions placed before them. Those who endured the Texas Revolution emerged from the crucible refined, with the first distinctly Texan perspective in such matters. But women never stopped arriving with more fuel for the flames as their families tried to find a place to settle down: some place with a little more room, where national destiny and personal dreams merged into a glorious whole. Northerner, Southerner, or European, these women had something substantive to say about the issues at stake.

It is to everyone's benefit that the work of these women remains available. By examining these sources, scholars can see a new depth to manifest destiny. True, such information remains in the background for the most part, never as prevalent as the *Democratic Review* or other journals or the orations of a Lewis Cass or Thomas Hart Benton. This does not detract from their value. While some may focus solely on the melody the loudest expansionists played, a more subtle harmony arises from those who did not always have the opportunity to take the lead. Harmony exists not to make itself known, but to color the work behind the scenes. As a result, it brings out the best in the melody by playing in concert with it. The resultant work becomes both more complicated and more beautiful. Such is the case with these women's writings.

That such sources exist is a credit to the women who provided them. Their presence indicates that these women desired to be heard and ultimately understood. Diaries were often passed down to one's descendants to share firsthand knowledge of a rough new world and the writer's place in it. In the same way, modern readers have an opportunity to indulge not only their own natural curiosity but also the wishes of the writers. The women—and their stories—speak for themselves.

2

Cultivating the "Garden of the South-West"

The December, 1829, edition of the *American Quarterly Review* contained an article on "The Public Domain of the United States." Within its pages it extolled the ever-improving situation for westering Americans as "the powerful arm of our government, and the mild influence of its pacific institutions," helped to shape the landscape into a place where even "on the remotest frontier the dwelling of the pioneer is sacred." Settlers could improve what land they had, leaving the rest for Native Americans whom expansion had pushed farther westward. The United States "would rapidly improve under such an arrangement," declared the *American Quarterly.* Simultaneously "a happy increase might be produced in the condition of the Indian tribes, by suffering them to remain stationary long enough to acquire local attachments, and encouraging them to make permanent improvements, and adopt civil institutions."[1]

In such a situation, according to the *American Quarterly,* all parties benefited from American expansion. Settlers would have land for their families and could work it to its optimal levels for the sake of the nation. Meanwhile, their presence on the frontier between American territory and wilderness would bring them into contact with the natives—or, more accurately, the natives would come into contact with Americans. Civilized behavior would rub off onto Indians until they too took up its mantle. In the end, native improvements upon the land would demonstrate their dedication to advancement and mark the spread of republican blessings across the continent.[2]

Such a view of expansion had two prongs. One focused on white improvements on the land, while the second emphasized the land's inhabitants. Each prong depended upon the other—two halves of the same whole. The wilderness awaited the benevolent touch of a civilized people to renew it, and for many Americans the wilderness necessarily included Indians. The United States' acquisition of territory destined it to become the Garden of the World, a new Eden that would distribute its blessings to all, including its own children. From this point, the blessings of freedom and civilization would spread throughout the world—if dedicated expansionists took up the responsibility. This axiom was as true of Texas as Louisiana or the Northwest Territories, and Texans took their duties seriously.[3]

Still, the first order of business upon arrival in Texas had little to do with discussion of esoteric issues. Those proved unimportant for families who, having left most of their worldly belongings behind to brave the trek into the wilderness, preferred to find things of substance. Their actions spoke clearly of their dedication to continental expansion—after all, they were there, beyond the Mississippi, not at home in Tennessee or Indiana or New York—but what took priority was the pioneers' desire to have a future of their own. Although they adhered to them in principle, nationalistic visions and goals took second place in comparison. A few acres upon which to grow crops or graze livestock, enough room to expand for one's children and grandchildren—this caught the imagination of emigrants before any call to patriotic duty. Only subconsciously did most settlers carry out their mother country's mission, but personal desires nevertheless managed to work in concert with nationalistic fervor.[4]

Needless to say, moving west to improve the land required labor and more than a little faith. Texas was not a recent discovery, having been part of New Spain and then Mexico since the sixteenth century, but it remained largely a rough-cut wilderness due to lack of interest and the seemingly insurmountable threat of "Indian depredations." Creating a new life here would prove difficult. There was much to be done—lands to clear, crops to plant, curious new neighbors to meet or, perhaps, to fend off. No one could be certain what awaited them. Then came the issue of recreating familiar institutions and patterns of life, if possible. Notions of community that had worked east of the Mississippi maintained their hold on the minds of emigrants, but they had yet to sink roots into the Texas soil.[5]

When examining the emergence of manifest destiny in the years prior to Texas' independence, it makes more sense to perceive it as the agrarian dream. The majority of land lay fallow in the Mexican province, which in the eyes of these new colonists was a waste, if not a sin. (The Mexican farmer did not generally figure into the Anglo-Saxon vision of a new Eden.) It became the duty of all new arrivals to do something with this wild terrain, to break it with the plow and tame it into a garden. While they did this, settlers often felt they had to remove the "weeds" from the garden—the Native Americans who already occupied the territory. Whites and Indians in the same territory made for uneasy neighbors, each concerned about what the other would do. Each made a few early, awkward attempts to cooperate with each other, even bartering for their mutual survival. Nevertheless, such efforts proved too complicated to achieve, and before long whites viewed their new neighbors as more a nuisance than a help. In order for civilization to proceed, Native Americans would have to go. Having fields or pastures, all free from native intrusion, would establish the foundation upon which manifest destiny could be built.[6]

But before expansion could stake its claim, emigrants had to be prepared. They had to rebuild their lives in a new location. Were this all the new arrivals had to do, it would be enough. Unfortunately, life in the wilderness offered additional challenges. Civilized life—meaning the life most had left behind in the United States—made a poor template. Transplants could not simply overlay traditional patterns upon the blank canvas and expect everything to proceed as normal. At the least, the environment varied substantially from eastern regions. Little could remain the same. Emigrants found themselves in a predicament. As historian Frederick Jackson Turner noted in his essay, "The Significance of the Frontier in American History," the frontier presented an obstacle that pioneers could not completely overcome. Something had to give, and what generally emerged was a compromise. Each side gave a little, allowing for change, but in return each required adaptation from the other. Settlers transformed their surroundings into something unique, but first they had to be flexible. Either they moved with the environment or else had to face the consequences as the land broke them. As a result, the culture pioneers brought with them changed to fit their circumstances and facilitated survival.[7]

Men and women alike had to meet the challenges the West presented. Starting anew with little or nothing proved difficult. However, women faced the bulk of the problems. Their fathers or husbands had, to some extent, cultural sanctions to go into the wild as frontiersmen or solitary hunters. For women, solitude and isolation seemed more a punishment than a blessing. As Noah Smithwick noted in his memoirs of early Texas life, women were less fortunate than their mates. "They—the women—talked sadly of the old house and friends left behind," he wrote, "so very far behind it seemed then. . . . There was no house to keep in order. . . . There was no poultry, no dairy, no garden, no books, or papers as nowadays—and, if there had been, many of them could not read—no schools, no churches—nothing to break the dull monotony of their lives." While the men went off to hunt and explore, women were left alone to consider their new situation. The *American Whig Review* agreed, noting the strain western life placed on women. "In thousands of humble cabins, by forest and prairie," it said, "are found pale, intellectual-looking women, broken down with unwonted drudgery." The journal expressed hope for these burdened souls by pointing out "a grand stock these Spartan mothers leave behind for the peopleing of future empires." Like "The Mother of the West," the *American Whig Review* awarded pioneer wives honor and respect through their offspring. Whether women took comfort in their frustrations as a result remained to be seen.[8]

The greatest ordeal for women was isolation. Women arriving in Texas in the 1820s and early 1830s had few neighbors in comparison to back east. Not only was the land foreign, it was devoid of familiarity, culture, or, most importantly, communities in which they could live and interact. Whereas men had the myth of the pioneering individualist, women did not. All their lives they had relied heavily on the cooperation and company provided by other women. Tackling life's events as a group, from the birthing room to dressing a corpse for burial, created a social network on which to rely. More importantly, it gave women companions to relieve their emotional distresses.[9]

Stressors multiplied when women transplanted to Texas. Friends and family lived hundreds of miles away, beyond the reach of a short visit, and weeks apart by mail. Even before her journey to Texas began, Virginian Elizabeth Cooley felt ambivalence regarding her upcoming move west. At first she wrote, "I am fixed to go to Texas, a country to which I had rather go than anywhere else, and to leave my *dear* old native land for a new and untried place of residence." But suddenly her tone changed as the uncertainty of the move settled in upon her; she would have to "quit my *old, true,* and long tried friends for new and untried love and friendship: at times my spirits are dark and gloomy as the grave, smothering, restless, uneasy." Her uneasiness grew when she reached New Orleans. "I feel bad, weary, out of spirits, for I feel I cannot like Texas," she mused. In fact, she did not stay long until she pressed her husband to take them both to Missouri. He had been ill, and her new neighbors had proved less concerned than Cooley would have liked. Their lack of hospitality finalized her decision. "I rue the day we ever thought of *Texas*," she complained, "for I fear it will end our happiness if not our lives." Many other women felt similarly about the journey west, but they persevered until they were able to establish a foothold. Nevertheless, ripped from their social tapestry, women initially felt disconnected from their new environment.[10]

Among those women who stayed in Texas, Harriet Ames also did not handle the isolation well. She lived for a year without any white women nearby, "in a country filled with Indians." Prior to settling in with her new husband, Ames expressed her concerns about the living arrangements. "There are no neighbors but the Indians," she informed him. "I don't see anyone living here. What are we going to do without neighbors?" Although her husband tried to assure her that "Indians make the best of neighbors," she remained dissatisfied until "we saw the country around us becoming inhabited by white people." Clearly local tribes seemed to be anything but neighborly to Ames. In fact, they did not even appear to be people, as she protested that no one lived nearby immediately after acknowledging the natives' presence. Native Americans signified to her a wilderness desperately in need of restraint.[11]

Mary S. Helm agreed with Ames's assessment of the situation. Texas was, for all practical purposes, on the other side of the world from her home and family. In 1829, the territory was "beyond the bounds of my own country, beyond the reach of our own mails . . . hemmed in by savages, and almost unknown." Not only did Helm still have obvious ties to the United States when Texas remained a Mexican province, she viewed her new home as a mysterious threat more than an exciting opportunity, and a threat dangerous to face alone.[12]

In a slightly different vein, Ann Raney Coleman viewed the dearth of white women with a little more levity than did Ames or Helm and turned it instead to her advantage. Coleman was still living with her parents when she and her family arrived in the early 1830s, and one of the first things she noticed was the favorable ratio of bachelors to available ladies. This worked to her benefit and that of her sister when attending dancing parties. They were good dancers, and because of the lack of girls in the area, both had "several admirers" from which to choose. Youth blinded Coleman to the future hardships she might have to face in such an environment; all she saw instead were potential beaux.[13]

This sense of life in a vacuum is crucial to understanding women's situation. As social creatures, American women believed themselves inseparable from society. Under the tacit expectations of the cult of true womanhood, women had a responsibility as mediating influences upon that society and their men in particular. As they tended to their homes, women were expected to ensure the stability of civilization nationwide; as went the household, so went the nation. In the West, in contrast, women had nowhere to begin. The foundation remained unlaid, and some wondered if it ever would be. Men frequently acted as if life beyond the Mississippi liberated them from rules for decent living, ignoring or rejecting the encouragement of their women. Often this left women with no sense of importance. Everything they had or believed in had vanished. These "moral missionaries" had to start over with a new foundation and build from there, something that few were prepared to do.[14]

The only remedy for this social malaise, this lack of belonging, was more people. As more families arrived, women would have more companions with whom to share their daily burdens. Together, they could work to rebuild civilization in the wilderness. Manifest destiny's call to the "multiplying millions" to make Texas home became women's call as well. As German immigrant Caroline Luise Baronin von Roeder wrote in a letter home in 1835, "Hurry, hurry and join us. This is truly the land of freedom and romance." Countless other immigrants shared the liberty von Roeder felt and urged their friends and family to do the same.[15]

Service to manifest destiny became the call of Mary Austin Holley in particular. Sister to early colonist Henry Austin and cousin to empresario Stephen F. Austin, Holley wrote one of the best-known guides to Texas in the 1830s after a trip to visit her relatives in 1830 and 1831. Widowed in 1827 with one child married and another mentally disabled, she came to

Bolivar on the Brazos River with her son Horace in tow. The Austins welcomed her eagerly, keeping her in their home for months. While she remained with her family, Holley spoke to the residents of Austin's Colony, learning as much as she could about the colony and the province as a whole. What she saw and heard about Texas impressed her so much that she decided to write a book lauding its beauty, its people, and especially its fecundity. *Texas,* when it was published in 1831, sang about the advantages of the landscape and particularly the "salubrity of the climate, the fertility of the soil, and the facility with which the lands can be brought under cultivation." In her work, Holley contributed substantially to the call for new emigrants. Although she never saw the whole region, relying frequently on secondhand information, the author impressed thousands of readers with the idea of moving westward.[16]

Primarily Holley intended her work to be an emigrant guide. Too many rumors existed regarding this strange new colony for Americans to know what Texas was actually like. Was it really a paradise on earth, where anything would grow without effort? Reports often made exaggerated claims, leaving unrealistic expectations in their wake. The author recognized that too often duped emigrants became "the certain victims of privation, disappointment and ultimate ruin," and Holley wanted to make amends for their losses. More importantly, she directed much of her work to women, a group that other published works ignored. Holley insisted that women understand the nature of their endeavor as well, because "the comfort of every family, and the general well-being of the infant colony" depended on their efforts. As a woman, she could provide "more hints for the judicious arrangements of the voyage and the indispensable attentions to the comfort and economy of an infant establishment, than could be gathered from the more abstract and general views of gentleman travelers." In a sense, *Texas* provided an impromptu community for emigrant women. No other women might have joined them on their journey, or perhaps none waited to meet them, but new arrivals had in Holley the voice of feminine experience to console and guide them.[17]

A primary concern for her readers was the state of culture and civilization in Texas. How much would new arrivals have to do to make Texas livable? Holley did her best to console them, lauding towns such as Brazoria, which by her visit was three years old and already had "some families of education and refinement." The houses in the area were admittedly rude and "temporary," but even within such cabins dedicated housewives arranged books, furniture, and other items "in perfect neatness about the room." Given the dedication of the current residents to progress, all the area needed was "neat white dwellings, to complete the picture." If "industrious mechanics and farmers and intelligent planters" were to emigrate, this land of bounty would "rival the most favoured parts of the earth."[18]

Despite her optimism, Holley realized that the colony was not perfect. She warned housekeepers to be prepared for anything, including a lack of available clothing and other sundries. "Ladies in particular, should remember," she counseled, "that in a new country, they cannot get things made at any moment, as in an old one, and that they will be sufficiently busy, the first two years, in arranging such things as they have, without occupying themselves in obtaining more." Here emerged one variation in true womanhood's credo. The emergence of separate spheres coincided with the commercialization of the marketplace. Although ancestors of middle-class women back east had once done for themselves, the contemporary women relied on stores and merchants. That was simply not always possible in Texas. Nevertheless, the chief tenets of domesticity still held, even in a territory in flux, and Holley tacitly encouraged her readers to excel at home by bringing along what they would need instead of spending on more.[19]

But even while encouraging her readers, Holley refused to allow them to remain deluded about the amount of work to be done. Presaging a later phrase from *DeBow's*, she noted that "the cows must be milked, and the honey must be gathered. Houses must be built and enclosures made. The deer must be hunted, and the fish must be caught." Texas had no place for those who shrank from "hardship and danger," insisted Holley, "and those who, being accustomed to a regular routine of prescribed employment in a city, know not how to act on emergencies." Anyone unable to meet the demands of rebuilding society in the wilderness "had better stay where they are."[20]

Holley's work became a brilliant success. In a letter to her daughter Harriette in December, 1833, she wrote that the book might soon see a second printing. She had made a name for herself while lauding her cousin and the flourishing province, as she had intended. Prior to its publication, she had written her brother-in-law, Orville, to help her find a publisher in New York while she remained in Bolivar with her family. "I think such a work is wanted and will be well received by the public," she wrote prophetically. But she did not stop there. "I think it will not only do me credit, but, what is quite as good in my circumstances, it may bring me a good sum of money, which I have need of to carry on my projects here." Her "projects" included the purchase of land of her own in Texas. "Wait until I am as rich as I mean to be," she told her daughter. "I shall have a league for you, one for Horace, one for myself with a good income besides."[21]

Clearly Holley had more than idealistic goals for Texas. Her plans required exploitation of the colony as well. In this the author had much in common with those to whom she wrote. Taming the territory had high priority largely because those emigrating did so for personal aggrandizement. Texas' position was "favourable for commerce," as Holley noted, and commerce motivated people to come. This created a synergistic relationship between land and emigrant. What benefited the individual benefited Texas as well. Even in her own ambitions, Holley remained in step with her audience. This helped to explain her publishing successes.[22]

Not all women had the ability to reach the general public as Holley did. Nevertheless, they could exercise some control over their surroundings. Their influence stretched only as far as their fingertips as they worked to bring the earth under submission. This proved crucial, as the land threatened not only the cause of civilization but women's stability. New arrivals often shuddered at an open wilderness too strange for words. When Millie Gray arrived in 1839 to tend the lands her husband had bought three years before, she expressed her own misgivings as best as she could to her diary. "My heart feels oppressed & it requires an effort to wear the appearance of cheerfulness," she wrote. "I could (if I were a weeping character) sit down & fairly weep." Yet even Gray did not know exactly what it was about Texas that upset her. She guessed that she felt unsettled "merely because all is strange & I fear to look forward." Eventually Gray forgot her concerns and settled into life in Texas with enthusiasm.[23]

Ann Raney Coleman had even more reason to feel unsettled. She arrived with her family from England in 1829, when she was a teenager. The entire continent, let alone Texas, was completely new to her. As she traveled inland with her mother and sister to join her father, who had arrived first, she found her environment more threatening than strange. She and her family spent their first night camped in the open beside a river, but according to Coleman they slept little. The proximity of the river prompted concerns of alligators rising from the water to make "a dainty morsel" of them all. Meanwhile, nearby panthers "were making night hideous with their cries," threatening danger from the woods beyond. Finally Coleman gave up on sleep and joined her mother and sister in sitting on the riverbank and considering their new circumstances for the rest of the night. Day would bring some relief, but the wilderness and its denizens would remain.[24]

For some women, Texas was not just a savage place, but an empty one. Mary Rabb saw "nothing but a wilderness" where her husband had decided to settle without "eaven a tree cut down to marke that plais." Dilue Rose Harris remembered that when her family arrived in Harrisburg in 1833, there was no "church, nor preacher, school house nor courthouse." The land bore few landmarks, whether natural or manmade, and had little aesthetic appeal for eyes accustomed to thick forests and glades or fine wooden houses. Even Hispanic women thought that Texas offered little, such as the Mexican wife of a customs inspector in Goliad. Someone "who had seen large cities could not live happily in such a banishment," she wrote, and declared her new home a "poor, out-of-the-world, ignorant village." This proved true even in 1848, when Helen Chapman arrived in South Texas with her soldier husband. Chapman quailed at the territory around the Rio Grande where they were stationed. "For what are we here?" she wondered. "For such a country as this why expend such blood and treasure?" Nevertheless, she chided herself for lack of vision: "But a region quite as unpromising met the eye of the Pilgrims at Plymouth, and this is no way to judge." First impressions meant little, she realized; it would take time to grow accustomed to more exotic surroundings. In fact, it did not take long before she wrote her son, who remained behind in Massachusetts, of the variety of fruits Texas offered lacking back home. "Our kind Heavenly Father loves all his children and divides his rich gifts equally among all," she noted. Texas had become a garden awaiting her approval and indulgence.[25]

Chapman's letter hints at a different perspective of the barren wilderness. If it appeared that Texas was empty, a little industry could soon fill it. Holley noted this in *Texas,* and other women took up the call. "If a healthy man is poor and homeless in Texas, it is because he is not manly enough to turn his hands to useful labor," insisted Jane McManus Storm Cazneau, who lived in Eagle Pass, a small settlement on the Rio Grande. She would have found Chapman's earlier observations short-sighted at best. German immigrant Ottilie Fuchs Goeth saw the same opportunity. "Here the prairies appeared to dominate everything without barriers of any kind," she said. The earth was "virtually begging for a hand to cultivate it." Teresa Griffin Vielé agreed in her 1858 work, *Following the Drum.* Vielé watched as "a very superior class of emigrants" poured into Galveston, "tempted hither by the rich, luxurious, easily-cultivated soil of this well-named garden of the South-West." With emigrants such as these, many believed, Texas was destined for ultimate prosperity.[26]

Both Cazneau and Vielé published their paeans to the fecundity of Texas land. Their enthusiasm was not limited to words alone. Not only did they move to Texas, providing material evidence, but Cazneau took matters a step further. She owned land in Texas as early as 1835 as she heeded her own advice. Then both women encouraged others to do the same. In doing so, these women helped promote cultivation. Only when settlers brought the earth under control would they have completed the first step in the process of civilization, a process that required both men and women for its full implementation. To tame the savage wasteland was to conquer it.[27]

But women's descriptions of their new home as an empty wilderness were ultimately deceptive. Texas had borne inhabitants for centuries prior to the arrival of any European. These Native Americans had taken advantage of local resources in their own way, establishing their own unique civilizations. Women played a crucial role in Indian society despite their subordinate status among most Texas tribes. Not only did they do traditionally domestic work in the household, they also tended to more strenuous chores, leaving their husbands free to hunt or fight as necessary. However, the newcomers tended to overlook or misinterpret native culture. In addition, many tribes' treatment of women as chattel appalled whites accustomed to some measure of chivalry toward the ladies. Even worse for emigrants, some tribes allowed female involvement in raids, such as one six-day visit to San Antonio in which Comanche men, women, and children raided the town at will. The two groups differed so much that it proved easier to label Indians as savage and start over without them if circumstances warranted.[28]

Such beliefs affected white-Indian relations in various ways. The view of Indians as "savage" was nothing new, going as far back as the seventeenth century. It did not help matters that Texas' Hispanic residents had struggled with Indian problems since first venturing into the region.

Although the quality of relations depended on the tribe, the presence of Apaches, Comanches, and others restricted growth and progress in Mexican Texas. Typically white women held a negative perception of natives, particularly in Texas where conditions proved more severe compared to other parts of the West. Simultaneously, women worked with Native Americans more often than men, forming a "collegial" relationship of trade and mutual assistance. Stereotypes frequently disintegrated in such an atmosphere. Again, this proved true less often in Texas because Indian warfare continued there into the latter part of the century.[29]

All these perspectives helped to motivate settlers with goals of taming the wilderness. For those who considered natives a blight on the land, the Indians' extinction would make the garden bloom. A more beneficent view of the situation stirred to action emigrants hoping to spread civilization across the entire population of Texas. Perhaps by their presence, Americans could teach their neighbors to become better people. One only needed to look at the position of women in native society to prove the need. Women who dealt with Indians on a regular basis saw how poorly Indian women seemed to be treated by their husbands, fathers, and brothers. Civilization presented a balm to heal native society, rescuing the women (and, in turn, their men) from the harsh taskmaster of savagery.[30]

But kind thoughts and words took time to sink into the American psyche. In the meanwhile, the traditional stereotypes of dangerous savages took preeminence in the white mind. Female emigrants to Texas began their relationship with their Indian neighbors with suspicion as early as 1822. In the winter of 1822–23, Jane Long, her two daughters, and her female slave, Kian, stayed at Point Bolivar, along the Gulf coast, in a fort her husband had built. He was away on a venture to claim Texas independence from Mexico, but Long had chosen to remain in hostile territory to wait for him. She did this knowing the reputation and temperament of her neighbors, the Karankawas. Widely regarded as vicious cannibals, the Karankawas offered little evidence to ease the mind of others in their territory.[31]

As the winter dragged on, food became scarce. This added to Long's concerns for her family's welfare. When it appeared that the natives might come too close, she quickly devised a plan to make it seem as if soldiers manned the fort. She ran a red petticoat up the flagpole as a warning to any potential intruders. Then, to back up her threat, she fired a cannon that her husband and his men had left behind. Every few hours, she would set it off again, hoping the noise might scare off any attackers. Similarly, whenever Kian went to search for shellfish or other food, she dressed in uniform to disguise her femininity and present a bold front of strength. Whatever the Karankawas thought of such displays, Point Bolivar remained secure until other Americans arrived the following spring.[32]

As Long's situation indicates, white women began their relations with natives at a disadvantage. Information regarding their new neighbors was scant and frequently contradictory. For instance, Long knew little about the Karankawas, basing her response on rumor rather than experience. Adding to the confusion, Americans' assumption of native inferiority aggravated an already tense situation. Still, emigrants sometimes began their stays in good standing with local tribes and worked to keep them in favor. Eliza Moore and Sabrina Townsend remembered decades later that the Tonkawas tended to be particularly friendly toward their families. Moore and her neighbors gave them food that they ate peacefully. But even Townsend knew that not all Indians were alike. The Tonkawas were kind to whites, she noted, but tended to plunder the tribes that "would kill our people and steal our horses." As peaceful as relations between whites and Tonkawas were for these two women, they recognized the fragility of the situation. Anything could change at any moment.[33]

Others insisted that there was no reason for concern in the first place. Holley wrote at length on the tribes in Texas as she tried to ease her readers' minds. True, the Karankawas were "reputed to be cannibals," but according to her research most settlers found them to be peaceful. The Kickapoos and Shawnees behaved "in a friendly and respectful manner" toward Texans, and even the feared Comanches were "a noble race of Indians," although they tended to wander and "not cultivate the earth." Above all, Holley noted that the number of Indians should not cause any concern. "They are either too few in numbers to be formidable," she said, "or so far civilized, as to provide well for themselves, without disturbing others." Such reassurance might lure emigrants who would otherwise have remained at home, where the Indians had become in essence extinct.[34]

Jane Cazneau took a different tack than Holley in discussing her native neighbors. Indians were savages, she acknowledged, but they did not have to be so. Cazneau called for Americans to teach civilized ways to Native Americans. After all, if Americans willingly sent missionaries to Asia, she asked, why not send others west to establish schools? Spanish missions had contained the Indians and helped them to settle down centuries before. In the same way, nineteenth-century whites needed to establish communities where natives could be taught and civilized. Cazneau's primary idea was to provide industrial education, basic work skills from which to begin. "In these communities, while the old and stubborn were held in peaceful submission," she suggested, "the young could be trained to habits of civilized industry, and their children again would rise still higher, and be good citizens and Christian examples."[35]

Cazneau's ideas adhered to the belief that man could progress from savagism to civilization. As bearers of civilization, whites had the responsibility to lead Indians to a more advanced state, leaving behind cultural detritus that limited them. Only by assimilating could natives survive. Later scholars have noted the irony of this philosophy; Native Americans might have persevered physically, but, culturally, assimilation would have exterminated them. Of course, nineteenth-century Americans would not have considered this worth discussion. In their eyes, the problem lay in the barrier "barbarism" presented to civilization. Unless the natives changed their ways, neither they nor the Americans would survive in any sense.[36]

Of all white emigrants, Germans had the best relations with neighboring Native Americans. Rosa von Roeder Kleberg and her husband arrived in 1834. Her first encounter with an Indian came soon after. A man came to their house carrying two large hams and crying, "Swap! Swap!" Nervously Kleberg presented a loaf of bread. The Indian took the bread and left the hams. Years later, she confidently said that "the Indians were in the main quite amicable." Louise Ernst Stöhr agreed. Her family landed at Harrisburg three years earlier than had Kleberg's, and in her experiences there she noticed that even the local tribes seemed to find it a "lonesome" experience. Simply to survive, natives and Germans would trade runaway horses and cows for milk and butter until more settlers arrived, and then the cycle of initial confusion and misunderstanding began again. Other Germans had less pleasant experiences. Clara Feller always believed "that the Indians' purpose was to impress us with their numbers and military efficiency." Once, when Feller had just finished baking bread for her family, an Indian came in and took it without a word. The experience left Feller shaken, but fear soon turned to rage—ingredients for bread were scarce at the time. After this event, she would never feel any affection for the "noble red man." Natives were friendly enough, Feller admitted, but too much so for her taste. Although she felt no hatred for her neighbors, she never had a good relationship with them like others had.[37]

At times the ambivalence white-Indian relations caused led to awkward situations. Harris was a child when her family arrived in the 1820s. Anglos had not lived in Texas long, and information about their surroundings was scarce. As a result, they preferred to remain on guard. Harris recalled that once, not long after her family had settled down, Indians came to trade for some of the community's corn. Their appearance startled the women and children, who had no idea what to expect. Fortunately the situation defused rapidly, and both sides departed happy. Mary Rabb did not feel so lucky. Her family had dealt with Indians before. Natives frequently stole the family's horses, so the group gave up and moved elsewhere. Once settled in a new location, locals visited again. Panicked, Rabb snatched up her children and hid from view. The Indians then entered her house, took assorted goods and food and left. For Rabb, and others like her, even nonviolent interactions had a hostile edge to them.[38]

The prevalence of such awkward encounters helped tinge Texans' view of Native Americans. Mary Sherwood Helm considered them hostile and sneaky and pronounced them filthy despite their bathing. Mary Maverick agreed after seeing her first Tonkawas on her way to San Antonio from Alabama. At this point, Maverick only knew Cherokees, who had adopted many white habits; as a result, her first meeting with Tonkawas repelled her. The warriors had painted themselves and "displayed in triumph two scalps, one hand, and several pieces of putrid flesh" that they intended for supper. When the passersby gathered around her infant son to "see how pretty and white" he was, Maverick feared for his life and brought her pistol and bowie knife into view. "That certainly was a narrow escape from a cruel death," she wrote later. Crisis was averted, at least in Maverick's mind.[39]

Many concerns stemmed from mutual misunderstanding, such as those mentioned above. Because of cultural and linguistic differences, whites and Native Americans could not meet each others' expectations. Native American dress and hygiene, which Helm admitted did exist, failed to reach white standards of decency. Their concept of personal space and property did likewise. When Feller stood in helpless rage as her bread walked out the door, or when Maverick quailed at Tonkawas' examining her baby, they could not communicate their frustrations. Women who did so frequently observed that the targets of their wrath merely laughed in response.

The fact that white-Indian relations often dissolved into violence did not help matters. One anonymous visitor in 1834 warned that Native Americans were attacking overland travelers. Kidnapping, murder, and other "depredations" occurred so often in Texas that, by the 1840s, papers like the *Texas State Gazette* compressed the news of the past year's difficulties in Corpus Christi in a single article to save space. Attacks continued into the 1850s despite progress made toward "civilizing" the state. Women had plenty of stories of their own to tell. Townsend, who recalled good relations with the Tonkawas, watched as warriors of another tribe killed one of her slaves the same year, fleeing with the dead woman's child. In March, 1840, sixty-five Comanches who had come to negotiate a treaty in San Antonio began a skirmish in that town instead. Maverick, who had held off the Tonkawas earlier, fled to her home and barred the door just as one Comanche reached it. She and her cook, Jinny, remained paralyzed while the fighting raged about them, although Jinny drew up enough courage to brandish a rock at one warrior who came too close.[40]

Nevertheless, Maverick could not help but feel some sympathy. Once she ventured into the street again, she saw one young Comanche dying nearby. Another man stood over him, ready to shoot him in the head. "Oh, don't, he is dying," she pleaded. The man agreed to placate her, although "it would put him out of his misery." Just what Maverick had intended is unclear. Was she shocked by the callous killing of a man who was already vulnerable? Or did she refuse to allow her enemy the satisfaction of a quicker, less painful death? Given the man's response, the former seems likely, but other women in similar situations hoped for as much suffering as possible.[41]

Emma Murck Altgelt had a similar experience to Maverick's. When she lived in Comfort, Indians raided the town and took "all sorts of articles . . . like kid gloves, soap, scarves" and other items. Eventually the raiding party was caught and brought back to town. As it turned out, one of the captives was a woman, a novelty for citizens. "She was led through Comfort," Altgelt recalled. "Everyone wanted to see her and she was worth seeing, half-naked, with long black hair and the vicious eyes of a beast of prey." There appeared no trace of feminine decency in her, which undoubtedly lent to the curiosity of the locals. The presence of a "savage" woman also challenged the ideal of womanhood and stressed the gulf between civilization and barbarity. What, if anything, did whites owe such people?[42]

The question was a complicated one. Texan women were familiar with the brutal treatment whites had received as Indian captives. Maverick remembered the return of fifteen-year-old Matilda Lockhart after two years of captivity. The girl told of beatings, and her own face bore the mark of her trials: the tip of her nose had been burned to the bone. Now degraded and humiliated, Lockhart only wished to go home, "where she would hide away and never permit herself to be seen." Maverick and others also helped a Mrs. Webster, who had also recently been released. According to Maverick, the Comanches had taken Webster's baby, bashed its brains out against a tree, and then took her older son from her. Only her daughter remained with her until finally the natives returned the boy in a captive exchange.[43]

Similarly, publishers released captivity narratives painfully detailing the ordeals each victim endured. Sarah Ann Horn, who came to Texas in 1834, provided one such narrative. The work held back nothing. Horn watched helplessly as Comanches killed her husband and, later, her three-month-old daughter. They then whipped and beat Horn, cutting off much of her hair to serve as an ornament, and dragged her away to endure mistreatment from a cruel Comanche woman. Her mistress "was an utter stranger to the feelings of humanity," Horn wrote. As far as she was concerned, no Indian, male or female, could be trusted. "Before I arrived in the neighborhood of the Comanches, they frequently gave me to understand that their women would kill me and burn me up," she related. She ignored their threats, "which I afterwards learned was the best way." Despite her outward passivity, Horn emerged from her ordeal shaken.[44]

Clarissa Plummer told a similar story, losing her husband only to become an unwilling concubine. As had Horn, she found her captor "callous to every human feeling." Her situation was almost too miserable for her to bear. "I found myself lying upon a filthy bed of leaves and moss," Plummer wrote, "and the only inhabitant, besides my child, of a miserable hovel, the internal point of which was wretched beyond the power of human conception!" When Plummer gave birth to a son, the Comanches threw him against a tree and then gave the corpse to the dogs. Tales such as Horn's and Plummer's admittedly exaggerated their ordeals, playing with their readers' sentimental urges and encouraging the removal of the culprits. Still, no decent American could stand by passively as women suffered at the hands of barbarians. In publishing the details of their captivity, then, women like Plummer called for the civilization of Texas in a different manner than Cazneau. No amount of education could tame the Indians in these women's stories.[45]

Yet Horn's narrative ended on a more optimistic note. She acknowledged the agony she faced as a captive. Nevertheless, although the Indians had brutalized her body, her spirit remained intact. The Comanches behaved this way, she wrote, because they lacked the spiritual understanding that only good Christians could provide. Were someone to minister to them, eventually the tribe would repent and join white Americans in the congregation of civilized men. "When shall the light of the Gospel illuminate the pathway of their return?" she wondered. "Saviour of the human race, hasten the blessed day!" Horn rejected the job herself—she had endured quite enough and preferred to return to New York—but her conclusion remained hopeful. More interestingly, Horn looked back at her experience with sympathy for the Comanche women she had observed. The men badly mistreated their women, she noted, in ways others could not fathom. "Never, until I was shut up in the horrible shades of pagan darkness," she declared, "did I see and feel the indebtedness particularly of my sex to the precepts of the gospel of Christ!" Her realization substantiated the idea that a civilizing moral influence could only benefit Native Americans, men and women alike.[46]

Horn was certain that, in the battle between civilization and savagery, the former would eventually triumph. Nevertheless, many other examples cast doubt on this concept, tending instead to point to the negative influence frontier life frequently had on its inhabitants. The best-known case study was that of Cynthia Ann Parker. Parker was nine years old in 1836 when Comanches attacked her family's settlement at Fort Parker. Her cousin Rachel Plummer tried to fend off the attackers but was knocked unconscious with a hoe and carried off, along with Parker and her six-year-old brother. Plummer's ordeal lasted two years; afterward she wrote a narrative of her treatment. Her captors whipped and beat her regularly. Her owner's wife and daughter joined in the torture, reinforcing the stereotype of the Indian savage. They took her six-week-old infant and threw it into a patch of prickly pear until it died. Her older son disappeared, never to return. Eventually traders on the Santa Fe Trail discovered her and took her to Independence, Missouri. Plummer returned to her family "ematiated [sic]" and "covered with scars, the evidence of the savage barbarity to which she had been subjected during her captivity." Rachel Plummer was never the same person again. As had Sarah Ann Horn, she hoped for the ability to pray for her oppressors, for "they knew not what they do," but she never went beyond such fragile sentiments. In 1839, one year after her release, she died, strained to the breaking point by her ordeal.[47]

In contrast, the Comanches adopted Parker and raised her as one of their own. This was a typical practice for Native Americans, who often took in captives to replace a child lost or killed in battle. When Texas Rangers finally found Parker twenty-four years later, in 1860, she had fully acculturated to Comanche ways. She had married and had three children, including a son, Quanah Parker, who eventually gained renown as Quahada Comanche chief. She only vaguely remembered her past and spoke little English, but the Rangers returned her to her overjoyed family. But Parker refused to stay. Too much time had passed for her to remember her former life, and the strain was difficult to bear. While among the Parker family, she maintained Indian customs, such as slashing herself in mourning for lost loved ones. She escaped from her relatives several times in attempts to rejoin her husband, and four years later she died, as had her cousin. Her death differed in that she died (according to legend) of grief and frustration at having been separated from her tribe. Although more than likely she actually died of flu, Parker always remembered her Comanche life fondly.[48]

The case of Cynthia Ann Parker challenged American notions of white cultural supremacy. According to contemporary wisdom, Indians would embrace civilization once exposed to it. Why, then, did people like Parker run the other way? She was hardly unique; Maverick remembered a girl returned in a captive exchange who begged to rejoin the Comanches. This is not surprising. Historian Glenda Riley proposes in *Women and Indians on the Frontier* that early interactions tended to be suspicious and fearful, but, after trading with natives and living so close to them, white women tended to change their perceptions and accept Indians as human beings. Therefore, captives also fit into their environment with little difficulty. Still, this happened more often outside of Texas; the constant conflict within the region lent itself more easily to traditional accusations of savagery. As a result, cases such as Parker's baffled the locals.[49]

Even more unusual were the stories of wild white women found roaming the Texas countryside. The details of the legend varied, but the theme remained the same. H. T. Houston wrote of the "Wild Woman of the Navidad," a naked woman covered in hair. Although people claimed to see her often, she appeared skittish, like an animal, and was never caught. The "Wild Woman of the Wichita Mountains" proved less elusive. In 1856 the *Dallas Herald* described her supposed capture as well as attempts to civilize her. According to the *Herald*, J. W. C. Northcott had gone gold hunting in the Wichitas one spring when he first saw the woman. Determined to get her, he later returned with his dogs to comb the countryside for her. She attacked him once he found her, he said, but he managed to get a rope around her neck and bring the savage back to civilization. The paper described the young woman as "a tall, gracefully formed, young white girl" with matted hair and no trace of "human passion." For the moment, she remained Northcott's "pet," but he said he hoped to teach the woman to speak one day so she could tell him her story. The *Herald* had its own hopes as to how the tale would end; "Romance Realized," the headline sighed wistfully.[50]

The seriousness with which the newspaper took this unusual story reveals the stark contrast whites drew between white civilization and Indian barbarity, particularly in women. Altgelt's recollection of the female Comanche raider depicts the gulf in colorful detail, contrasting the rational but curious gaze of the observer to the dark, animalistic eyes of the captive. But there was more to the situation than simply standing apart and castigating the primitives. Thanks to the nurturing, encouraging role women bore, the gentler sex felt obliged to serve as "moral missionaries" to the wilderness. Not only did they have a responsibility toward their husbands and children, but some assumed toward Indians as well. Captivity narratives suggested that women who endured this ordeal could reform even their own captors by their behavior. The ending of Sarah Ann Horn's narrative reveals this obligation; although she considered herself unable to do anything personally, she expressed her hope that someday her captors might set aside violence and take up the standard of civilization as well. Understandably, then, those captives who rejected their former lives insulted whites everywhere. Stories of wild women presented the same problems. How could white women, the epitome of all that was good in America, become savage or even bestial? The idea seemed illogical to early settlers.[51]

Such tales also reinforced the need to tame the wilderness into a perfect garden for settlement. The wild women of the Navidad and elsewhere were anomalies that reinforced the need for the presence of even more women in Texas. Perhaps if more women arrived to anchor civilization, such stories would disappear into folklore (as indeed they did). Clearly much work remained to be done.

Most importantly, the shocking stories of white women run amok proved cautionary to female pioneers. A whole new landscape awaited the touch of women to shape it into its proper form, but those called to work had to beware the seductive call of the wild. Were they to try their hand alone at adapting their environments to something more familiar and acceptable, there might be no guarantee of success. Women needed the help of their neighbors and friends to tackle the problem before them collectively.[52]

This concept contradicts the traditional notion of the lone individualist bending the land to his will. Frederick Jackson Turner's frontier thesis prefers to focus on this aspect of westward expansion, declaring that western life developed "that dominant individualism," and although it did to an extent occur (no one can deny the presence of trappers and traders, regardless of how scholars portray them), it neglects the crucial phase that emerged with pioneer families. Trappers and traders led a nomadic lifestyle, traipsing across the wilderness as they pleased. No need existed for them to remain outside the pale of civilization, although sometimes that did occur.[53]

But settlers moved west with a different worldview. They arrived as groups, not individuals, demonstrating a reliance upon collective social frameworks. These in turn required civilized behavior in order to function. As such, families proved to be the harbingers of manifest destiny for the remainder of the continent, and, as families, men and women worked to realize it. For the most part, civilization required individuals willing to work for its establishment. In Texas matters proved more complicated by ever-worsening political circumstances. The conflict between Texas and its mother country would eventually lead to war, which in turn created a need for a different tactic to tame the frontier.

Women
and Texas
Independence

In February of 1836 Mexican forces under General Antonio López de Santa Anna laid siege to the mission of San Antonio de
Valero, better known as the Alamo. Some of Texas' best-known warriors
gathered inside the mission's walls, preparing for the worst. The story is
a familiar one. Countless schoolchildren today learn the names of some
of those involved: William Barret Travis, Davy Crockett, Jim Bowie. These
men and nearly two hundred others defended the Alamo in a doomed
struggle against a much larger force. Their martyrdom on March 6 inspired generations to come and continues to kindle imaginations to the
present day.

Other stories are less renowned. Take, for example, the story of San
Antonio resident Andrea Castañón de Villanueva. In 1836 she ran a hotel
and was well-known by the locals. One day she received a letter from Sam
Houston, who was then in charge of all Texan forces. Jim Bowie had taken
ill with pneumonia and desperately needed aid. Would Villanueva come
and serve as his nurse? The innkeeper could not help but know of the
ongoing struggle between Texans and the Mexican government. Like other

Hispanics in the province, she harbored ill feelings of her own against the latter; the Mexican army had killed her first husband years before. No doubt the bitterness she had swallowed came rushing back as she made her way toward the Alamo and her patient.[1]

While Bowie lay helpless, with Madam Candelaria (as she later became known) faithfully by his side, the struggle for the Alamo reached its peak. Its defenders urged the woman to leave, but she refused to abandon her charge. Later she recounted the final battle. She recalled Colonel Travis's charge to his men as he drew a line in the earth with his sword and how everyone swore loyalty to the end. The battle was brutal. Finally Mexican soldiers entered Bowie's room, ordering her aside. Protectively the nurse instead placed herself between Bowie and the intruders. Years later she showed reporters the scars she received from bayonet strikes to the arm and chin in that confrontation. Although she managed to survive, her efforts for Bowie came to a bad end; he died as did all the defenders of the Alamo. Nevertheless, Madam Candelaria's story became a local legend.[2]

Many historians would take this a step further and say that the entire story is myth. After all, for this woman to have been there, Andrea Castañón de Villanueva would have had to be more than 113 years old when she died in February, 1899. Such longevity is possible, but it stretches the limits of probability. Some eyewitnesses claim that other women such as Ana Esparza and Juana Navarro Alsbury cared for Bowie, not Madam Candelaria. Typically scholars declare her story—or, more accurately, stories—the ramblings of a liar and a glory-seeker or simply a mentally imbalanced geriatric. Even her contemporaries debated the validity of her tales. When the Alamo Monument Association asked to add Candelaria to the list of heroes as well as that of pensioners, not everyone was willing to do so. Eventually she received a monthly stipend of $12 for her work among yellow fever victims in 1836.[3]

Whether or not Madam Candelaria's story is accurate is irrelevant to a larger truth. She represents an archetype: traditional histories largely overlook women at the Alamo. Their stories muddle an assortment of fact and fantasy, but women were indeed present when the Alamo fell. In fact, women played several critical roles in Texas as it fought to become a republic separate from Mexico, and they had done so for nearly twenty years before Candelaria and her compatriots watched events in San Antonio.

This evolution from wilderness to province to independent nation was one of the early success stories for manifest destiny. Texas' Anglo settlers tied ideology to their endeavor from the beginning. One letter dedicated "to the people of the jurisdiction of Columbia" reached *Niles' Weekly Register* in October, 1835. "Your cause is a good one," declared the writer, "none can be better, it is republicanism in opposition to despotism; in a word it is liberty in opposition to slavery." Observers compared the late revolution with that against Great Britain in their discussion of "just rights" and "struggle for freedom." In Texas, such words kindled a hope that someday the United States might extend its "fraternal affection" and take them into the Union.[4]

This underpinning for American expansionism was not and could not be merely theoretical. It required action to achieve that glory to which Texans aspired. Rather than developing in a vacuum, the simultaneous goals of expansion and nationalism emerged from the crucible of hard-fought revolution. Expansionism could not simply happen. It took the dedication, sweat, and even blood of its devotees to erect a living shrine to manifest destiny.

Madam Candelaria and others reveal that the liberation of Texas was not merely a masculine affair. Women helped to secure the land they called their own, and the avenues for assistance were many. Regardless of whether they followed traditionally feminine routes or helped men more directly in the fighting of the Texas Revolution, women never remained passive, content to let the menfolk shoulder the burden of the future. Given the nature of this war, women had to act, even if simply to gather the children and flee the coming onslaught to keep the family alive. For the sake of posterity as well as livelihood, American life and culture had to be preserved. Efforts of Texan women made this possible.

In a sense, Mexico found itself in a losing situation even before Moses Austin requested the right to settle in the desolate northern province of Tejas. Americans had expressed interest in this region and had worked to try to appropriate Texas as early as 1806. These early attempts coincided with Mexican revolts against Spain and were short-lived. Still, one last filibuster movement pushed into Mexican territory in 1819, led by Mississippian James Long. As the leader of a group championing the independence of Texas, Long not only moved his troops from the United States to Mexico but eventually allowed his wife Jane to join him.[5]

Jane had asked to go earlier, being as enthusiastic about the endeavor as her husband, but he had refused. After all, she was pregnant and already cared for their young daughter. He did not want to expose mother or child to injury in the move to the wilderness. While she waited out the remainder of her term, Jane Long sewed a white silk flag with red stripes and a white star for the expedition. (Women frequently contributed to such endeavors in this way. Rather than going to war themselves, women throughout this period created banners for the men going to meet the enemy in battle.) At last the anxious mother delivered her second daughter, Rebecca, in June, 1819. Within twelve days she traveled to Nacogdoches with two small children and her servant, Kian, in tow.[6]

After living in eastern Texas for a year, the Long family and entourage relocated to the peninsula opposite Galveston Island in December, 1820, where they erected a fort at Point Bolivar. This fort was to be James Long's base camp for the rest of his life. In September, 1821, the filibuster heard that San Antonio intended to rise up against the Mexican government. Promising Jane that he would return in three weeks, he and his men left Point Bolivar. However, within that time they surrendered to the Mexicans. The Mexicans then sent their captives to Mexico City, where Long died under mysterious circumstances in April, 1822.[7]

Mrs. Long remained unaware of the party's fate throughout the winter. Still optimistic regarding her husband's cause, she maintained the fort with only Kian and her daughter Ann to help her. (Rebecca had died before leaving Nacogdoches.) To complicate matters, Long was pregnant again with a third daughter, ostensibly the first white child born in Texas, in December, 1821. Long fended off the supposedly cannibalistic Karankawas while waiting for word from the ill-fated group. Nothing would remove her from her location until word came that her husband had been captured. Only then, in March, 1822, did she move farther inland. Four months later, she learned that she had become a widow at age twenty-four.[8]

Harris Gaylord Warren describes the Long expedition as proof of "the futility of filibustering." Regardless of the approval of the U.S. government, whether tacit or explicit, small groups of enthusiasts could not an independent state make. There is some truth to this. However, these early movements had more staying power than is evident at first glance. Proof of this lies with Jane Long herself. Rather than fleeing back across the Sabine River to a safer environment, as did many, Long remained in her newfound homeland, persevering there alone for the rest of her life. She first moved to San Antonio. On her way there, the people of Goliad learned of her presence and threw a ball in her honor. Long enjoyed the festivities from the sidelines, as she was still in mourning and unable to participate fully. Governor José Felix Trespalacios proved difficult to deal with upon Long's arrival in the city in October. Although Trespalacios had helped her husband in 1820 as part of Long's "Patriot Army," the governor refused to give Long remuneration for the loss of her husband. She negotiated with the governor for days until he finally agreed to relinquish her husband's old arms and ammunition. Like her husband, she was unafraid to fight the authorities for her benefit.[9]

In 1825 she left San Antonio for San Felipe de Austin, where she lived until 1832. Noah Smithwick remembered her as the leader of the local social set, although he admitted that at the time "there was a scarcity of ladies of any kind" in the town. Long moved again, this time to Brazoria, where she opened a boardinghouse. There she became acquainted with many of the up and coming settlers who had arrived after her, including future presidents of the republic Sam Houston and Mirabeau Bonaparte Lamar. As calls for revolution grew louder in the 1830s, Long opened her doors to insurrectionist meetings, revealing her own revolutionary feelings. As in Madam Candelaria's tale, there was no love lost between her and her husband's suspected murderers.[10]

Admittedly, filibustering expeditions such as James Long's were on their face extravagant failures. Nevertheless, enough patriotic enthusiasm for such projects carried on in those who remained behind, such as Jane Long. Freedom for Texas, specifically freedom from Mexico to embrace American republicanism, maintained primary importance in her thoughts and the thoughts of others. This fervor grew exponentially as more settlers came bearing similar beliefs. Once the process began, it could only conclude in conflict.

Much of this conflict resulted from cultural differences between the Anglos and their Mexican government. Understandably, Anglo settlers struggled to bridge the gap between Hispanic and U.S. politics. Scholars have already outlined in depth the passage of property laws and laws against slavery that alienated Texans and helped to spark the revolution. In addition, the Mexican brand of republicanism—one that wrestled with autocracy from time to time—often confounded Americans. Even before her arrival in Texas, Millie Gray noted what a "ruthless tyrant" Santa Anna was and criticized his unrepublican ways. Nevertheless, much of the lan-

guage settlers used to defend their actions extended beyond simple questions of law. As one visitor commented in 1834, it made sense that feelings of independence should arise in such an open land as Texas. But in
dealing with Mexicans, writers took their vitriol a step further, accentu-
ating cultural and racial differences to justify their insurrection.[11]

To begin their attack, Anglos questioned the viability of Mexican government. As late as 1850, the *American Whig Review* tried to fathom why
Hispanic republics seemed to fail consistently. To the editors, Mexico and
other Latin American states bore the oppressive burden of their Spanish
legacy. As had the colonial government, these new republics faced "the
corruptions of a powerful court and of an arrogant aristocracy." The
American Quarterly Review had noted the same thing while attempting
an analysis of Mexico after its independence from Spain. As much as they
wanted to, the writers could not praise the new nation, because they could
not yet tell if it would develop in the right direction. Instead, they noted
that Mexico's "degredation [*sic*]" under Spain had so stunted its growth
that, eighteen years after Father Hidalgo led his revolt against Spain, it
was "too soon to expect the moral and intellectual improvement we are
supposed to require." Had the Mexicans had English antecedents, matters might have been far different. As it was, most Americans believed
democracy an impossible goal for Latin Americans.[12]

Therein lay the problem. Texans were generally Anglo-Saxons, while
Mexicans came from a corrupt Hispanic heritage at best. Tyranny was
their birthright, determined Mary Helm. When they declared their independence in 1821, they were "a semi-barbarous people" with no understanding of republican government. Little wonder, then, that progress had
eluded them. Ultimately Helm traced their failures to race. "Mexicans are,
as it were, the debris of several inferior and degraded races," she pronounced. In Mexicans, "African and Indian crossed and mixed, and even
the old Spanish blood was mixed with the Moorish and demoralized by
a long course of indolence and political corruption." Race and corrupt
government ruined the rulers of Texas, setting them in complete contrast
to Anglo Americans.[13]

Most Texans agreed with Helm, going so far as to declare racial differences the primary reason behind independence. "*We* separate from a
people half of whom are the most depraved of the different races of Indians," declared the *Telegraph*. By absorbing inferior races, Mexicans had
become "a people whose inert and idle habits, general ignorance and

superstition, prevents the possibility of our mingling in the same har-
monious family; and if possible, could only be done by self-degredation
[*sic*]." Here the paper depicted Mexicans as lazy and self-absorbed, ut-
terly different from and inferior to their Anglo colonists. How could a
proper Anglo-Saxon subject himself and his family to a people who could
not even control themselves? The idea contradicted the premise of republican virtue, which required a self-possessed, mature government of
people of like mind. As far as the Texan revolutionaries were concerned,
Mexico was simply incapable of such a feat.[14]

Another difficulty the *Telegraph* identified was the "general ignorance
and superstition" of the Mexican people. Here the writers referred to
Roman Catholicism. The vast majority of Americans in the early nineteenth century were Protestant and distrusted "Popery" wherever they
found it. When Mexico allowed emigrants to settle Texas, they did so with
the insistence that all settlers profess Catholicism, a faith that many
Anglos considered heresy. To gain the desired land, emigrants frequently
"converted," although they privately remained true to their Protestant heritage. Helm mourned the loss of her beloved Protestantism but said she
nevertheless felt "free from the interference of Romanism, being hundreds
of miles from any Romish spies." That thought helped to sustain her until
after the revolution, when she embraced Episcopalianism instead.[15]

Still, Catholicism made a considerable impact on Texan society. In her
memoirs, Dilue Harris recalled one year when no one in the vicinity got
married, because no priest was available to perform the ceremony.
Couples who married outside the Church would have to remarry, and
no one saw the point of duplicating their efforts. This situation was more
a matter of inconvenience. Harris also remembered a Father Muldoon
who had the Protestant Sunday school in San Felipe de Austin shut down.
Unfortunately for Father Muldoon and other Catholics like him, what
benefited the Church ultimately hurt the state, as concerns of theocracy
filtered into the province.[16]

Others rejected Catholicism because they believed it could not survive
in a republican nation or vice versa. Catholics subjected themselves to
church hierarchy, which violated the spirit of republican government.
Catholicism could only bring repression and tyranny to its subjects, Texans believed. "Both cannot have at once the ascendancy," one writer noted.
Mexico became a case study for church-state difficulties. Clerical interests had already suffered because of Mexican republicanism. This pat-

tern appeared to have no stopping point in the 1830s. Either religion or politics would have to give, and observers could not tell which would emerge triumphant. Usually they feared the worst. As it was, religious enthusiasm still appeared to have the upper hand among Mexicans in 1837, one year after the revolution. Anti-clerical rhetoric from the government carried little weight in the rest of the nation, particularly in Texas, and made even less difference after independence. Nervous colonists guarded their liberties closely, uncertain of when they might be revoked.[17]

All of these factors figured into the rapidly deteriorating relations between Texas and Mexico. In fact, only a few years later, in the spring of 1832, tensions exploded into violence in the short-lived Anahuac War. Under Governor Manuel de Mier y Terán, Mexican forces filled the province, including one hundred men garrisoned at Velasco, at the mouth of the Brazos River, under Colonel Don Domingo de Ugartechea. The presence of increased forces angered some of the newer emigrants who had been unable to gain land and were feeling the strain of Mexican law. Soon John Austin, a member of the original Long expedition (and no relation to Stephen F. Austin), led his men across coastal Texas to retrieve ammunition and arms and strike out at the Mexicans. Eventually Austin's forces attempted to reach the town of Anahuac from Galveston Bay, but Velasco blocked their path. The Texans launched a two-pronged attack on June 26, with a schooner attacking from the river and riflemen assailing the garrison on land. Finally Ugartechea surrendered and fled south to Matamoros, ending the Anahuac War.[18]

Local women put their own patriotism to work when the war began. Ann Raney Coleman remembered hearing the cannon fire in Velasco from her house. She and other local women applied themselves as best they could to help their relatives and neighbors in their fight. Coleman and a friend spent two nights "moulding bullets and making bullet patches" for ammunition for the men. Later she heard that in nearby Brazoria, ladies occupied themselves in the same way. Women might not have been allowed to fight, but, given the situation, they made it easier to do so by their efforts. As their ancestors had done during an earlier revolution, they poured their patriotism into more acceptable ventures such as home manufacture of matériel. In that way, both the thirst for involvement and prescriptions for gender were satisfied.[19]

Coleman's term of service had not yet ended. Years later she wrote her memoirs to send to the Texas Legislature. She was running low on income and thought that, given her service at Velasco, she deserved a pension or some other form of compensation. Coleman had "performed services when a girl before my marriage . . . but because the men are dead who know I performed these services, I must go without reward," she explained. Her actions provided evidence of her dedication. Not only did she help to make the bullets the Texans used, Coleman rode halfway out to the battleground to leave the ammunition in a hollow tree for the soldiers to retrieve. Even though she did not venture farther, she was no less in harm's way. When she returned home, she was followed by "two Mexican spies and it was a race for life." She added, not without some pride, "Had I not the best horse they would have caught me." Prior to this, her pride in her accomplishment had served as reward enough; it was not until old age that she requested compensation for services rendered.[20]

Coleman and the women at Brazoria already felt patriotism for the Texan cause by 1832. From there, anti-Mexican sentiment continued to build until the crisis reached its peak in late 1835 and 1836. As before, women served the province in several ways. Even newspapers acknowledged the role women could play in fomenting revolution. At first, however, they presented this role as being more passive than active. Editors used women and children to provide a rationalization for war. Texas had to be separate for their sakes, the *Telegraph and Texas Register* said. Otherwise their land would be overrun with dark forces that would destroy their freedom and livelihood. "Figure to yourselves, my countrymen, the horrors and misery that will be entailed on you, should the ruffians once obtain foothold on our soil!" the writer declared. "Your beloved wives, your mothers, your daughters, sisters, and helpless innocent children, given up to the dire pollution, and massacre of a horde of barbarians!!" Mexico represented every sort of evil Texans despised; in contrast, women and "helpless innocent children" displayed all that was good in the world. To be true men, settlers had to take up arms against the oncoming threat and defend the life they had established in Texas.[21]

This perspective makes it appear that the *Telegraph* upheld women as a symbol of threatened liberty, nothing more. Too gentle to fight for themselves, ladies required careful protection. Such rhetoric paralleled the ideal of true womanhood. But the paper—and the ideal—did not stop there. If women symbolized purity and freedom, they also set a standard for action that their men would do well to follow. Some Texans, said the *Telegraph,* had so far refused to defend their families. To shame such backward men, the newspaper set up women as the epitome of dedication during the revolution as well. "Even the women are nobly contributing all the services in their power in defence of our country." Many examples existed. One old woman provided invaluable intelligence for the Texan cause. Others donated clothes "and other articles of equipment for those going to the field." If ladies gave all they had within their power for the cause, implied the *Telegraph*, what sort of men would shirk their responsibilities for their country? Dedicated women and backward men contrasted one another starkly, revealing what true patriotism entailed.[22]

The Texas Revolution elicited a flurry of similar support from the United States. Typically women offered their sewing for the cause, sending clothes and other items. Mary Austin Holley solicited support to aid the cause. She wrote a letter to the *Lexington Intelligencer* in Kentucky, asking all women to help her and Texas in their fight. Women did not participate in battle, but they could still sew for the "holy cause of Texas," providing uniforms for the threadbare armies. Another woman, Joanna Elizabeth Troutman of Georgia, made a more renowned contribution. A group of men from that state had volunteered to fight for Texas in 1835. Wanting to help, Troutman created a flag for the Georgia volunteers. A lone blue star sat proudly in the center of a white field, with the words *Ubi libertas habitat, ibi nostra patria est* (Where liberty lives, there is our fatherland) emblazoned across the bottom. Soldiers in Texas drew encouragement from her work. "Your flag shall yet wave over fields of victory in defiance of Despotism," Lieutenant Hugh McLeod wrote her. The Lone Star flag, as it became known, later flew in Velasco and eventually became the first flag of the republic. Although Troutman never saw Texas, her efforts demonstrated women's deep feelings for revolutionary efforts.[23]

Jane Cazneau was equally unwilling to sit on the sidelines. In 1835 she owned one thousand acres in Texas, part of the original Austin's Colony. Land rich but money poor, Cazneau decided to sell what she could to contribute to the Texan cause. "As a female," she wrote, "I cannot bear arms for my adopted country, but if the interest I possess in her soil, will be a guarantee for any money, I will with joy contribute my mite to purchase arms for her brave defenders." In lieu of fighting herself, Cazneau easily decided which direction to go. Ultimately she believed it to be the duty of all those who lived in Texas to support its cause. "Every Texonian will be called on to yield his utmost assistance to the cause of freedom and justice," she insisted. And she was not alone. Cazneau later recalled "a glow of pride" when she heard "of the exertions made by her citizens here, to supply her with men and arms."[24]

This evidence reveals the level of dedication women in Texas had to preserve their interests. It was not enough to sit idly by and care for one's own family alone; the welfare of the country required the attention of all its inhabitants. Mary Helm noted this peculiarity of the period. "The females were in sympathy with all state affairs," she wrote. Politics played a larger role in a woman's life than it would later. Helm believed this to be the case because life in the colony was difficult. "They had no time or opportunity to think or care for the last fashions or discuss the merits of the latest improvements in cooking," she stated simply. Instead, "common and necessary sense was the everyday business of the day." Clearly, although government was presumably within the male sphere of influence, affairs of state could not help but affect women's lives. Then women responded from within their prescribed roles to effect change.[25]

Of course, interest did not always translate into service directly related to the war. Life went on, and, with the men away fighting, women shouldered the daily chores for the entire family. Harris remembered that in the fall of 1835 "every man and boy that had a gun and horse went to the army, and the women and children were left to finish picking the cotton." Women remained behind to care for household duties, but this was as important a task as the one their husbands, fathers, and brothers had undertaken. Texans waged a war for independence to maintain their way of life; if anyone or anything disrupted that, the result would be no different than losing the battle.[26]

Given the situation, women understandably allowed their husbands to go and fight. Some women were more willing than others. Harriet Ames followed her first husband to Brazoria to find that, while he awaited her arrival, he had gambled away everything they owned. Infuriated, Ames insisted that he go to town and buy food for her and their children. The husband later returned with nothing; he had taken the money she had given him and bought "some clothes to go to the war in; he said that everybody was volunteering to go and that he did not want to be called a coward." Ames let him go freely, sending him off with a prayer "that the first bullet that is fired will pierce your heart." The revolution proved beneficial to Ames in two ways; not only would it provide freedom for her family, but for herself as well.[27]

While for the most part women supported the revolution on the periphery, others found themselves face to face with conflict, side by side with men. The story of Madam Candelaria provides one possible example. According to her tale, Mexican soldiers did not preserve her from injury while she defended Bowie. A better-known story also emerged from the siege of the Alamo, and, unlike the San Antonio innkeeper, her story was well documented by contemporary sources. Susannah Dickinson became the most famous of the survivors of the massacre, providing grim notoriety for her and her daughter for years to come. Dickinson and her family had lived in Texas since, at the latest, 1831. Her husband, Almeron, took her and their daughter Angelina into the Alamo when he learned of the attack on San Antonio and remained there until his death.

Details beyond this are sketchy. Dickinson told at least two versions of the story afterward. In one, Dickinson watched her husband die along with the others; later she described the Mexican soldiers throwing the body of Bowie in the air from their bayonets. In comparison, in an 1876 interview, she said that she hid in a back room and never emerged until the massacre had largely ended, seeing only one person killed. According to *Niles' Weekly Register,* Dickinson "begged to share the honorable fate of her husband." General Santa Anna refused, stating that he was not "warring against women." He released her to a servant who took her as far as Washington-on-the-Brazos. Other sources say that General Juan N. Almonte led her and her baby out of the Alamo. Regardless of the fuzziness of details, Texans such as Noah Smithwick remembered Dickinson and Angelina as the "sole American survivors" of the Alamo.[28]

The story of Susannah Dickinson was tragic but fueled the fire of the Texan cause. First, Dickinson represented the severity of the situation for citizens of the rebellious province. While newspaper editors could only hint at the potential dangers for men and their families, Dickinson and her infant demonstrated in the flesh what could happen. They provided the patriotic motivation to defend Texas. She also used and exacerbated racial tension with her story. She asserted that Juana Navarro Alsbury, wife of a prominent doctor, and her sister-in-law were also in the fort and that they gave the Mexicans vital information in the last days of the siege. Alsbury later requested aid from the Texas Legislature, not mentioning any possible dealings with the enemy, instead outlining how she nursed and cared for the sick in the Alamo. Still, Alsbury and other Hispanic witnesses at the Alamo remained in the background as Dickinson's story spread across the Anglo countryside. It was too difficult for white Texans to sympathize with a Juana Navarro or an Ana Esparza.[29]

Dickinson's ordeal elicited sympathy across the United States, but in the aftermath of the Alamo, Texans were more concerned with their own fates. Santa Anna's victory set off a panic across Texas as the Mexican army moved east. Fearing what might happen if they fell into Mexican hands, settlers took their families and what belongings they could and fled the region in a pell-mell race for safety later known as the Runaway Scrape. Lucinda Gorham recalled the desperation of the times years later. "The fall of the Alamo was a great shock to all of us," she said. "We knew there was nothing for us to do but run." Mary Rabb got word of the approaching army from her brother-in-law, who served with the Texan forces. "Uncle Tommy would keep telling old Sam Houston that he had better fight the Mexicans and not let them invade," she later recalled. Tommy's wife was one of many who did not survive the flight. "There were many births and deths [sic] on that road while we was running from the mexicans [sic]," Rabb said. Harris walked away from her home as she and her sister wept for the martyred Colonel Travis and prepared for the days to come.[30]

Ann Coleman's husband kept her and their young son on the farm until he knew for certain the Mexican army had crossed the Brazos. Only then did he allow his panicked spouse to pack up their belongings and their child and leave. The family traveled as far as Louisiana, at which point Coleman's husband announced that he would never live in Texas again. He refused to live in such a lawless land, he declared, where soldiers could force such an evacuation and others could do nothing about it. Coleman tried to dissuade him but was unable. It was only in 1855, after Coleman divorced her second husband (the first had died years earlier), that she returned to Matagorda. For Coleman, evacuation was only temporary; she saw no need to abandon her adopted home because of war. To surrender land to the enemy was counterproductive, violating the unspoken tenets of manifest destiny.[31]

That Coleman's husband remained at home to dictate the family's actions is surprising. Women organized much of the escape. Mary Helm recalled black men being their protectors in lieu of absent husbands, fathers, or brothers, while Dilue Harris recalled their men rejoining them at the Trinity River. Meanwhile, women helped dictate the actions of those in flight. Gorham's group paused to vote on whether or not to continue after Comanches stole their horses along the way. "The women voted too," she added, a striking comment in an era before women's suffrage had even become an issue. Still, the Runaway Scrape was a domestic matter—the survival of home and family—so it was not a stretch to allow women to participate in decision making, especially with the heads of household away at war.[32]

Almost all families lost something in the Runaway Scrape. Rosa Kleberg remembered returning to her farm to find everything that they had abandoned destroyed. Even the books they had buried for safekeeping had been dug up and burned. "We had to begin anew, and with less than we had when we started," she said. Others were more fortunate. Caroline von Hinueber recalled that the Ernst homestead remained untouched throughout the revolution. The Mexican forces had left it alone, she said, because the Ernsts had placed large crosses in their garden. The Ernst family was Catholic; that fact alone appears to have saved their home and their belongings. But the loss rankled women like Helm. It would not have been necessary to flee, she complained, had the Mexican army been civilized.[33]

Panic held the countryside until the revolution ended at the battle of San Jacinto on April 21. Once hostilities had ended, women and men celebrated the victory together. Some did this more literally than others. Leo Roark took Harris to the San Jacinto battlefield only days after the battle had ended. Santa Anna and other Mexican prisoners of war were still on the site when she toured it. Harris was only days shy of her eleventh birthday at the time, yet Roark saw nothing wrong with allowing the child to see dead soldiers not yet removed from the scene. Considering all she and her family and friends had endured, it probably seemed sensible to allow her the chance to partake in the conclusion as well. Age meant little in this case; what mattered was the independence of Texas.[34]

But Harris could not claim to be the first woman on the field after the battle. Sophia Sutton Porter declared that honor for herself. Porter's past is a mosaic of stories, some of which undoubtedly are true. Like other women, she fled during the Runaway Scrape, but she apparently remained in Texas instead of heading to Louisiana as so many had. Her exploits at San Jacinto, on the other hand, remain open to debate. Porter said that she helped nurse hero Sam Houston back to health on the battlefield. This tale is shaky due to lack of witnesses; it adds some credence that Porter gained renown during the Civil War as the "Confederate Paul Revere," placing herself in harm's way for a cause she deemed worthy, but ultimately no one can prove or deny her account.[35]

Regardless of the veracity of Porter's account, her supposed foray into nursing would have allowed her to enter the masculine arena of war in a decidedly feminine way. Care for the sick or injured required both a knowledge of basic medicine—which often appeared in contemporary recipe books—and a tender heart. The true woman had both. A woman could move freely around a battlefield with mercy as her aim. One poem, "The Poor Soldier," noted the "magic power" women wielded over their patients:

> *She draws from sorrow's breast the dart,*
> *And heals the anguished wound.*

For the poet, physical care coincided with attention to emotional pain. After Texas' violent separation from Mexico and the terror that followed, women would prove necessary to recognize the new nation's accomplishments even while mending its wounds.[36]

Other women commemorated victory in more traditional ways. Eva Catherine Sterne opened her home to the public on San Jacinto Day for a banquet and ball. At this point, balls provided a way for both men and women to celebrate together without too much concern for propriety. (There was no alcohol present, sparing the ladies any untoward behavior.) Kleberg enjoyed a ball as well in 1838, again to commemorate the anniversary of San Jacinto. But Jane Long outdid them all, hosting a party in October, 1836, on the anniversary of the Texans' victory at Concepción. She invited veterans of the battle to attend, along with the president of the new republic, Sam Houston. Her ball merited two notices in the *Telegraph and Texas Register*.[37]

Mary Love commemorated the end of the war in a more somber fashion as she remembered those who had died for the cause. As Long had done for her husband's expedition years before, Love sewed a flag for the veterans with the motto "THE HERO OF SAN JACINTO" and presented it in a public assembly. A Captain Burrough received the flag and the address that accompanied it with warm appreciation for what Love and other women had accomplished during the course of the revolution. To Burrough, the flag served as proof "of the chivalry of the American ladies, that spirit which shone so brightly in the dark and trying hour of the revolution."[38]

The events of 1835 and 1836 lingered long in the collective memory of the Texans. At the beginning of the U.S.-Mexican War, Holley wrote a poem published in the *Telegraph* lauding Texas for its tenacity against injustice and for the cause of American republicanism:

> *We are thy children; doubt it not—*
> *We've proved our birth in many a spot,*
> *Where cannon-thunder pealed—*
> *'Twas Saxon heart that dared the fight,*
> *'Twas blood of yours that gave us might*
> *Upon Jacinto's field.*

The "Saxon heart" and blood that aided in the revolution struck a clear blow for manifest destiny. The Texans had rescued the land from tyrannical forces, making it more available to those who pursued liberty across the continent. Women such as Holley considered land, liberty, and citizenship inseparable.[39]

As women continued to hail the victories, they also remembered their own contributions and their roles in Texan independence. At the same time, they tended to forget the roles played by non-Anglo participants. While the enemy was clearly Hispanic, many allies were as well, a fact that frequently faded in the light of Anglo accomplishment. More than four thousand Mexicans lived in Texas by 1836, although Anglos outnumbered them ten to one, overshadowing their presence in the province. Hispanics were as concerned with the independence of their land as Anglos and sacrificed as much. Ana Salazar de Esparza and her husband Gregorio offer two examples of many. Gregorio fought alongside more familiar men such as Travis and Crockett at the Alamo and died with them. The revolution was not merely a race war, pitting Anglos against Mexicans; the truth proved far more complicated.[40]

There are few, if any, written sources from Hispanic women in this time period. Mexican women rarely wrote diaries or could even read. Such women contributed within the sphere of the home as "mothers and supplementers of family sustenance." One visitor noted such submissive behavior in the Mexican wife of an Anglo man. Not feeling equal to eating dinner with him at the same table, she ate with her fellow Hispanic "domestics," squatting on the floor in the kitchen for her meal after her husband had completed his dinner. None of this is to say that

Hispanic women had no other roles; at times, they substituted for their husbands when they were away. They were also allowed to retain their own property after marriage, which differed from Anglo law. More often than not, however, they remained in the background of Hispanic society.[41]

Still, Tejanas made their presence known during the revolution. Salazar de Esparza was in the Alamo when Mexican forces penetrated its defenses. She watched as soldiers killed her husband and almost two hundred others. Jim Bowie was married to a Mexican woman, Ursula Veramendi. Guadalupe Ruíz Durán was the wife of patriot "Deaf" Smith. She endured the strain of the Runaway Scrape as did the other settlers; in fact, were it not for the kindness of her neighbors, Ruíz Durán could not have escaped. As the flow of panicked Texans surged around her, she remained in a cart with her two young twins at her side, unable to get out and push. Finally some passersby helped to pull the cart out of harm's way.[42]

Although race became a greater issue between Texans and Mexicans at this point in Texas history, prior to this Anglos and Hispanics endured little conflict. This was primarily due to lack of contact. About 2,500 Tejanos lived in the province by 1821, and their numbers did not increase as drastically as those of the Anglos; by 1836, whites outnumbered Hispanics by nearly 10 to 1. The case of Bowie and Veramendi demonstrates that the marriage of Anglo men to Mexican women was not unusual in this period. Noah Smithwick observed without further comment that Captain Philip Dimmit had a Mexican wife. Prior to the Civil War, there were far fewer women from the United States for men to marry. More importantly, according to historian Jane Dysart, many well-to-do Hispanic families married their daughters to Anglo men with land or influence in the hopes of maintaining their social positions. Once the couple married, they lived and moved about in Anglo culture. Their children would not be considered Mexican, but Anglo, as the wife helped to Americanize her sons and daughters. For the time being, race paled in comparison to the call of nationhood; citizens were Texans, not Mexican or American. The struggle for independence created a nationalism that often overcame questions of ethnicity.[43]

After the revolution, in the early days of the Texas Republic, race created greater problems within the new nation as Texans and Tejanos were thrown together, in a sense for the first time. The process of Americanization restricted the amount of Hispanic culture that children of mixed-race marriage received. Instead, they received Anglo names and education at American schools, where they were taught an Anglo American perspective. Hispanics who did not assimilate became separate from "mainstream" Texas culture and were subject to harassment. Such hostility increased as more Americans emigrated to the republic. Soon Mexican Americans found themselves in an inferior position socially, and their part in the Texas Revolution disappeared behind the gilded tapestry of Anglo accomplishment. Manifest destiny had once more allowed for the conquest of territory for the Anglo American worldview.[44]

American emigrants paid little attention to the cultural havoc they had wreaked. They knew that Indians were losing ground, but they attributed their demise to racial or cultural weakness. Whites viewed Hispanics in a similar fashion. Natives' failure "was because civilization had more of the principles of endurance and progress than barbarism," said the *Democratic Review*, "because Christianity was superior to paganism; industry to idleness; agriculture to hunting; letters to hieroglyphics; truth to error." The triumph of civilization took precedence over the "hord [*sic*] of barbarians" that had once ruled the land. Any threat from an inferior force had been eliminated, at least for the time being. The Texas Revolution had demonstrated the superiority of Anglo-Saxonism over other races as well as reinforcing the place of American republicanism in Texas and—they hoped—elsewhere. Their proof was self-evident: the Lone Star Republic had emerged where before there had been a subservient Mexican province. Settlers had improved the land, held back the menacing Indian savages, and fought off the tyrant's armies. A new Texas awaited them as their reward. What other evidence did they need?[45]

Julia Sinks offered some of her own in her memoir, *Chronicles of Fayette*. Not only had the revolution proved the ability and tenacity of Anglo men, but it also put women in their proper place in society as a result. "Mingled with that seemingly rough hardihood that was required for a handful of men to stand firm amid Mexican change of government," she wrote, "there might be found that feeling that honors the highest state of social refinement,—a universal respect for females." All this bloodshed had a purpose, Sinks maintained. In chivalric form, the warriors of Texas had placed women on a pedestal, lauding them as the inspiration for all their actions. This admiration of women proved Texas both civilized and ready to evolve beyond its prior status.[46]

As Texans wound down from their revolutionary fervor, they returned to their hopes of civilizing the republic. Their early steps were admirable, but they were not enough. Sinks's words, written decades after the revolution, reflect the shift from a wartime to a peacetime understanding of expansion. In lieu of force, Texans relied on subtler means of advancement, and in this war against perceived barbarism, women held the front lines.

4

Fighting
for the Cause of
Civilization

The excitement brewing since the Texas Revolution still stirred the hearts and minds of Texans when an unusual "memoir" of the war appeared in 1843. Entitled *The Female Warrior,* it purported to tell the thrilling and sordid adventures of Leonora Siddons, a young woman who joined the Texan army dressed as a man after her father died. The plan only made sense to Siddons, who believed fervently that every citizen had a duty to defend his—or her—country to "erect the noble standard of liberty, from which the banner of freedom triumphantly may wave o'er all the land." Assuming that no one suspected—although she gleefully reported "some very flattering compliments relative to my beauty"—Siddons enlisted with no difficulties.[1]

The story would be difficult enough to believe for a nineteenth-century reader to this point, but Siddons continued even deeper into implausibility. She and her cohort met the enemy on the plains outside San Antonio in a gallant fight. Siddons managed to shoot one Mexican soldier through the heart before she was wounded and left for dead on the field. Later that night, as she tried to escape, she was captured and taken to Santa

Anna himself. The "bloodthirsty" general sentenced her to 150 lashes, which his henchmen would gladly have inflicted, had they not removed her shirt and discovered her secret. According to Siddons, Santa Anna refused to whip a woman, but he was crude enough to offer her freedom for sexual favors. Fortunately Siddons did not elaborate much beyond this point. Finding a saw and file cleverly hidden in her jail cell, she escaped to the United States to relate her thrilling tale of adventure.[2]

Siddons's account flirted heavily with reality, but its numerous errors declared its origins in fantasy. According to her book, she and her father emigrated to Texas after "the great money pressure of '37" (the revolution took place in 1836), and apparently the fight for the Alamo took place on an open plain in the forested Hill Country. Contemporary critics took little time to fall upon the work as a masterpiece of nonsense. "Judging from the portions of the narrative that we have seen, she ought to have returned to her friends and regaled them with her narrative on the first day of April," chided the *Telegraph and Texas Register*. "For it seems more like an 'April fool story' than any other tale that we have seen for a long time." In fact, contemporaries did not even have enough resources to determine whether or not Siddons was actually a woman. The entire story remained suspect.[3]

The *Telegraph* went further, using *The Female Warrior* to express its disgust with the narrative's unfeminine premise. "If the story were true, a *lady* should have too much regard for the dignity of her sex to publish it," it declared. The gruesome details of Siddons's attacks on Mexican soldiers or, even worse, Santa Anna's attempted solicitations were unbecoming any female author. Such myths did not deserve publication in any medium with a mixed audience: "A just sense of delicacy would prevent any *lady* from reading it when published." The entire work was an embarrassment not just in style and syntax, but in content that violated acceptable moral and social standards.[4]

The Female Warrior used the Texas Revolution for its stage at almost the wrong time. As critical as the fight had been for the cause of civilization and manifest destiny, the set was already changing to new scenery as war gave way to less pressing matters. The army had defended their homes; now the call went out to build stronger homes upon a surer foundation. The Lone Star Republic had emerged from the battle, carrying with it the hint of future glory. Texas needed time to allow the seeds of manifest destiny to germinate and expand. Tawdry tales meant little, whereas the actual goals of civilization—and the roles of women within them—meant everything. During the revolution, masculine virtues such as bravery and fortitude received the most emphasis. Their job having been completed, women and their more "feminine" virtues took a larger role in reshaping society.[5]

Women had already contributed substantially through their efforts during the revolutionary period. But as Texans of both sexes tried to focus on stability in their new republic, women shifted their efforts in a different direction. These tactics stretched back to the late eighteenth century to the concept of republican motherhood and its nineteenth-century heir, the cult of true womanhood. These philosophies had served well in the days of the early American republic; they did the same in Texas. Relying upon familiar patterns of domesticity and influence, Texas women worked to create a more civilized nation.

Their work stemmed in two directions. First, women fulfilled the traditional call to transform society through their duties at home toward their husbands and children. However, although their influence on their families appeared limited to their immediate audience, it proved to be far-reaching. As feminine influence grew, it expanded into benevolent societies and in other, more public, directions. Both branches of domesticity assisted in spreading the benefits of civilization across the country and provided a stronger foundation from which to work in the future. Simultaneously, women took part in public ceremonies and rituals, both as observers and participants. Female involvement helped to bolster the growing nationalism of the young republic. Republicanism had social ramifications as well as political; by promoting the former, women also contributed to the latter.

According to scholars like Barbara Welter, the cult of true womanhood provided at least a semblance of stability in a drastically changing world. By adhering to traditional virtues such as piety, purity, submissiveness, and domesticity, women contributed to the smooth flow of society and supported men's activities. Welter determined that the separation of spheres prevented women from becoming fully involved in American life. The cult of true womanhood restrained them from masculine activities, which at the time included politics and full participation in the democratic process. Only by going outside the home could women find more satisfaction. Other historians disagree with this concept. Rather than weakening women by their separation from men, domesticity allowed women to consolidate their energies in homosocial groups and exercise an even greater influence than they would have otherwise. By banding together within their separate spheres women became not oppressed but dignified, and they worked jointly to effect change in their society.[6]

The moral implications of true womanhood also challenged notions of female inferiority and oppression. Adherents to the cult of domesticity considered women morally superior to men. Their presence in the home both protected them from the defiling ways of the marketplace and allowed them an arena in which to shed a purifying light. "Woman's mission, then, is to cooperate with the Redeemer of men, in bringing back from its revolt, the same world which was lost by another species of cooperation on the part of Eve," wrote William Alcott in 1850. Although Eve had tarnished the earth first, women had the opportunity to remedy the situation she had created through their Christian actions. Anything women accomplished with this in mind would benefit humanity for eternity. In *A Treatise on Domestic Economy,* Catharine Beecher agreed that women's role was not simply to transform society, but to be like Christ, rescuing the world from its dissipation. Within these boundaries, women had an "acknowledged empire" the likes of which man could never know, and well-applied female piety would win all concerned a crown of life in the future.[7]

The home remained the best location for women to exercise their purity and moral superiority. It provided them an unstained platform that laid out plainly feminine responsibilities. Women excelled in areas like "the nursery and the pantry," the *Southern Quarterly Review* opined; "the proper place for a woman is at home." While such phrases might seem demeaning at first glance, later issues insisted that domesticity remained a position of honor. After all, from home women could nurture and educate their children to become mature, moral adults. From there, women could extend their influence throughout the world. "You may hence see that you have power," declared Alcott, "that you do, as a matter of fact, rule the world." Poet Alexander H. Everett added a spiritual dimension to women's roles as he lauded their ability to ease the tormented minds of men in "the temple of Home," which represented a welcome refuge after a long day waging war in the marketplace. For many, women held positions of power as queens of America and, simultaneously, its priestesses.[8]

Such assertions did not seem overstated at the time. Homes contained children, and children held in their hands the destiny of the nation. "To aid in educating a child," insisted popular author and poet Lydia Sigourney, "is one of the most commendable and profitable designs." Catharine Beecher expressed this concept more prosaically: "The mother writes the character of the future man; the sister bends the fibres that hereafter are the forest tree; the wife sways the heart, whose energies may turn for good or for evil the destinies of a nation." From this vantage point, remaining at home with the children became a patriotic as well as a moral issue. Other writers discussed the importance of mothers not only teaching basic literacy, but training their own daughters "to habits of domestic industry" while teaching their sons the habits of republican virtue. One generation passed down such valuable lessons to the next, spreading the gospel of domesticity and extending the rule of domesticity for a few more years. In a sense, the future rested on the able shoulders of the true woman.[9]

Clearly, prescriptive literature stood on the side of the cult of domesticity. Yet how often did Texas women adhere to such rules and principles? As historian Elizabeth Jameson notes, circumstances differed greatly in the West from mainstream American culture. According to Jameson, such works as those mentioned above ignore differences in class and ethnicity, lumping all western women together without concern for social differences. What about those who were not writing at the time? Those who could not? Not everyone "fit the prescriptions of true womanhood," she declares. Jameson also accurately points out that what Americans wrote does not necessarily reflect what they did.[10]

Jameson's point is that the picture of western women as meek civilizers is a partial one at best. Eastern niceties meant little when leaving behind family or struggling to make a living in the wilderness. Nevertheless, in stressing the rugged aspects of women's lives, the author slights those women who did trust in the cult of true womanhood and practiced its tenets actively. Even if they did not use the standard terminology, Texans recognized the call of domesticity on their lives. Mary Helm staunchly defended separate spheres in her book, although she utilized into three branches instead of two. "God has given us three institutions: The Family; the Church; the State," she declared. "The duties of each harmonize and commend themselves to our instincts and our reason." Helm's three arenas remained distinctly separate, but they worked together for the good of society. Women clearly fell under the umbrella of Family and perhaps Church, to a lesser extent; that will be discussed below. But Helm never complained about the separation of women's activities from those of men.[11]

Admittedly, most diaries and letters offer little hypothetical discussion of true womanhood. Scholars can glean more information from Texans' actions than their words. It would be unfair to consider women's home lives as evidence of their faith in domesticity, as society expected all women to raise children and care for their families. However, some avenues existed to measure feminine response. This evidence comes from activities outside the home. Belief in domesticity actually prompted more public involvement than one might expect. The difference between expectations and practice came from an incomplete understanding of the ramifications of true womanhood. The most obvious departure from the "norm" resulted from the relationship between the cult of true womanhood and religion. Women were morally superior to men—focusing primarily on their homes allowed them to remain so. They therefore had a spiritual obligation to their families and, less directly, to society. Soon the link between home and church became clear, and women ventured into the life of public faith.[12]

Sometimes women's church activities remained closer to the sanctuary walls, focusing on internal improvements. Such was the case for the ladies of the Episcopal Church in Houston. In May, 1845, they planned a "ladies' fair" to raise money for their congregation. They sold "useful and fancy articles" to other women, keeping their benevolent interests within reach while extending their influence beyond their own homes. Women both organized and frequented such fairs, maintaining a semblance of separate identity and dignity. Nevertheless, the community understood their presence and the benefits of their actions.[13]

Still other women worked to raise money not just for benevolent ministries of their churches, but to have a church at all. The Austin Female Benevolent Society formed in the 1840s with a goal to construct church buildings for the young town. Their activities garnered more than $1,200 in donations in Texas alone, but their work extended to the United States as well. In February, 1842, James Schott of Philadelphia sent a letter to Hannah Burnet, president of the benevolent society and wife of David G. Burnet—the future governor—and other society members, thanking them for their tireless efforts. Similarly, Margaret Houston, Texas first lady;

her mother, Nancy Lea; and her sister, Antoinette Bledsoe, became three of the seven founders of the Concord Baptist Church in Washington-on-the-Brazos. Then, after Houston moved to Huntsville, her desire for a church continued. When one minister caused dissension between denominations in town, she offered her own home as a more peaceable place for meetings. In all these situations, women saw a need they could satisfy without violating standards and stepped forward to act. Apparently they did not feel encumbered by any potential restraints true womanhood might have presented, nor did they deny its presence—or its uses. Perhaps their femininity presented a persuasive argument for donations to their cause rather than a hindrance.[14]

The Austin Female Benevolent Society, as well as Houston and her family, provide useful examples of women's potential. Yet their joined efforts paled in comparison to that of one woman, Helen Chapman, who arrived in Texas in January, 1848. Chapman had married a soldier who fought in the Mexican War and was transferred to Fort Brown on the U.S.-Mexican border. She was from Massachusetts, and her experiences in the new state at times overwhelmed her. Above all, she expressed surprise that so few churches existed in the area around the Rio Grande. She once found herself in conversation with Isaac Bigelow, chief justice for the county. He pointed out the new courthouse with its refined and "handsome" construction. Chapman agreed readily, then asked, "But where are you going to get a handsome Protestant Church, Judge? You know a city can't pretend to much respectability until it has schools and churches." She pressed the justice until he acquiesced and agreed to support her efforts to build a "respectable" town, complete with churches for its citizens.[15]

Chapman's movement was soon underway. Churches and schools would provide not only a semblance of civilization and decency but would help to rescue the town from its vices. "My dear Mother, I have given up my dreaming and become a more practical woman," she wrote excitedly. She had decided to take her opportunities where she could find them, planning to use "my energies, my position, and my influence in any cause where they may be made availing." Grandiose schemes meant little to Chapman in a region barely civilized enough to be livable. Instead, the simple task of establishing a few churches and schools could only benefit the region "not because it is right, but because they have such things at home and because they help to make a country respectable and prosperous." (Remember that, for Chapman, "home" meant New England.) This army wife desired to create a more American land out of Texas, to spread American civilization to the barbarous frontier. Paralleling those settlers who went before her, she desired to build a garden oasis in the desert. Temporary discomfort did not discourage her. "Our destiny is the frontier and I am not sorry for there we are most needed," she said.[16]

Her mission continued as she accosted friends and even strangers with her plans to establish familiar institutions. "I catch people on highways and byways and lost no opportunity of saying church and schools," she announced. She left the reaction of her unsuspecting audience up to her readers' imaginations. By this point, in fact, she had added the development of a local Sunday school to the list, crusading to improve not only the landscape but also the people within it. Chapman achieved one of her goals in 1849 when she established Brownsville's first Sunday school. It had seventy students, half of whom were Mexican and spoke little English, but for her it represented a triumph for the cause of civilization and, to a lesser extent, the cause of women. "The moral influence of women cannot be overrated," she determined.[17]

Chapman's words accentuate a crucial aspect of her work and the goals of other benevolent societies. It was not enough to present a landmark for civilization. Women desired to spread a missionary influence beyond churches and across the countryside. The gospel of civilization needed evangelists, and women lined up eagerly to participate. Margaret Houston began her work at home, with a husband more interested in politics than morality. Not only did she eventually persuade Sam to attend church, but also to be baptized by 1854. The Houston Ladies' Depository helped to spread the news to the public at large. As did the earlier ladies' fairs, the store offered for sale "fancy articles," except this time the profits went to orphans' asylums and mission work. "Such an establishment is well deserving of public patronage," declared the *Telegraph*, "to relieve the sufferings and wants of the destitute widow and orphan or to rescue some benighted heathen from the thraldom of Paganism." Whether this mission took place overseas or among regional savages or even nearby towns remained unsaid. The missionary impulse changed little whether it affected the Far East or far western Texas. The result would ultimately be the same. As Julie Roy Jeffrey notes in *Frontier Women*, "With growth came the opportunity to carry out the civilizing mission implicit in the concept of domesticity." Where that civilization occurred meant less than that it occurred at all.[18]

Church work was only part of women's benevolence. As did men, early-nineteenth-century women became caught up in the tempest of reform sweeping the continent. Dedication to religious principles carried over into the secular arena as reformers strove to improve their surroundings however they could. Whether in new standards for prisons, asylums, or even personal hygiene, reformers hoped to create a better world in which to live. The movement borrowed language from religion along with a millenarian hope to bring about an earthly paradise. In part, this spiritual veneer across the face of reform gave women their opportunity to act within its circle.[19]

Of all reform movements of the period, the most notable (aside from abolitionism, which deserves more space in a later chapter) involved the question of temperance. Prior to the nineteenth century, alcohol consumption merited little discussion. With market capitalism, consumption patterns shifted until Americans were drinking more than ever. Some scholars have estimated that, per capita, Americans drank more than five gallons of distilled spirits each year. The rapid changes that Americans endured contributed substantially to this jump; many citizens had difficulty handling their new life. Simultaneously, the nation went through the evangelical upheavals of the second Great Awakening, in which those who had not fled to drink fled to the church pew instead. Borrowing from revivalists and their methods, the new teetotalers launched their own campaign against sin, specifically drunkenness.[20]

This dedication to stamping out liquid vice became known as the temperance movement, although most advocates preferred to abstain completely. Temperance societies sprang up across the nation, offering support for penitent drunks. One such group was the Sons of Temperance, organized in 1842 as an alternative to the more renowned and expansive Washingtonian movement. In addition to club-like camaraderie, the Sons of Temperance added ritual to help the reformed along their way (that is, until one outside observer noted similarities between their rites and those of the Masons). Women served as the majority of temperance advocates, involving themselves heavily in temperance groups such as the Daughters of Temperance, which had almost thirty thousand members by 1850. Millie Gray attempted to form her own society to wage war herself.[21]

That women took such a commanding role presented no surprise to contemporaries. Drunkenness was not just a solitary social evil, but one that lashed out at everyone in its path. Women frequently became its victims without tasting a drop. The poem "The Lament of the Widowed Inebriate" told the sad tale of a drunk who regretted his mistakes after they killed his wife. A few years later T. S. Arthur helped promulgate this idea in his bestseller, *Ten Nights in a Bar-Room* (1852), which followed the stories of several barflies as they staggered collectively down the road to ruin. Several female characters served as Arthur's collateral damage, from a doomed daughter to a loving but haggard wife and a beleaguered mother, searching the local taverns every night for her lost son. Innocent bystanders served well as propaganda for the cause of temperance; women were more aesthetically pleasing and therefore served even better. Wives, mothers, and daughters all struggled against the demon rum. In a striking move of solidarity, other women took up their burden as well and crusaded for the elimination of this threat to home and family.[22]

Texas was not immune from the dangers of alcohol. Chapman recoiled in disgust as she watched soldier and civilian alike indulge. Drinking shops and gambling tables—and the two necessarily went together—filled the town and brought its citizens to ruin. "Billiard tables, eating and drinking make up the lives of a great many," she noted. Had there been any churches, she said, "I believe they would consider it as a necessarily preliminary to invite a friend to take a drink before going to or upon departing." To her mind, the evils of Texas paralleled those of California, except "on a smaller scale." Yet Chapman was uncertain what to do about it. Women carried a strong moral influence, but how that would help she did not know. "The best wife cannot keep her husband from intemperance," she exclaimed, "but if she be a woman of commanding and elevated character, she can prevent her parlor from being turned into a barroom as is too often the case." Whereas she moved boldly into the construction business, lobbying for churches and schools to decorate Brownsville, she remained oddly timid insofar as individual vice went.[23]

Other women knew exactly what to do. Margaret Houston believed that the condition of her husband's soul lay in her hands. It was no small secret that the president had a liking for alcohol; before he met his young wife, he had already become renowned by one of his less-flattering Indian names, "Big Drunk." Her greatest concern therefore became Sam's "moral reformation." Her influence over the years made such an impact that her husband largely refrained from drinking after marriage. This came as a shock to many, who could only acknowledge Margaret's hand in Houston's ultimate salvation. Margaret's efforts mirrored the sentiments of the *Texas State Gazette,* which declared it was better to be near a woman than a tavern. Contemporaries confident in the positive influence of women would have seen Sam Houston as a case in point.[24]

Women also offered their support to groups such as the Sons of Temperance. A letter to the *Texas State Gazette* in 1849 discussed the value of "Female Eloquence" displayed at a ceremony for the organization. Eliza Pitts and Mary Johnson presented a banner to the Austin branch while H. Maria Haynie gave them a Bible. According to the journalist recording the scene, both Pitts and Haynie delivered elegant and moving addresses. "It's to be hoped that the Sons of Temperance will give the fair daughters of Texas throughout the State, wherever the Order is established, an opportunity to display their talents, and zeal, and interest in this able cause," he urged. Apparently the Sons took the writer's advice. In May, 1850, the Cameron Sons of Temperance received a banner with the motto "Love, Purity and Fidelity" emblazoned on it as well as a Bible from Margaret Chalmers and Margaret Ross, and later that year the ladies of Caldwell planned to donate similar gifts to their own local branch.[25]

By presenting banners and Bibles, these women presented a united front against the evil in their midst. As had their wartime predecessors, their flags encouraged their warriors and armed them with the sword of the Spirit to strike down sinners with a ready verse. Such practices might appear to be only moral support, and admittedly moral support was part of the rationale behind the women's actions. But by publicly decrying the dangers of drink and urging their neighbors to take a stand for sobriety, women exercised their own form of social control. As models of piety and purity, women had considerable clout with which to pressure the community. Their efforts did not always succeed—not everyone considered intemperance a vice worth eliminating—but female solidarity helped to create an atmosphere of decency in the republic.[26]

Of course, not all women relied on rhetoric to make their point. Others made their case more directly. In 1855, residents and temperance activists met at a public meeting in Rockwall to protest the opening of a new grocery store. The owner had already determined he would sell liquor and opened for business as local reformers protested to no avail. Not long after the store opened, a group that the *Texas State Gazette* called the Kaufman "girls" raided the store, seized the barrels of alcohol, and poured out their contents in the street. As unusual as the scene appeared, the *Gazette* approved of the women's actions. "We would rather witness this, than see the liquor emptying men's pockets of their money, and their minds of its reason," it determined. Still, violent reactions against drink proved rarer than subdued banner presentations.[27]

Another area of benevolence, one in which women had considerable clout, emerged in the obvious need for education. As settlers tried to establish civilization in their midst, they bewailed the primitive conditions in which their children were growing up. "Is Texas to have no literature, no science that she can call her own?" asked the *Telegraph*. "Truly we are a youthful State, and much cannot be expected of us at present; but none can say it is too soon to lay the foundation of liberal institutions to organize and call into action the intellectual capacities of our people." Chapman agreed, waiting patiently for an educational system that seemed never to appear. Texas desperately needed education "as a means of restoring pure religion to a Christian nation." While the *Telegraph* hoped for full-scale institutions to improve Texas, Chapman hoped only for a line of primary schools along the frontier to protect the region from its less-educated southern neighbor.[28]

Women had the distinction of being natural teachers of children. If they had the responsibility to teach their children—and possibly the children of others—then they also had the responsibility to ready themselves for the task by learning as much as they could. "Let the women of a community be made virtuous and intelligent," declared Catharine Beecher, "and the men will certainly be the same." Beginning in the late eighteenth century, Americans established female academies to train their daughters for their future careers as wives and mothers. This tradition continued into the next century. When Texans organized schools, they included female institutions and seminaries to train the next generation of teachers. The two developed almost simultaneously.[29]

When the *Telegraph* published its plea for public education in 1847, schools had existed in Texas since 1835 at the latest. On January 1 of that year, Frances Trask began her boarding school at Coles Settlement. Two years later it became Independence Academy, the first school to be chartered in Texas. Others followed Trask's example and began schools of their own. Mrs. Ayers and Miss McHenry opened a boarding school of their own in 1836, and later that year Ann D. W. Splane opened a female academy in Brazoria County "to teach all the polite, useful and ornamental branches." Splane's emphasis on the "polite" sciences reveals the differences between female and male education. For example, the female academy of the Masonic Collegiate Institute taught their young women everything they taught the boys except political economy, but they also added subjects such as painting, music, and embroidery. With the extra benefit of the gentle arts, women not only raised their sons to be good men, but their daughters to become good mothers in their stead.[30]

Education proved vital to the perpetuation of the republic. In his address to the Kaufman Female Institute in 1859, B. J. Osburn lauded its efforts in the valiant assault against barbarity. Only twenty years earlier, he noted, Indians had roamed the land where the school now stood; now civilization had claimed the territory for its own, expanding its empire peacefully, thanks to academies like Kaufman's. As for the future, Osburn said, no one could say what might lie ahead. To be sure, the graduates of the institute could only help spread its feminine influence across the countryside. For Osburn and his audience, the "development of mind" reigned supreme, for women as well as men. Still, female education carried a slightly different tone to the speaker: "The American woman is the happy companion of the American freeman, gladding his heart by her smiles of confidence and love; and cheering him on in his duty, by her voice of counsel and approbation. Glorious as our institutions are, their fruits would turn to dust and ashes without the lovely association of the softer sex, fitted by education to be the friend, the joy, the pride of the American patriot." Were it not for "the good sense of American ladies," men's efforts to bring about the reform of religion, government, and other areas would come to nothing. In other words, he saw female education not so much as an opportunity to create feminine patriots, but rather helpmeets for the primary actors in the cause.[31]

Not all Texans viewed female education this way. In fact, as women graduated from such institutions, they carried with them the seeds for future societal discord. If women had the intelligence to get an education, they reasoned, why could they not participate fully in the political process and elsewhere? Elizabeth Cady Stanton's Seneca Falls Conference had taken place eleven years prior to Osburn's speech, and across the continent supporters advocated rights for women. Lucadia Pease, wife of Governor Elisha Pease, considered herself to be a "woman's rights woman." Other Texas women shared her view. Some felt the strain more than others. Elizabeth Scott Neblett expressed frustration at her inability to satisfy her personal ambitions. "I can never gain worldly honor," she wrote. "Fame can never be mine. I am a *woman!* a woman! I can hardly teach my heart to be content with my life." For Neblett, her only hope was to focus her ambitions on her fiancé, an attorney. It is ironic that schools built to assist women in their domestic efforts would kindle the flames of future conflict, but this fact only demonstrates the narrowness of the gap between men's and women's spheres.[32]

Meanwhile, these various aspects of domesticity continued to assist women in their push for Texas' development. Yet their call for the spread of civilization did not stop with cultural matters. Manifest destiny meant nothing without nationalistic underpinnings. Proponents of civilization depended not just on culture or even Western culture, but Anglo American culture. The bulk of emigrants to Texas were heirs of American republicanism, the epitome of political development in the world. Lydia Sigourney urged her readers to remember "the country that gave you birth" and give back to it as they had received. "Are you not willing for a season to devote yourself to the culture of her children, as some remuneration for the privilege of dwelling safely under her auspices?" she asked. "Will you not at least, become the instructer [*sic*] of all in your own family, who may be made better by your influences?" To Sigourney, domestic devotion hinged on patriotism and vice versa. Although it began in the home, it would be only a matter of time before it spread to other areas.[33]

Leonora Siddons's tawdry pamphlet reveals this thread of nationalism. Here the author declared it the duty of all citizens of the country "to drive back her tyrannical invaders." Clearly, not only men felt a desire to serve their country directly. One of many problems with *The Female Warrior* is that it leaned too far in the other direction, abandoning conventional notions of feminine behavior to embrace martial spirit. Still, Siddons felt strongly enough about the duties of citizenship to publish her views on the topic. She also attempted to aid the cause of civilization, albeit in a distinctly different manner than that to which Texans were accustomed.[34]

The Texas Revolution presented a glorious fight that no Texan could study without some measure of personal pride. By achieving independence, the young republic demonstrated its strength as well as its superiority. It also sparked a sense of nationalism for its inhabitants, binding them together with shared experience. In this way, Texas nationalism conveyed not only pride in country, but in self. The two were combined in history as well as destiny; as went Texas, so would go its citizens.[35]

But Texas itself had little history compared to those countries that surrounded it. Texans looked not to Mexico for its heritage, but to the United

States. If Mexico had allowed Texas to grow to maturity, it served as little better than a foster parent. The United States—its people, its culture— had given Texas birth. The roots connecting the two remained tight, particularly because the majority of emigrants to the Lone Star Republic came from the United States. They shared racial characteristics, the same blood, which separated them from their neighbors. They also shared the same legacy of republicanism. When the Texas Legislature developed a constitution, they patterned it after that of their eastern relatives, creating yet another republic on the continent. Republicanism made both countries what they were. As such, it also intertwined with the rapidly developing concept of manifest destiny. The republican ideal deserved the attention of the entire world; its successes at Philadelphia and Washington-on-the-Brazos demonstrated its efficacy and its merits. The creation of Texas gave an added boost to feelings of exceptionalism as well. By triumphing over tyranny, Texan patriots proved the supremacy of democratic rule; a people's army had arisen and conquered the foe, and now those people had built a new nation on a proven foundation and made it work.[36]

Nationalism was crucial for the young republic to survive. It provided a sense of unity of purpose that would aid in its protection from future attackers. Texans—both longtime inhabitants and newcomers—felt like a part of the country, participants in the drama unfolding before them. As a result, they would be more willing to sacrifice to reinforce their homeland. Because of their belief in Texan superiority, residents would work to promote the expansion of their culture and beliefs, to reach into new territory and repeat the civilizing process all over again.

The problem with measuring nationalism lies in its ephemeral nature. Mental processes are hard to quantify. Scholars must rely on extant writings, such as diaries or memoirs. Not much evidence exists in these media, but there is enough to get a general idea of how people at the time thought and lived. Many women did leave behind thoughts that could shed some light on the importance of nationalism. But these ruminations were rarely esoteric in nature. Women required something to write about to free them to explore their beliefs concerning the value of the nation. For this reason, another aspect of this study requires examination of the symbols of nationalism. As anthropologist Clifford Geertz has noted, symbols—whether in everyday life or in elaborate rituals such as those accompanying ceremony or celebration—provide the only real understanding of a culture.[37]

One example of nationalism made concrete is the celebration of holidays such as the Fourth of July. As several historians have noted, festivals and celebrations reinforce a sense of community into their participants. This worked particularly well in the early republic, when parades and public orations lent a patriotic air to the proceedings of the day. The process worked so well, in fact, that political factions and even regions of the country used the holiday in different ways to reinforce different aspects and create a distinct identity from others around them. What is interesting about Independence Day celebrations in this period is that even while they remembered the glories of the past, they also "celebrated not their past, but themselves," creating a national consciousness through an ever-growing tradition.[38]

Earlier discussions of balls and barbecues thrown to remember San Jacinto Day fall into this category. Such celebrations continued decades later; Henrietta Embree and many other ladies witnessed a "sham battle" to recreate the event in 1859. "'Twas quite interesting," she noted, "as well as animateing [sic]." Clearly women shared in the swell of patriotic fervor following the revolution and indulged in it however they could. Still, these were not isolated incidents. Women had enjoyed national holidays since Texas had been a part of Mexico. Beginning in 1825, colonists even celebrated the Mexican holiday of Diez y Seis (September 16), which commemorated the independence of Mexico from Spain. Still, Anglo settlers focused primarily on more familiar American holidays such as Independence Day. On July 4, 1834, colonists held a barbecue and ball as the women gathered together to quilt. Above all, the holiday provided a social occasion for everyone in the region. "The ladies spent the day in conversation and work, the young people dancing in the yard, the children playing under the trees, and the men talking politics," said Dilue Harris. But the situation was not as patriotic as it otherwise would have been; no political speeches occurred, as Mexican officials were present. Any nationalistic fervor that might have arisen remained underground. Nevertheless, it is telling that both Diez y Seis and the Fourth of July focused on familiar republican themes: liberty and independence.[39]

America's Independence Day held the greatest regard among settlers. Coming from the United States themselves, that holiday had a stronger appeal than one commemorating a Mexican declaration. Texans participated in festivities enthusiastically, sometimes staying all night, as Mary Baylor recalled. Years earlier, Millie Gray watched the Milam Guards and a group of Sunday school children parading down the street in honor of the day. Later someone gave a speech, but Gray could not remember the speaker's name by the time the information reached her diary. Parties, dances, and quilting appear to have taken priority over parades and speeches, but women participated regardless. Only later did women find themselves squeezed out of some celebrations. For instance, Harris participated in the last ball on an election day in 1836. "After that," she said, "there was too much whiskey drunk for ladies to be present." Were it not for the presence of alcohol, celebrations would have continued as they always had during elections.[40]

Baylor also described how distinguished heroes and patriots were frequently invited to Fourth of July celebrations. Men like Sam Houston and Mirabeau Lamar would come to town and give speeches, and people would swarm in to be in touch with local celebrity. Still, there was more involved in such orations than star power. Houston and others represented Texas at its best, heroism incarnate. As George Washington symbolized the American Revolution, so Texan dignitaries stood for Texas and its own struggle for freedom. Texans wanted to be nearer to these paragons because they made Texan nationalism more concrete. Embree understood this after reading a biography of Houston. "I do so much regret not reading it soon[er]," she wrote. "I might then have known more about the struggles of our *Lone Star State* [that] she had in dashing of the galling chains—that the Mexicans had bound her with." Once she comprehended this, Embree felt more sympathy for Texas as well as patriotism for its cause.[41]

Anna Hunt had more opportunity to absorb her country's history. Her husband, Memucan Hunt, was a hero of the Texas Revolution. Hunt's diary mentioned several guests who had fought alongside him. Having so much living history in her parlor seems to have motivated Hunt to pursue a greater understanding of their cause. One evening, after spending a cold and nasty day reading history by the fire, she expressed her enthusiasm for the discipline. For Hunt, history primarily provided "striking instances of virtue, enterprise, courage and generosity." Such reading inspired as well as entertained, uplifting the soul and enriching one's character. Aside from this, it also portrayed "the history of the first civil government ever established upon the genuine basis of freedom." Notably here she referred to the United States, although she also spent considerable time reading Texas history. Her newfound hobby soon made its way to her pen; not long after taking up the discipline she spent most of one day writing fervently on the "important [*sic*] of history." The time Hunt spent indulging in historiography had motivated her to recommend it to others. With this information, Texans could have a better understanding of as well as a fervent patriotism for their home.[42]

Evidence of feminine nationalism is frequently circumstantial. Nevertheless, it helps to demonstrate that matters of state did rest on women's minds from time to time, even if domestic matters overwhelmed them. Much of their silence can be attributed to a lack of personal political interest; because women did not have the right to vote, they focused more on matters within their capabilities. This, however, did not mean that they had no interest in Texas—merely that their interest became apparent in less obvious ways. The enthusiastic promotion of domesticity is a case in point. Women could not speak at the ballot box, but they could at the breakfast table.

Simultaneously, European immigrants displayed their own nationalism proudly. Arriving from the Old World often sparked a newfound patriotism that manifested in diaries and letters home. In Texas, the best example of this pattern emerges among German women. Germans were the largest European group to immigrate to Texas; from 1844 to 1847 more than seven thousand arrived, prompted by social upheaval and overpopulation at home and the establishment of immigration societies to the United States and Texas. The best known of these, the *Verein zum Schutze deutsche Einwanderer in Texas* (Society for the Protection of German Immigrants to Texas, *Verein* or *Adelsverein* for short), began encouraging migration in 1842, although individual German families began arriving as early as the 1820s. To Germans, Texas appeared to be the ideal location for farmers seeking "economic independence," new markets, and that greatest of Holy Grails for the politically traumatized Germans: liberty. Men, women, and children alike looked to the New World for opportunity and worked hard to achieve it once they had found it.[43]

Ottilie Fuchs Goeth first heard stories of the faraway land of Texas when she was nine years old. All the descriptions provided her and her brothers and sisters a glowing image of the republic—only months away from statehood—as "a kind of paradise." With great anticipation she left Germany and traveled with her family to their new home, arriving in early 1846. Earlier immigrants felt the same way. "Hurry, hurry and join us," Caroline Luise Baronin von Roeder wrote friends in 1835. "This is truly the land of freedom and romance." The Fuchs family joined hundreds of others ready to make Texas their new home. Their homeland, not yet unified, faced a host of trials and obstacles in the 1830s and 1840s that made the promise of freedom in the New World that much more tempting. Open land, available for farming, presented an opportunity too good to ignore when coupled with the republicanism that many Germans, both men and women, desired.[44]

Nevertheless, as Goeth later noted, "the reality was a bit different." After building their dreams on stories from friends or relations, these new immigrants frequently found their ideals collapsing under the weight of life on a barely restrained frontier. Nothing was as it had seemed in Europe. Like American-born women, German women discovered that life on the periphery offered challenges before unknown. Even more problematic, they faced a language and culture barrier.[45]

But the Germans remained undeterred. In order to build a decent life, German women worked to establish a strong cultural foundation in their new home. They also had to reconsider what it meant to be German, Texan, or eventually American. By redefining their sense of nationalism, they Americanized and adapted to their environment. Simultaneously, they stressed the benefits of German *Kultur* in the hope of making Texas a better place to live for all its inhabitants.

The "civilizing" process for German women began with the concept of nationalism—specifically, German nationalism. This brand of political philosophy was still young in the 1830s, emerging from a flowering of regional pride in the late eighteenth and early nineteenth centuries. Borrowing heavily from liberal ideas such as those prompting the American and French Revolutions, German nationalists placed faith in republicanism. Unfortunately, the governments under which they lived did not indulge such radical ideas and repressed public opinion to restrain them. Rather than remain in Europe to face certain persecution, many Germans looked west to the birthplace of liberal thought for their satisfaction. American equality promised a better way of life for nationalists.[46]

Texas held an even more compelling charm. Not only had Texans recently cast off the fetters of Mexican tyranny, but the Lone Star Republic offered land and opportunity. As immigrant Viktor Bracht declared in his pamphlet on immigration, *Texas in 1848*, "It is self-evident that in a country so sparsely settled, profitable employment is always to be had by those who wish to work." Bracht primarily meant being hired out, but the prospect of farming proved no less alluring. As Elise Willerich wrote, all Texas needed was enough hands to turn the virgin earth "into rich garden soil." For immigrants, the prairies would become the Garden of the World, a fertile testament to the Jeffersonian ideal of the agrarian republic, as they had for Anglo settlers. Whatever happened, as Ida Kapp noted, Texas offered a much better life than the one they had left behind.[47]

It did not take long to shift allegiance to American nationalism. When Willerich heard of the violent revolutions occurring in central Europe in the late 1840s, she expressed hopes "that the revolution may drive others here to these parts." Enthusiasm for republicanism proved more important than zeal for one's native land. Soon after arrival, German men joined the rest of Texas in fighting off Mexico in the Texas Revolution and, ten years later, the U.S.-Mexican War. German women endured the panicked Runaway Scrape alongside their American counterparts, losing homes and fields as well. Louise Stöhr expressed her dismay that, after the battle of San Jacinto, the retreating Mexican army killed her family's best milk cow. No one escaped the crucible from which the Lone Star Republic would emerge. Then, when the battles ended, German women rejoiced as eagerly as their neighbors. Rosa Kleberg recalled enthusiastically a ball celebrating Houston's victory at San Jacinto, complete with barbecue, cakes, and visitors from as far away as forty miles. Celebrations such as these carried meaning even for newcomers, meaning that they were eager to absorb.[48]

Above all, the drive for nationalism encouraged Germans to reach out to their new neighbors for stability and unity. They included even Native Americans in their endeavors, as John Meusebach's 1847 treaty with the Comanches demonstrated. Kleberg frequently sewed clothes for them in exchange for moccasins, and both sides traded for necessary goods. Cooperation proved a necessity for survival, creating a strong bond between neighbors. Although Germans usually had a better relationship with Indians than other Texans had, at times the tribes taxed the immigrants' patience. Auguste Wiegreffe recalled the first—and last—time her community served the Indians dinner. The women provided all they could scrounge, having barely enough for themselves. Then their guests arrived, digging into the meal with their fingers. This appalled the townsfolk, who "could hardly stand to be near them." After the Indians ate a nearby dead horse for dessert, the matrons concluded that inviting the neighbors over was a very bad idea. Clara Feller agreed, noting that the Indians, while friendly, were almost too much so, using "all their spare time coming to town." Although Germans acknowledged the kidnappings, robberies, and murders committed, they were unique in observing the downside to good relations.[49]

Also, although many Germans did not own slaves, others took on one or two in order to run the family farm. Slave owners like Amanda Fallier von Rosenberg justified the practice by casting it in the light of American freedoms. "It is said negroes are often treated inhumanly," she wrote, "but those are single cases, from what I can see the negroes are better off than your poor Lithuanian workman." Nevertheless, slavery remained for others a strange and paradoxical institution.[50]

German women gladly related their improving relations with Americans for friends and relations in Europe. Kapp and Kleberg noted how hospitable and polite they were. Emma Murck Altgelt went into more detail, describing the kindness of an American family that nursed her back to health for days after she fell from a horse. That people whose language she did not speak would care for her impressed her favorably toward her neighbors, and also her adopted country. Differences in language meant little to these pioneers; as Goeth declared, "Racial prejudices [against Germans] did not yet exist."[51]

Unfortunately, such glowing reports of good neighbors and good experiences coexisted alongside experiences that made many German women uncomfortable. Their discomfort stemmed from the nature of German nationalism itself. Because Germany did not yet exist as one country, Germans struggled to unite however they could, primarily through language and culture rather than politics. This focus on culture created problems in the New World. Language clearly presented a barrier, albeit one that immigrants expected. Culture, on the other hand, was something that Germans sorely missed—Americans did not appear to have any. Caroline Luise Baronin von Roeder missed the opera and theater, which existed in some parts of the United States but nowhere near her new home. Similarly, Louise Romberg Fuchs and others avoided American schools because they felt such distaste for the apparent lack of culture in Texas. As a result, they learned English with difficulty. Hospitable or not, the cultural vacuum inhabited by some Americans repelled some immigrants and threatened to staunch the naturalization process.[52]

Even worse, many Americans seemed uninterested in embracing a refined lifestyle. Europeans did not know what to think. They viewed

Americans' excessive drinking and swearing with disgust. Tobacco chewing—and the concomitant spitting—even among women baffled the Germans. "The women sat before the fireplace," wrote Fuchs, "smoked corncob pipes, and spat into the fire; that did not tempt us to become better acquainted with them." Altgelt also reported events following her first dinner at a plantation. Here the "lady of the house" smoked while her husband chewed and spat. For the meticulous Germans, such lack of couth and cleanliness, particularly from women, made no sense.[53]

Observers recognized that much of this behavior stemmed from difficult frontier conditions. Pioneers dealt exclusively with the "practical side of life"; some rough behavior was to be expected. Ida Kapp recognized the transforming influence of the wilderness. "The further one comes inland, the more civilization ceases," she noted, "but one changes with it and begins to think it must be so." This realization came after her own disgust upon her arrival in Galveston the year before, when she criticized the lack of trees, unpaved streets, and shoddy architecture. It took time to accept the rustic charm of the wilderness, as Altgelt learned after a sleepless night en route to Victoria. Listening to the howl of nearby wolves, expecting Indian attacks at every moment, her first night inland "was just a little too much romance for me."[54]

Altgelt was not alone in feeling disoriented in Texas. Other German women felt so, often long after arrival. Seemingly stranded in a foreign country with few means of survival, they quickly turned to familiar German ways not only for comfort, but to help bring civilization to their new home. As historian Crystal Sasse Ragsdale notes, they added *Kultur* to the traditional call for *Kinder, Kirche und Küche* (children, church, and kitchen). Goeth, for example, declared that, without culture—specifically German culture—"a nation cannot maintain itself and must eventually fall." For the sake of their newly adopted country, German women took up the task of instilling civilization into their surroundings.[55]

But how could they accomplish their ambitious goal? Goeth had a simple answer: through family. "From generation to generation," Germans would teach their children the rudiments of civilized behavior. To have new generations to teach, of course, required marriage, which they pursued in droves. Early attempts proved problematic. In the early stages of colonization, women were vastly outnumbered. Young men became so desperate that they would swarm to incoming ships to see if any women were aboard. They frequently learned to overlook German concepts of class to marry whomever they could find. "Any girl who wants a husband should come to Texas," asserted Kapp. Immigration then became a sign of patriotism as incoming women helped to pass on traditions and civilization to a new crop of children.[56]

Not all German women embraced this at first. Emma Altgelt considered herself a modern young woman. Preferring a career in journalism, she rejected offers from neighbors in New Braunfels to help her find a man. Altgelt was not alone. When she first arrived in Texas, she witnessed the fruitless efforts of a local baker as he tried first to hire a pretty blonde arrival, then propose to her. "To be married is exactly what I do not want," she retorted, much to Altgelt's "secret satisfaction." Nevertheless, Altgelt eventually capitulated to tradition, marrying a young man with whom she fell thoroughly in love. For whatever reason, the call of *Kinder, Kirche und Küche* continued in her life.[57]

Music provided another means of taming the savage wilderness. Germans stood resolutely by their love of music and their belief that it transmitted a sense of culture. Valeska von Roeder, for instance, insisted on bringing her piano to Texas from Europe. It took two years to arrive, but the benefit to the community seemed worth the wait. Immigrants also quickly formed singing societies as they had in Germany. Wiegreffe recalled such groups in New Braunfels in the 1840s. By 1853 the city had a singing festival, and Fredericksburg soon created a similar, three-day affair.[58]

Much of this love for music stemmed from the nationalistic overtones it contained. In Europe, Germans used singing societies to communicate ideas, hoping to sway public opinion indirectly. By the 1840s, they provided both entertainment and a platform for nationalistic sentiment. Singing societies provided German immigrants a comfortable atmosphere and a way to transmit patriotic fervor. They also created an opportunity for all German immigrants to unite under the banner of song.[59]

Germans' attempts to make Texas a better place in which to live, then, served a double purpose. Immigrants carved a secure niche for themselves in Central and West Texas. Communities like New Braunfels, Fredericksburg, and Boerne gave those with similar backgrounds the support they needed to persevere in difficult surroundings, providing the means for survival. In turn, these new towns populated the Texas interior and brought it under the control of republic-minded citizens. Both helped to civilize the wilderness for future progress.

Despite conflicts between German and American women, the two actually benefited each other. Both wanted better lives for themselves and their families and wanted to tame their new land. In fact, conflict between Germans and Americans produced a stronger society as a whole. Texans gladly welcomed them for their "high souled love for liberty" and their eagerness to "become good republicans, good citizens, from the moment they set foot on American soil." Although the editors who wrote these words could not fully understand the deep roots of republicanism in the new immigrants, they recognized it and publicly embraced it. By their presence, let alone their agricultural or cultural contributions, German women contributed substantially to the realization of manifest destiny in the new state. When they finished, Texas had become for them and others a new "kind of paradise."[60]

Both Anglo and German nationalism made Texas what it eventually became. Of course, their efforts owed much to the inheritance they had received from the United States—the working modern republic, the pattern that Texas and other countries hoped to follow. As Texas evolved, its citizens became more interested in annexing themselves to their mother country, placing a substantial piece of geography upon the altar of manifest destiny. Once that had been accomplished, Texans—now Americans—joined the rest of the nation in expanding the country's reach to the Pacific for an even greater prize. The enthusiasm that nationhood created found its perfect outlet in the events of the mid- to late 1840s as women and men looked west to pursue the ideal republic.

5

A Feeling of Destiny

As noted earlier, holidays such as the Fourth of July carried with them an innate patriotism that stirred the emotions and renewed the dedication of their participants to their country. Sometimes, celebrants came away with more than that. Helen Chapman took part in an especially moving Independence Day in Brownsville in 1849, one year after the Treaty of Guadalupe Hidalgo ended the Mexican War. She listened intently as someone read the Declaration of Independence at the government hospital. "I was most agreeably surprised with the whole proceedings," she said. Never had she heard the document read this way, in a section of territory recently brought into the Union, surrounded by men who had just fought for it in the war.

Viewing the event with eyes that had so recently viewed the repercussions of battle, the occasion sparked within Chapman "a feeling of Destiny, a kind of prevision that was overwhelming." Prior to this, she had expressed reservations about the efficacy of such a war as that between the United States and Mexico. It had been too bloody, too brutal for its purpose. Only when she heard the speaker and saw the audience could she understand "how good might come out of evil." This section of Texas, south of the Nueces River, had been contested territory before the war;

now it rested safely in the bosom of the republic. Where barbarism had reigned, civilization had begun to filter into the lives of its residents. Perhaps American efforts had not been without meaning. Thanks to "their blood, misery and moral desolation, this former part of Mexico is fairly launched into the great confederacy of States." Rather than decrying the Mexican War and its participants, future analysts "and the children's children will see only the blessing" and not any potential curses. Chapman felt more than excitement; she felt purpose.[1]

Chapman believed that she saw, for the first time, the benefits of manifest destiny in the celebration at the hospital. How clear it seemed in that brief moment for a woman who earlier had seen South Texas and asked, "For such a country as this why expend such blood and treasure?" At first the landscape had promised only dust and discomfort; when coupled with manifest destiny, it inspired. From that moment on, Chapman's writings focused more on the potential of the West in the hands of the Union than on the bloody necessities of war. Manifest destiny no longer meant simply taming a land for the cause of civilization. Territorial expansionism had staked a claim in her mind and created a new convert to its cause.[2]

Since its occurrence, many Americans—scholars and citizens alike—have criticized the Mexican War, although not so much for its military excesses. They focus instead on the goals of the war, primarily the absorption of more territory. The events of 1846–48 represent greed and selfish ambition, and the contemporary reference to manifest destiny appears more like rationalization than divine permission. Manifest destiny's racial aspects also bring criticism, as portrayal of the Mexicans as indolent and half-savage helped Americans justify encroachment. As a result, the war receives little emphasis except as a shameful example of the more base aspects of American character.[3]

This perspective of the war has its origins in contemporary debates. Not all Americans supported the annexation of Texas or expansion of any sort, let alone a military endeavor to achieve it. The president had endorsed a war of conquest, his opponents complained, and their charge of territorial aggrandizement was admittedly accurate. Nevertheless, emphasizing the negative perceptions of Polk's maneuvers skews the historical picture. Such a representation of the facts obstructs attempts at objectivity. Modern diplomatic considerations tend to emerge from a less obvious ideological bent than did those of the mid-nineteenth century. This is not to say that the United States has ever relied solely on the machina-

tions of *Realpolitik;* the philosophy and mindset underpinning most de-
cisions are more understated than in days past. As a result, the actions
and reactions of men like Polk may appear more melodramatic than diplomatic. Although a study of contemporary opinion still appears unpleas-
ant to modern eyes, at least it can provide a historical perspective and,
hopefully, a greater understanding of the situation.[4]

One way of doing this is by examining manifest destiny through
women's eyes. Women in Texas had a unique vantage point from which
to observe its effects. They, no less than men, had a stake in annexation
and expansion and contributed to the discourse. Some even stepped over
their thresholds to speak publicly on political matters, offering their words
as encouragement to proceed and take that course which Providence had
allotted the United States. Much of this support for expansion stemmed
from earlier events. After fighting for independence from Mexico, women
felt a strong sense of nationalism and patriotism for their home. In the
1840s, feelings of nationalism often translated directly into politics, and
women followed along with that change according to their individual
perspectives. No invisible sphere restricted their movements in such instances; they found enough freedom to support the flow of westward
progress.

Events soon tested women's resolve. Although Texas had declared itself the winner in the Texas Revolution, Mexico did not acknowledge its
separation from the mother country. In the eyes of Mexican officials, Texas
was still a province, albeit one in a state of rebellion. This belief prompted
occasional skirmishes between the two nations into the 1840s. Had the
continuing battles across the Nueces been merely a matter of defense, the
Southern Quarterly Review determined, Texas would have Americans'
"active sympathies" and little else; however, many Texans took the offensive and therefore merited disapproval. The U.S. government appeared
to tolerate an offensive strategy, as it allowed the republic to fight its own
wars without interference or support. As a result, Texas remained a dangerous place to live throughout its time as a republic. Only by fighting
could Texans maintain their sovereignty.[5]

The best-known of the battles between Texas and Mexico was the Mier
expedition of December, 1842. Designed as a counteroffensive to General
Adrian Woll's capture of San Antonio that year, the Mier expedition
planned to strike back at the Mexicans and reclaim their territory. Upon
arrival at Mier, a small town on the Rio Grande, Texan forces requested

ammunition and other supplies from the alcalde, taking him hostage for leverage. The delivery never came; instead, Mexican and Texan armies fought until Texans surrendered under a deceptive flag of truce. Mexicans captured 176 prisoners. What followed became known as the "black bean" incident. The victors forced their prisoners to draw beans out of a jar; those who drew black beans were executed. One in ten prisoners died as a result. Those who survived remained in Mexico until 1844.[6]

Woll took Mary Maverick's husband, Samuel, captive during Woll's September 11 invasion of San Antonio. According to Samuel Maverick, the "invading army" had mistaken him and his cohort for robbers and had held him until March, 1843. After his capture, he wrote his wife to let her know what had happened. Regardless of how bad things might have appeared, he wrote, "I nevertheless feel confident that I will meet my own dear Mary & our dear little ones provided she takes care of herself & them." The best thing she could do would be to continue living as she had, caring for the household without fear, but at the same time acting with more than a little caution. "Be calm & do not run too fast," he cautioned. Clearly he was concerned for the safety of his family, but he remained sure that all would be well under her supervision. Mary's diligence at home represented her contribution to a successful end to their crisis.[7]

Other women helped more directly with military efforts while still using feminine skills for this purpose. Primarily this meant offering aid to those who fought, both living and dead. During the debacles of 1842, many men received posthumous honors. Captain Nicholas M. Dawson and his men faced death that same year when they surrendered to Mexican forces near Salado Creek and were killed. In *Chronicles of Fayette*, Julia Lee Sinks drew examples of the casket trimmings for the Mier soldiers as well as the Dawson massacre victims from memory. "I made the trimmings," she added, "therefore am able to distinguish them." Here domestic skills were put to patriotic use, inspiring funeral attendants with embroidery to more valiant action against the enemy.[8]

Mary Holley preferred to face danger not with needles but with a rifle. In 1837, in a letter to her daughter back in Kentucky, Holley described the steps she and her friends had undertaken to defend their country. "We have been out this morning firing at a mark with a rifle, under Capt. Dolrocha of the army," she announced. Drill practice began after Holley and a Mrs. Franklin and Mrs. Ancheros heard of a young lady in Matagorda who was "a superior marks*man*." Not to be outdone, the three warriors proposed "to form a corps of *rifle men*—as an army of reserve." With her granddaughter, Henrietta, carrying the Lone Star flag as ensign, Holley and her sisters in arms indulged in some target practice to prepare for potential attack. Apparently their first attempts were not ideal. "We did not exactly hit the mark," she confessed (she had only managed to split a clothesline), but her attitude remained optimistic. The writer recorded her experiences with a vein of humor, but she knew that life in Texas was far from secure. Both Holley's band and the sharpshooter in Matagorda felt a responsibility to serve in Texas' defense, and neither wanted to stand by idly and watch the newborn republic—and the sanctity of their home life—disappear without a fight.[9]

Here Texas and manifest destiny collided in history. The Lone Star Republic represented the triumph of civilization over the wilderness, although that civilization still struggled to maintain a foothold on more remote areas. It possessed abundant resources that the United States could use. The process proved the value of Anglo-Saxon efforts on the continent. It only made sense that Texas annex itself with its spiritual mother, expanding American territory and sovereignty across the continent. In fact, many Americans believed that the issue was not annexation, but reannexation. Had officials forced the issue against Spain in 1819 when John Quincy Adams negotiated the Transcontinental Treaty, they maintained, the region would have been part of the United States decades before. Texas became, in a sense, a test case for manifest destiny.[10]

Texans themselves had considered annexation as an option as early as the fall of 1836. A canvass in September disclosed that only 61 of 6,000 voters believed Texas should remain separate from the United States. Newly elected president Sam Houston made annexation the emphasis of his administration, asking Andrew Jackson for recognition of the new republic. As did many Texans, Houston believed that recognition would serve as the first step toward unification. Nevertheless, Jackson and his successor, Martin Van Buren, were too concerned with possible sectional repercussions as well as Mexico's reaction to the Lone Star Republic's independence to move quickly. Finally Houston could wait no longer. The economic and political situation in the United States had worsened, thanks to the panic of 1837. The new republic at last had gained recognition from England and France. Nationalism had also begun to swell among Texans as their situation seemed to improve. Texas' first request for annexation was withdrawn in 1838.[11]

Still, many Americans had confidence that other opportunities would arise to include Texas in the Union. From the beginning, Texas appeared to have great potential as an American territory. Texas had not even declared its independence before Americans wondered if it would be a useful addition. The *American Quarterly Review* decided to withhold judgment in 1830, protesting that the time was not right to consider such matters. Discussion did not begin in earnest until the mid-1840s. Among other reasons, the United States noticed the surge of attention on the republic by European nations. What if Texas should fall under German influence? Everyone knew that German immigrants had flooded the region. Worse, the British—still antagonists after the bitter Revolution and War of 1812, as well as fervent abolitionists—had expressed interest in Texas' being "slave free." The Lone Star Republic was weak and still struggled against the natives within its borders. Would the United States stand by and watch Britain become the country's champion?[12]

Suddenly Americans began to note the similarities between Texans and the Founding Fathers and called for reunification of the two nations. Even Jackson, who had rejected recognition earlier, urged annexation by 1844. Cultural and political similarities, as well as geography, linked the two nations. "The very configuration of the earth, annexed Texas to the United States," declared Charles Jared Ingersoll in *Niles' Weekly Register.* The *Democratic Review* observed how "this valley region" appeared "symmetrically planned and adapted to its grand destiny." The rivers and mountains urged unity between the two. It would only be a matter of time until they joined in perfect harmony; in fact, it was the responsibility of all Americans to come to the aid of the lost colony and reattach her to the republican body. "Who will refuse to heal the bleeding wounds of the mutilated West, and reunite the veins and arteries dissevered by the dismembering cession of Texas to Spain?" cried the editors. If Nature seemed predisposed to joining the two, could governments keep them separate?[13]

For a while, it certainly seemed so. Despite the rationale for annexation, some Texans viewed such arguments with skepticism. Debate raged between devoted annexationists and those who, although they liked the idea in theory, believed that Texas could not give up its sovereignty to the United States on the latter's terms. National pride ran strong: annexation would annihilate "*our identity as a country*" and diminish diplomatic clout in dealing with other nations. Thomas Jefferson Green agreed with those who endorsed caution. His main concern lay in future expansion. As part of the Mier expedition, Green had seen the Rio Grande and was convinced that the destiny of the Anglo-Saxon race was to the south and west "as surely as that has been the course of former conquest." If annexation occurred, expansion would as well; if not, Green asserted, Texas' own push to the southwest would happen that much faster. After all, Texas was much closer to Mexico than the United States and had that much more to gain in trying.[14]

Others disagreed sharply. National security motivated many as they eyed their former masters to the south. Even after the revolution, Texas had found it necessary to continue fighting for freedom. With the help of U.S. presence and more troops, perhaps Mexico would not be as daunting an enemy. Besides this, nationhood proved difficult for the Lone Star Republic; for many years the nation teetered on the brink of economic collapse. As proannexationist sentiment grew in the United States, it likewise spread in Texas, especially after John Tyler created an offer for Texans consideration in March, 1845. Despite overwhelming support for annexation, the battle over security versus national greatness raged.[15]

The *Telegraph* expressed its opinions on the subject in verse. "The Girls and Annexation" presented a short, pithy argument for unification, complete with a loosely veiled threat to men across the republic:

Our village maids all vow and swear,
It gives them great vexation
To hear a "nice young man" declare
He's not for annexation!

They're all for union to a man,
And go the whole for Texas;
And say to all who ain't, "git out!
"You never shall annex us!"

Like the women in *Lysistrata,* these fictional "maids" used their feminine wiles to endorse unification. They might not have been able to express their views at the ballot box or from the podium, but women watched events as did their husbands, fathers, or brothers.[16]

One woman willingly overstepped societal boundaries to fight for annexation. Jane Cazneau had limited opportunities as a woman with deep political interests. Such a person was not supposed to exist in nineteenth-century America, where women ideally remained above the fray of diplomacy and intrigue. Nevertheless, Cazneau knew what she wanted to do. Only two options remained to her, according to Anna Kasten Nelson: shaping public opinion "through the men she could dominate"—and Cazneau was a charismatic individual, from all accounts—or "through the power of her pen." The latter won her the most attention, although frequently indirectly, because she used pseudonyms to avoid bringing excessive attention to her private life. Her ideas, not her name, deserved praise or criticism.[17]

Cazneau's first love was the expansion of the United States in any way possible. She originally became interested in Texas in 1832, when she met with Aaron Burr regarding settlement in Austin's Colony. She, along with her father and brother, became involved in a plan to bring German immigrants to Texas. Their plan fell short of their expectations when the immigrants preferred to remain on the coast rather than moving inland, but her attachment to the colony was already in full bloom. As noted earlier, she owned land in the area, contributing the profits from the sale of part of it to the Texas Revolution. From the 1830s until the 1850s, when her attention moved elsewhere (a subject for a later chapter), she carried a banner for Texas in every publication to which she contributed. She wrote several letters promoting annexation, some of which found their way to the *Telegraph and Texas Register* office. Throughout the 1840s she wrote for the New York *Sun,* then edited by expansion enthusiast Moses Y. Beach, focusing on the question of annexation. According to Linda Hudson's biography, Cazneau also wrote for the *Democratic Review* on the topic, including the famous article "Annexation" from July, 1845, which coined the phrase "manifest destiny." Certainly Cazneau had more than a passing interest in Texas' future.[18]

Eventually the proannexationist arguments persuaded Texans and Americans alike. President John Tyler, nearing the end of his administration, hurriedly manipulated Texas into the Union. Mary Maverick expressed her relief at the event in her diary. "Thank God, we are now annexed to the United States," she wrote in July, 1845, "and can hope for home and quiet." The chaos that had erupted over annexation was too much for Maverick, who longed merely to return to everyday business. The Lone Star Republic became a state on February 16, 1846, and Texans hoped to settle into their new position with little difficulty.[19]

The United States was not so fortunate. As Texas embraced statehood, American troops set up camp in the disputed region between the Nueces River and Rio Grande, directly opposite the Mexican town of Matamoros. On April 24, a group of infantrymen was running reconnaissance there when they stumbled upon Mexican soldiers who were searching for them. Eleven U.S. soldiers died on what Polk called "American soil." This encounter spurred entry into the Mexican War on May 13, the final confrontation between Mexico and the United States over territorial issues. By the time both countries signed the Treaty of Guadalupe Hidalgo in February, 1848, the United States had extended its reach across the entire continent, from ocean to ocean. For many Americans, manifest destiny reached its peak with the absorption of the Mexican Cession. At last, the United States possessed the land set aside for them from the beginning.[20]

The Mexican War receives little attention compared to other American wars. The Civil War, for instance, overshadows it by thousands of volumes. Scholars of that great conflict have countless primary sources to work with as well, particularly journals and diaries. Mexican War diaries also exist, but for the most part they are descriptions of battle rather than perspectives from nonparticipants. Women's diaries in particular seem lacking. Even Texas newspapers that eagerly detailed women's efforts during the revolution said little about women's roles during the war. This fact is interesting, as Robert W. Johannsen has noted that women played an active role in the Mexican War. Not only did they sew and make ammunition, but they often followed the army to cook, do laundry, and sometimes even fight. "The involvement of women in the war," he notes, "was an index of the world's advancement." Samuel Reid, a Texas Ranger serving under Ben McCulloch, confirmed this in his memoirs of the 1846 campaign. As soon as Texans heard the call to battle, everyone eagerly volunteered "amid the encouraging smiles of mothers, wives, and sisters, who cheerfully came forth to lend their aid, making wallets, and moulding leaden messengers of death." As many Americans saw the war as one for civilization, it made sense that women participate in their country's efforts.[21]

Women also felt the impact of the war on their everyday lives, sometimes more directly than they liked. In San Antonio, an old woman called Tía Bonita complained to a neighbor that army volunteers had accosted her at a *baile* one summer evening in 1847. They robbed her of the $6 she carried and left her badly injured. A friend wrote of her predicament to the *Telegraph and Texas Register,* which published the letter in English and its original Spanish to express disgust. Americans' fight was with Mexico, not Mexican Americans, the article implied. Such brutal attacks on American women, regardless of race, merited only scorn.[22]

Why is there so little information in Texas women's diaries? Two possible reasons exist. First, by the late 1840s domesticity could have taken such complete hold over the populace of female diarists that they felt little interest in masculine affairs such as war. Given the American emphasis on true womanhood, a well-kept house and well-behaved children undoubtedly captured the bulk of their attention. Others would have to take control of military matters. A second possibility could be that a fight for Texas may have been more important than for the United States at large. The threat was more immediate when citizens struggled not only for territory, but survival. Therefore, women had less to say about the war. This latter view makes less sense when considering the ongoing dispute between Texas and Mexico after the revolution. Annexation provided some security, but proximity to the fight could easily have negated it. Still, Texas now had soldiers from every state for protection. The concept of safety in numbers might have come into play in this case. Also, the war was in Mexico, not in their front yards as in the past. Most settlers at this point still felt more threatened by Indian rather than Mexican invaders. Why worry about distant rumors when a more immediate threat camped outside town?

Both of these theories have some merit. History is rarely an exact science, and maybe neither—or both—ideas are correct. Possibly some felt constrained by decorum to avoid such brutal topics beyond their ken, while others simply ignored an affair that took place for the most part beyond their borders. Regardless of the reason, lack of information requires considerable creative analysis on the part of the historian. Examples of both perspectives exist and can be gleaned from available information. For instance, Holley demonstrated in another letter to her daughter that not all women shunned political thinking. As was frequently the case, she hinted at larger matters without addressing them directly. "You can hardly think of what excitement we are in," she wrote. "If it were not that I have to use my time and my mind with my *delightful tasks,* I could fill these sheets with stirring things." Holley's land interests still took precedence over the war—personal business was more immediate—yet recent events filled her thoughts. Mary Maverick also recalled local enthusiasm after the battles of Palo Alto and Resaca de la Palma, although she contributed little detail otherwise.[23]

In fact, Palo Alto and Resaca de la Palma became symbolic of the entire war effort for Texans. Teresa Vielé commented at some length on the need for a monument at the sacred sites. To have no memorial, she said, would violate the memory of those who died there for American freedoms. Simultaneously, Vielé recognized the battlefields for another reason. Both sat on what had been purported to be Texas soil—the primary reason behind the war. The battles deserved a monument to recognize the state's role in the conflict as well as to foster pride in both state and country.[24]

For other women, however, war translated as the loss of family and structure rather than a call to patriotism. Martha Barbour moved to Galveston from Kentucky when her husband, Philip, went to Mexico with the infantry. The ties between husband and wife were so strong that she expressed more displeasure than he when his promotion was denied. Still, Barbour's primary longing was not out of ambition for Philip's career. She primarily wanted to see the war's end and her husband back home. Politics paled in comparison. "I look forward with *almost* certainty that we will be settled this fall," she wrote in 1846. "How happy we will be when sitting around our 'own fireside' and talking over the events of '45 and '46." Apparently war meant more for Barbour in retrospect than as a present reality. At the time, her husband faced too much danger for her to rest easily. Unfortunately, her dreams of domestic bliss died with Philip on September 21 when he was killed in battle. Her diary does not record her feelings regarding war; any negative emotions she felt after being notified of his death never made it into her writing, which ceased before she received the news.[25]

But not all women in Texas approved of the war. Even while they supported the expansion of civilization over Mexico, they rejected violence as appropriate. These women represent what Frederick Merk would label a quiet, almost passive form of American expansion. As he elaborates in *Manifest Destiny and Mission in American History,* the United States emerged as the first nation of its kind in the world, a radical experiment in republicanism. As such, the country was unique, a model for the rest of the world to follow. Two methods of application emerged from this exceptionalist mindset. Merk labeled one method an impulse toward "mission." Proponents of this concept hoped that by remaining the celebrated "city upon a hill," silent but emitting the brilliant light of liberty, Americans could demonstrate the values and benefits of republican society so others might emulate it.[26]

Other Americans developed their own biases into an enthusiasm for expansion. Rather than waiting for other people to accept such critical ideas on their own, enthusiasts endorsed physical and political expansion, taking the philosophy beyond the nation's borders and putting it to work, by force if necessary. Those who cherished mission found such blatant displays offensive and even contrary to the ideals that they claimed to support. This did not deter expansionists from proclaiming their gospel of American destiny and gaining countless adherents across the country. Although by the 1840s the two camps had largely hardened into partisan positions (specifically the Whig and Democratic Parties), prior to this the ideas simply existed as an undercurrent to discourse.[27]

Some women did speak out against the war as an unfitting means to an end. Expansion was a worthy goal, but they stressed less violent methods. In an article for the New York *Sun,* Cazneau wrote that "the sword was not an appropriate 'implement of republicanism.'" Still, she supported the war effort, as she hoped that the "rough attention" of U.S. troops would motivate Mexico to embrace more civilized politics. Regardless of her feelings toward the war itself, the U.S. mission in Mexico remained of primary interest to her. She even tried to bring about a practical, peaceable solution to the conflict. Thanks to her friendship with Moses Y. Beach, editor of the New York *Sun* and friend to President James K. Polk, Cazneau was able to join him on a secret mission to Mexico. Government intelligence implied that "certain political and clerical elements" might accept a settlement. As a result, President Polk had appointed the editor to travel to Mexico, observe conditions there, and attempt to organize a truce with the Mexican government. Beach arrived in Mexico City in 1847 along with Cazneau, whose fluency in Spanish benefited him tremendously. Cazneau was not currently married, having been divorced from her first husband and not yet married to William Cazneau, a vital figure in Texas politics at the time. (They married in 1849.) Her independence allowed her to travel with Beach without attracting too much criticism.[28]

Later, when Beach's son, Moses, described his father's adventures in Mexico, he mentioned Cazneau only in passing. (Had she not drowned the year before when the ship she was on sank in the Caribbean, Beach would not even have mentioned her by name.) According to the son's letter to *Scribner's Monthly,* Cazneau joined the party as a "companion" to the editor's daughter so the group would appear less suspicious. The presence of the two women made it appear as though they had traveled to

Mexico purely for "pleasure and observation." Her work nevertheless had some impact, as Beach noted. As the editor of the *Sun* worked his way toward an amenable peace, he sent Cazneau to Veracruz to tell General Winfield Scott of the possibility of an end to the war. Scott responded poorly to the news—it came from a woman—and did not accept its veracity until Beach completed his mission and reunited with Cazneau in Veracruz. Reportedly Scott then jokingly warned Beach "never to send messages of such importance by a 'plenipotentiary in petticoats.'" Although the general had not taken her role seriously, Cazneau was deeply involved in Beach's trip to Mexico.[29]

Helen Chapman shared Cazneau's concern with the Mexican War. Chapman's antiwar protests were ironic, given her husband's military career. The couple would never have come to Texas if not for the U.S. Army. They arrived in the Rio Grande valley in 1848 after the signing of the Treaty of Guadalupe Hidalgo. Her husband was part of the occupying force in Matamoros, where she lived for some time before they were transferred to Fort Brown on the northern bank of the river. Prior to this, he had fought in the battle of Buena Vista. His wife remained behind in Massachusetts with their son. As a result of her experiences in New England, Chapman brought a unique perspective to Texas, one educated by reformist thinking. Not only did she vocally prefer the verdant Massachusetts landscape to the dry, rugged terrain of the borderlands, but she also openly advocated temperance, abolitionism, and pacifism. Her ideological heritage saturated her letters home, particularly at first. However, the longer Chapman remained in Texas, the more her experiences shifted her thinking until she tentatively embraced the cause for which the war was fought.[30]

At first, Chapman recoiled at the shadowy legacy that war had bequeathed to both countries. "Tell all my friends that I have seen the Elephant, not in his improved condition after traversing two or three thousand miles of civilization but fresh from the camp," she wrote home. The experience left a bitter taste in her mouth. "The more I see of war," she insisted, "the more it seems to me unmitigated evil." As far as Chapman was concerned, the fruits of war were rotten from the branch out. An American presence in the valley had created moral dissipation among the soldiers, a lamentable loss of life on the battlefield, and a responsibility for questionable territory that no one could envy. Carnage had left its bloody mark at Buena Vista. There, more than a year after the battle had occurred, "arms and legs are found with the skin dried upon them and the clothing still on them," she wrote. No one could approve of such cruelty, she was certain. She only hoped that God might forgive the United States "and bring good out of evil."[31]

This prayer never changed completely, but the perspective from which it sprang shifted the longer Chapman lived in Texas. She had several opportunities to tour the area, including the battle sites of Palo Alto and Resaca de la Palma, and she observed locals on both sides of the Rio Grande. Eventually she gained some insight into the minds of those who had caused this war, and for one moment she understood what they had tried to accomplish. "We frown very justly on the idea of Destiny being made the excuse for this rapacious invasion of our neighbor's rights," she mused, "and yet it is impossible to live among a people so morally, physically and intellectually degraded without feeling assured that a more powerful race must before long subdue them." As delightful as she found Mexican women in Matamoros, Chapman fell prey to the same racialist sentiments as her fellow Americans. Since their first incursion into Hispanic territory, Anglo-Saxons (and others who lumped themselves into this admittedly obtuse category) had maintained their superiority to the politically and culturally backward Mexicans. Still, the opinion sat uncomfortably on her conscience at first; her idea had little logic to it, merely "intuition or impulse."[32]

Soon manifest destiny had found its beachhead in Chapman's philosophy. After her epiphany on Independence Day at the government hospital, in a town that only a year or two before had been in Mexican territory, she allowed herself to imagine good emerging from the evils she had witnessed. Not long afterward, this bud of enthusiasm blossomed into a full-scale endorsement of the triumph of American civilization over an inferior people. "There is something in seeing barbarism and civilization side by side, that affects you strangely," she said. "You feel the irresistible necessity that one race must subdue the other and, where the moral precepts are not keen and delicate, they, of the superior race, can easily learn to look upon themselves as men of Destiny, impelled to conquer and subdue by the great design of Providence." No longer did Chapman think it a bad thing that the conquerors of Mexico loved their conquest. The Mexican Cession was at last "in the hands of the Yankees," which could only benefit it. As "knowledge and freedom" seeped into the cultural fabric of the region, all its citizens would benefit. "Nothing escapes their ambition," she noted. The price of freedom, then, deserved any means.[33]

Chapman took her thoughts a step further, ironically joining with the most ardent expansionists. Many Americans, she noted, viewed the cession as "the first step to Annexation" of the rest of Mexico. During the war, some citizens lobbied for what became known as the All Mexico movement. The United States deserved more than New Mexico and California, advocates insisted; by virtue of its racial and cultural superiority, it deserved the entire continent. This idea gained more support in the North than the South. Many southerners quailed at the thought of racial mixing between Anglos and the "mongrel" Hispanics. Nevertheless, *DeBow's* exulted in the thought of spreading across the hemisphere for the greater glory of the republic. "We have New Mexico and California!" it declared. "We *will* have Old Mexico and Cuba!" Chapman agreed. "I may seem visionary in saying that if I should live to an ordinary age," she wrote, "I believe I shall see the whole southern part of North America included within the United States." Dreams of a United States reaching to Central America never saw reality, although Americans later attempted to realize them of their own volition. (This will receive more attention in a subsequent chapter.)[34]

Americans across the nation contemplated the land that had become theirs after the Treaty of Guadalupe Hidalgo. Citizens had distinctly different ideas about how to use it. As they had during the discussion of Texas annexation, sectional arguments flared in Congress. Would the cession become slave territory, as dictated by the Missouri Compromise of 1820, or would it be free? David Wilmot, a Pennsylvania congressman, sparked a new round of controversy when in 1846 he tacked an addendum onto an appropriations bill. "As an express and fundamental condition of the acquisition of any territory from the Republic of Mexico," the amendment read, "neither slavery nor involuntary servitude shall ever exist in any part of said territory." In other words, Wilmot effectively hoped to negate the Missouri Compromise. Ultimately most Americans believed the arid geography of the region made slavery untenable; however, that did not matter on the ideological battlefield. Southerners vehemently protested the Wilmot Proviso, insisting that it meant the destruction of political balance between North and South. The bill passed in the House of Representatives, but the Senate adjourned before it broke its deadlock. Northern hopes, for the moment, remained unfulfilled.[35]

Despite the failure of the Wilmot Proviso, the congressman had brought to the forefront an argument over slavery that had boiled in the background of American politics since the framing of the Constitution.

Since the late eighteenth century, when northern states began to pass manumission laws for slaves within their borders, a discernible split emerged. By the 1840s, the rise of abolitionism had expanded the gap between North and South until it had become a chasm almost too wide to bridge. A country originally unified by a desire for liberty had become two distinct cultures within one border, one reliant upon free labor and the other upon slaves. For the South, attacks on its economic and social structure (as they saw northern condemnations of slavery) threatened not only its internal stability, but the South's role in the nation. Southern states had built their economy and society upon slavery; Texas was only the most recent example. It followed, then, that expansion of the peculiar institution would continue to create a strong America. The next twelve years would test this idea.

6

Slavery and Expansion

When Jane Long followed her husband to Texas, she was not alone. She had her two young daughters with her, along with a female slave named Kian, or Kiamatia, the first known slave in Texas. Usually stories focus more on Long than on her companion, but Kian played a larger role than many people recognize. Originally the Longs had to mortgage Kian so they could finance their upcoming expedition, but Jane Long refused to let her remain in such a situation. She soon bought Kian back. When the women remained at Point Bolivar, awaiting James's return from his ill-fated expedition, Kian ventured outside the fort dressed in a man's uniform to gather firewood and food. Due to their fears of possible attacks by Karankawas, she also served as lookout and undoubtedly helped Long handle the heavy weaponry of the fort when the women set off the cannon at regular intervals. Perhaps it was Kian who first saw the party approach that told Long of her husband's capture. Despite her legal status, Kian and Long were partners and even friends in their battle for survival on the peninsula. After she died, Long mourned her and gave her "a decent funeral."[1]

Kian did not simply serve a mistress. Primitive and threatening circumstances complicated her situation, affecting her as an individual and not just as property. As part of a preliminary expedition, Kian was as isolated as the rest of the family. Her own survival depended on her work on the beach at Point Bolivar. She also needed food and fuel as well as protection from unknown enemies. Had she chosen to flee or not respond to the needs of the group, she would have suffered as much as those she had been bought to support. She and Long struggled together in the cold wilderness of the Gulf shore. The fort they occupied was the lone outpost representing American society, and their responsibilities there implicitly included holding out against the perceived threat of barbarism by natives and repulsion by Mexican forces. Texans revere Long in part because she held the fort, refusing to abandon her station despite all obstacles, and Kian contributed substantially to their success in that regard. Both women inspired later emigrants and strengthened the American presence—both Anglo and black—in Texas.

That blacks lived in Texas alongside whites, Native Americans, and Hispanics must not be forgotten. Blacks had accompanied Spanish explorers on their journeys through North America since the sixteenth century and had arrived in Texas from the United States since 1803. Despite this, historically they often become invisible settlers or are simply labeled as unwilling participants in American expansion because they arrived as slaves. This perspective is both incorrect and incomplete. Not all black emigrants to Texas came enslaved, and some who had did not remain so. Others already had their freedom and came anyway, hoping for the same opportunities as other Americans. These lesser-known emigrants' contributions to Texas' development are as noteworthy as anyone else's. They, no less than whites or Hispanics, worked to transform the wilderness for the greater glory of manifest destiny.

How this happened nevertheless carried considerable irony. Blacks, whether slave or free, fought alongside whites for liberty against Mexican oppressors in the Texas Revolution, yet at the same time what was for colonists a question of liberty was also a question of slavery. Texans fought simultaneously for both; one disagreement between Texans and Mexicans dealt with the right to own slaves in what Mexico had decreed to be a free territory. For many settlers who came from the South, manifest destiny championed both. This clash between two opposing concepts continued until the Civil War, when the conflict became far more deadly.[2]

Regardless of the situation's complexities, blacks joined others to bring a familiar culture to the wilderness. This occurred partly because of the innate benefits of selfish ambition in such cases; as settlers flourished, so would the country. Slave or free, black Texans had personal interests in this new land and strove to realize them. At the same time, the presence of blacks in Texas amplified a grim facet of expansionism. As noted earlier, the rationale behind the concept carried with it a racist element that focused on blacks as one more "other" with which to deal. How would their neighbors—Americans, Europeans, Hispanics, or otherwise—relate to this distinctly different segment of society? Citizens had to come to terms not only with racial differences, but those that life in slave territory imposed. The place of slavery in manifest destiny received considerable discussion, particularly in the 1850s, when sectionalism overwhelmed national politics. Blacks in antebellum Texas as a result could not be ignored.

Unfortunately, finding primary sources for black women in this period is difficult if not close to impossible. Little information exists for scholars for two reasons in particular. First, because many blacks in Texas were slaves, they did not have the opportunity to write letters or memoirs. Some left slave narratives, thanks to interviews with WPA historians in the 1930s, but these leave many questions unanswered and often merit suspicion regarding their facts. Another difficulty was that many blacks, free or not, were illiterate and therefore not able to record their thoughts for posterity. According to Ruthe Winegarten, only about five percent of slaves in Texas could write in 1860, and this number is undoubtedly high, compared to earlier dates. Of course, neither could many other Texan women read or write; Susannah Dickinson, the survivor of the Alamo, had to ask friends to write her petitions for aid to the legislature and signed them with her mark. But illiteracy presents only part of the problem. The combined effect of illiteracy, lack of opportunity, and population (whites outnumbered blacks by about six to one in 1836) squelched the voices of blacks in Texas. As a result, scholars must use either anecdotal evidence about blacks or white perspectives on blacks to determine what happened in the lives of this otherwise silent segment of society.[3]

One black woman who stands out does so as both fact and legend. Emily D. West became famous not because of what she did so much as where she was at a given time, although later storytellers attributed more action to her than she would have liked. West became better known as Emily Morgan, the "Yellow Rose of Texas," who delayed General Santa Anna enough with her feminine charm to allow Sam Houston to catch the Mexican army off guard at the battle of San Jacinto. The last name of

Morgan came from her employer, Colonel James Morgan, who had hired West to come to Texas from New Haven, Connecticut, to work as a house-keeper at a hotel in Morgan's Point. Texans assumed that she was his slave, one of many incorrect assumptions surrounding her story.[4]

In April, 1836, General Juan Almonte seized West and several others and held them captive. West soon found herself en route to Buffalo Bayou, where Santa Anna was preparing to attack Houston and his army. From here, said the legend, Emily (usually with no last name) became an unwilling consort of the general's. He was so distracted by the affections of his new concubine that he became completely unaware of his surroundings and ran out of his tent undressed and unprepared when the battle began. In reality, there is little evidence that West intentionally delayed Santa Anna, although it is likely that not only Santa Anna, but other Mexicans, took advantage of her while she remained in captivity. Nevertheless, rumors abounded afterward, and West's tale—or others' stories about West—were at the center of it all. West clearly did not enjoy her newfound celebrity. She stayed in Texas only until 1837, when she managed to procure a passport to leave.[5]

West's fame for her part in the emergence of the Lone Star Republic is ironic. All she did for her notoriety was fall captive to the enemy. She was literally in the wrong place at the wrong time. In contrast, blacks who lived in Texas for far longer and who contributed far more to the advancement of American civilization largely remain anonymous. Certainly none had songs written about them. As entertaining as the "Yellow Rose's" story was for later generations, its ultimate value pales in comparison to efforts of those who worked for years to create a viable place to live and to expand American influence beyond its current borders.

When examining the role of blacks in expansionism, it makes sense to begin with the slave population, the majority of blacks in Texas. Slavery gave the settlement of the territory a distinctive flavor that other western regions, such as California or Nebraska, did not have. Randolph B. Campbell calls Texas "an empire for slavery." This means that slavery shaped the nature of the expansion taking place in the area. Most emigrants were born in the South and either owned slaves themselves or were simply accustomed to a plantation-based culture. Moving west into Texas extended southern culture and expanded southern political and economic clout. About ninety percent of Texans were southern in 1850 and 1860, which meant that the emphasis on traditional southern ways—namely, slavery—would overshadow other perspectives. Plantations in the state produced ninety percent of its cotton, the state's primary export. As a result, slaveholders also dominated the state's government up through the Civil War. Slavery quickly became the distinguishing characteristic of this area of the West.[6]

Understandably, whites portrayed this arrangement as the ideal in Texas. At the same time, they promoted the peculiar institution as one benevolent for slaves as well, bringing them civilization and direction that they otherwise would not have. Slaves also hoped for better lives in Texas, although not in the same manner as their owners. Obviously they had little control over their immediate circumstances, but they utilized available avenues to better themselves. Some slaves worked not only for their masters, but to an extent for themselves, creating a more palatable environment in which to live. Kian's story provides an excellent example of this perspective. This in turn contributed to the idea of Texas' becoming the Garden of the World. Prior to the arrival of the agriculturalists, Anglos regarded Texas as merely a vast empty expanse; thanks to farmers and slaves, that had changed. One significant step in the process of manifest destiny had been completed: the cultivation of the land. Even if they did so unwillingly, slaves contributed to agricultural expansion by their presence.[7]

Despite the supposed benefit of slavery to Texan development, few settlers actually owned slaves. In 1850, only about one in four families and thirty percent of the heads of household in the state owned slaves; in 1860 the percentage had dropped to twenty-seven. The number of slaves was also low in comparison to states in the Deep South. Only 444 slaves lived in Texas in 1825; the number had grown to 5,000 at the time of the revolution; 58,000 in 1850; and 182,000 in 1860. Those who did not own slaves farmed the land themselves and thought little of it, but they never considered the possibility of using hired hands. It was simply too expensive to be practical in Texas.[8]

White settlers also dealt with other slavery-related problems prior to the revolution. The law in Mexico forbade slavery; some whites believed that this was because the Mexicans themselves were of mixed race, often including European, Indian, and African simultaneously. This made the idea of taking another race captive deplorable. More than likely, the Mexicans also remembered their own peonage under the Spanish. Regardless of the reason, the Mexican government sought to prevent settlers from bringing slaves into the province. Under the Imperial Colonization law of 1823, Mexico allowed colonists to bring slaves in with them, but any children they had enslaved had to be manumitted when they reached the age of fourteen. The Mexican government later found this decree too lenient. The Constitution of 1824 did not mention slavery explicitly, but a decree issued during the constitutional convention prohibited the slave trade altogether. Nevertheless, immigrants could still bring slaves with them. This state of affairs did not last long. The 1827 Constitution of Coahuila y Texas prohibited entry of slaves under any pretext, although later that year the government relented and allowed for the sale of slaves already in the state. Finally, on April 6, 1830, President Anastacio Bustamante prohibited all immigration from the United States into Mexico, whether slave or free.[9]

Colonists managed to work around the system, including empresario Stephen F. Austin's cousin, Henry. When inviting his sister Mary to come to Texas in 1831, he advised her to bring one or two slaves along to make her life easier. Because of Mexican law, he urged her to be circumspect in how she brought them. "Black Servants must be indented to work at low wages until their pay reimburses the money advanced for their liberty and the cost of clothing and other expenses as certify'd [*sic*] by the Mexican counsul [*sic*]," he informed her. "This is good title and agreable [*sic*] to Mexican law." By requiring "servants" to work off debt for their freedom, blacks frequently found themselves in the same situation as laborers later in the century, who owed increasing amounts of debt to the company store. Austin put a limit on the amount spent, but it would be easy to increase the amount due thanks to ever-increasing amounts of money spent on food and clothing for the slaves.[10]

Texans like Austin who indentured slaves this way had no intention of releasing them. This practice was an exercise in semantics for many colonists who refused to allow the law to interfere with their lifestyle. Instead of owning slaves, Texans now had "indentured servants for life," hiring out people for longer than their life expectancy. Because of Mexican law, many settlers became lawbreakers willingly, although, according to their reinterpretation of circumstances, they had broken no law. By working around the system, Anglos were subtly able to continue their practices and perpetuate the southern system of plantation agriculture. The charade ended quickly after the revolution, when the new republic permitted slavery, and the system continued into statehood.[11]

Whether their situation was labeled indefinite indenture or slavery, slaves still negotiated a difficult situation. Not all slaveholders treated their people humanely, but, even if they did, servitude compared poorly to the liberty that Texans had lauded so loudly and for so long. When slaves' circumstances proved too harsh to bear, they chose several different avenues of resistance or rejection. Many simply chose to escape, whether it be to join a loved one nearby or to Mexico, where freedom awaited. (Mexico rarely returned fugitives and usually protected them from those who would enter the country to hunt them down.) One mass exodus occurred in 1844 when more than thirty slaves fled across the Rio Grande to Matamoros. Whites frequently mocked this idea, doubting that the grass truly was greener on the other side of the river. Mary Helm had seen several former slaves flee south only to regret their decision later. Her opinion was patronizing, as she claimed blacks missed Texas because there they would be cared for when sick, and in Mexico they had to care for themselves. Her perspective was not uncommon.[12]

Although the majority of runaways were men, female slaves also fled when they could. Twenty-five-year-old Emily fled Houston in November, 1842, and was not found for some time. In the same way, Melissa, a seventeen-year-old mulatto, fled six years later; the advertisement for her recapture ran for months in the *Telegraph and Texas Register*. Still, the lower frequency of female runaways did not mean that they did not resist their circumstances, as historian Deborah Gray White notes. Women could easily appropriate other methods of resistance, such as sabotage of farm implements, poisoning the family's food from the kitchen, or simply playing sick. Any of these techniques could break down the plantation system for some period of time, granting even a brief respite from the strain of work.[13]

It is understandable that slaves frequently felt the need to abandon a life in Texas for one of liberty elsewhere. Nevertheless, others found themselves in situations more like that of Kian, where they faced the same dangers as their owners and joined them in the struggle against such threats. This occurred particularly when dealing with certain tribes of Native Americans. For Kian and Long it had been Karankawas, purported cannibals that lived on the peninsula. Years later, Comanches perceived black and white settlers as alike. Neither was Indian, and both were interlopers, and as such deserved attack or worse. When Comanches raided San Antonio in 1840, Mary Maverick's cook, Jinny, helped her barricade the door to the house just in time to prevent a warrior from entering.

Jinny then threatened another with a rock, defending herself as well as the Maverick household. Lizzie Atkins remembered Indians as being a constant danger in Texas prior to the Civil War, slaughtering livestock and stealing everything else. She rarely had the chance to go to church, because "if we left home to stay very long the Indians would steal and burn everything." Destruction of property or loss of life affected everyone on the farm, regardless of social status or race.[14]

Blacks also viewed other tribes with suspicion, not because they were hostile but because they also owned slaves. The practice of slaveholding existed primarily among "civilized" tribes such as the Choctaw and Chickasaw. As these tribes struggled to adjust to white standards, they frequently took on American habits and patterns, including owning slaves. Generally, mixed bloods began the practice within the tribe, because they had more interests in the white world, but it often expanded from there. Still, the behavior of Indian slave owners differed substantially from that of whites. Creeks and Seminoles, for instance, had too much mixed blood to consider blacks inferior. (Many Seminoles, for instance, had black ancestors, former slaves who had fled to Florida before removal.) Instead, these tribes treated their slaves as equals, often freeing them and intermarrying with them.[15]

As this indicates, the relationship between blacks and natives proved to be a complicated affair. Blacks often had sympathy for Native Americans as well, whether due to their own heritage or the fact that the two races shared an antagonist: whites. Amelia Barnett had an Indian grandmother (as well as a white father), and Catherine Green believed that she also had some native blood. Genealogy helped to foster understanding between the two groups, especially between blacks and mixed-blood Indians. At the same time, both blacks and the less adversarial tribes understood their situation. Both contended with Anglo settlers in less than ideal circumstances: blacks under slavery and Native Americans due to removal and other conflicts over land and culture. Blacks and Indians often shared an informal community of understanding. In contrast, blacks who felt threatened by Comanches and other hostile tribes supported the elimination of such barbarism from Texas and the triumph of American civilization. Ultimately, response to Indians depended on perspective.[16]

This notion proved true regarding Mexicans as well. During the period of the revolution, slaves could perceive Mexicans either as people to despise or to depend on for rescue. Many Tejanos saw slavery as a means to populate their province with willing Anglos, whereas others agreed with their government's ban on the practice. Either way, slaves were primarily interested in their own improvement, whether among Anglos and their dreams of manifest destiny or Hispanics and the promising hint of freedom under a questionable regime. As most slaves by the nineteenth century had been born and raised in an American culture, the choice was more difficult than the simple question of slavery versus freedom. For instance, Sarah Ashley worked as a domestic for an old, disabled woman until the woman's death. "Mistus Betsy" treated Ashley like her daughter, and Ashley remembered her kindly for it years later. In comparison, Nellie Hall suffered brutally at the hands of her owner's son, who liked to whip slaves with peach tree branches. Such drastic differences in treatment naturally affected how slaves viewed their circumstances and opportunities.[17]

For a time in the young republic, slaves had an opportunity to become free. Free blacks had lived in Texas since the early nineteenth century; although their numbers were few (in 1860, 355 free black Texans compared to more than 182,000 slaves), they contributed substantially to Texas' development. Among the free black community, blacks contributed most significantly to manifest destiny, creating a role for themselves within the nascent Americanized civilization in the republic. Tamar Morgan acquired such an opportunity for herself when she bought her freedom, along with "a considerable amount of Real Estate" in Brazoria County, in 1834. Later she married a free black barber and lived comfortably for some time.[18]

Most free blacks arrived during the colonial period, attracted by the antislavery position of the Mexican government and the lure of available land. During this period, the only other options available to them were either to face prejudice and discrimination where they were or to join the growing colonization movement and move to Liberia. Although they were African Americans, they were not Africans—the possibility of moving there did not appeal to many. Emigration to Texas allowed them to continue living within a familiar culture and in what they hoped to be better social circumstances. At the same time, as George Ruble Woolfolk suggests, free blacks viewed the frontier not just as physical, but also cultural. In the borderland between civilization and the wilderness—Texas in this period—free blacks could help reshape society into something more beneficial to their interests.[19]

One cultural gray area for free blacks lay in the realm of interracial marriages. Such unions faced harsh criticism in the United States; removing to

Texas originally provided a more lenient atmosphere. For instance, Harriet Newell Sands moved from Michigan in 1834 with her white common-law husband to escape their former neighbors. Even slaves were known to marry whites in Texas, the best-known example being that of "Puss" Webber and her husband, John. Webber was a slave when John married her but then became free. Known for her kindness to neighbors and even local Tonkawas, Webber nevertheless faced discrimination from other women who appreciated her kindness but could not consider her as an equal. If women came to visit her, she would serve them and then sit to the side, never eating with them. Similarly, if she chose to return the visit (the appropriate response in the etiquette-conscious world of true womanhood), the women were obliged to feed her, but did so in the kitchen, where she ate alone. In his memoir of life in early Texas, Noah Smithwick asserted that he urged the Webbers to move to Mexico, where they would not face such offensive behavior. They did so in 1851. For the Webbers, life in Texas ultimately proved as constricting as elsewhere in the States.[20]

Although some free blacks settled in East Texas and became farmers, most settled in urban areas, including San Antonio, Austin, Galveston, and Houston. There they established their place in society. Free women contributed as much as their men; contrary to the rules of domesticity, in which women stayed home and were unstained by the pressures of work, black women had to make money to support themselves and their families or else starve. Still, they usually took jobs in domestic areas not far removed from the ideals of true womanhood. Zelia Husk, Diana Leonard, and Fanny McFarland were washerwomen, and Charity Bird became a baker. (McFarland had lost everything she had at San Felipe during the Runaway Scrape.) One woman by the name of Margaret even ran a boardinghouse. Although these jobs were less acceptable socially, they provided necessary services in Texas cities. Such responsibilities supported and promoted the civilization that earlier settlers had begun to establish. In this way, free blacks effectively added to the success of manifest destiny in Texas.[21]

Texas' independence from Mexico brought problems for free blacks. Once it became a republic, Texas passed laws banning their presence. Under President Mirabeau B. Lamar in 1840, all free blacks were told to leave by January 1, 1842, or become slaves. In 1841, Houston changed the date to 1845, but the tension remained for those who had no desire to leave the lives they had created for themselves. The only option for those who wanted to stay was to request help from the state legislature and hope for a reprieve. One example of this is the case of Harriet Arnold, a young woman whose father, Hendrick, was a veteran of the Texas Revolution. In 1846, Hendrick gave his daughter over to a neighbor to become his slave on condition that she be manumitted in five years. Three years later, both her father and new master died of cholera. Two possibilities remained open for Arnold. One of her former owner's relatives requested to take her in as his slave. At the same time, other friends asked the legislature to allow Arnold to live as a free woman of color instead. Eventually the law ruled in Arnold's favor. Usually blacks' principal request was to remain free in Texas. They did not want their current opportunities taken from them. Tamar Morgan's white neighbors in Brazoria County petitioned the legislature on her behalf for this reason. (The legislature granted their request, and Morgan remained in Texas until at least 1844.) Free blacks had contributed to society as well as benefiting from it; a restriction of their liberty would have been, in their eyes, a violation of the rights they had worked toward alongside other citizens.[22]

Although their numbers were few, free blacks helped considerably in establishing a viable civilization in Texas, but typically other Texans tended to think of all blacks as curiosities. Slave or free made little difference to most, partly because so few free blacks lived in Texas at the time, but also because their color created a gap that was difficult to bridge. How different individuals treated blacks depended on their background: their race, ethnicity, or culture. Each factor added a new perspective to race relations in Texas. Considerable discussion but little action resulted, due in part to the political and cultural strength of local slaveholders.

Of all groups involved in the discussion over blacks' roles in society, Hispanics made the most efforts to act on their beliefs. Tejanos felt sympathy for blacks, who frequently faced as much discrimination as Hispanics themselves. Anglos in Texas saw Tejanos as inferior, as they asserted that Hispanics descended from Indians and blacks. As a result, they classed Mexicans and blacks together in some respects, always below Anglos on the racial and social hierarchy. Such attitudes helped create a bond between the two groups, a desire to look out for each other and help whenever possible. The anonymous Tejana wife of Ben Simpson's master certainly felt this way. She tried to give her slaves more food when she thought that her husband had not given them enough. The slave owner whipped her for her indiscretion, something Simpson remembered long afterward.

Tejanos also recognized their ties to their southern kin in Mexico, a free country. Thanks to Mexico's antislavery policy, Hispanics knew that blacks who traveled there could procure a better life for themselves than they frequently had.[23]

Because of this, many Tejanos helped slaves escape to Mexico. The country's proximity made such a practice easier, particularly due to the disputed territory between the Nueces and the Rio Grande. Anglos considered this "Negro-stealing" and harshly criticized the practice. In 1842, several local Anglo men captured a Mexican who had tried to escape south with a slave woman "with whom he had been living as his wife." Their marriage meant little to her owner; chances were that he prohibited slave marriages in the first place. Of more importance was the loss of property and the affront to his authority. The newspaper reported the incident as a warning to other planters. They needed to be "on their guard lest their slaves should be enticed away." Despite incidents such as these, sympathetic Tejanos could not do much for slaves. The institution was too large to challenge.[24]

Regardless of their impact on the slave system in Texas, Mexicans' obvious concern for blacks was evident. In *Following the Drum*, Teresa Vielé expressed her own disgust with Tejano compassion and favor. "In spite of philanthropy, Christian charity, and liberal views," she wrote, "I do not believe that the colored and white races can ever by any possibility amalgamate to an equality!" Holding to the racial beliefs then in vogue, Vielé not only considered blacks unable to reach white levels of civilization but also lumped blacks and Hispanics into one group. Their feelings of solidarity were justified, in her eyes: neither could attain superiority.[25]

German immigrants also sympathized with slaves. Few Germans owned slaves; only about nine percent had slaves in 1850 and four percent by 1860. These immigrants approached extra labor from a more European perspective, either hiring workers (usually German) to help, or, if no one was available, doing the work themselves. "The getting of female household help appears as yet quite a vexatious problem in this land," noted Ida Kapp. "I have not made any inquiry into the problem and do not know of anyone in town who has a maid." This problem emerged because when unmarried women arrived in Texas they frequently got married and quit working. "There is no one to help" in New Braunfels, Kapp complained; at least in Galveston families had "Negro girls" to assist them.[26]

Anglos tended to view Germans as abolitionists, but this perception was overly simplistic. Slavery presented Germans a serious dilemma that they could not easily resolve. Many immigrants were indeed antislavery; many intellectuals who had fled Germany after the revolutions of 1848 and settled across Central Texas became staunchly and vocally anti-slavery. The idea of holding other people captive sat poorly on their consciences; it contradicted the liberty they had gladly embraced upon arrival in the New World. Other Germans, who were afraid of being considered abolitionists, voiced pro-slavery opinions for their own protection. The projection of Germans as abolitionists still carried, due in part to an 1854 convention in San Antonio in which participants emerged with a resolution against slavery. Still, convention participants never intended to speak for the entire German community. Their statement was primarily rhetorical and received minimal reaction from the larger community.[27]

Theory meant little in such instances. In fact, in practice many Germans ignored such resolutions. Some emigrants became slave owners as early as 1840. Caroline von Roeder's family owned "domestics" (she disliked the term "slave") by 1835 as substitutes for "your good German servants." To von Roeder, blacks were nothing like the more familiar German help and merited description in letters home. "They are big-hearted, humble creatures," she wrote, "and learn our way of life readily." As unusual as slaves were to German eyes, von Roeder believed that her friends and relatives would "soon accept" the practice with little difficulty. Amanda von Rosenberg found her two slaves "absolutely necessary," given the amount of property her family owned. When writing her sister-in-law in 1850, she tried to describe how slavery differed from Europeans' perception of it in order to explain her participation in the peculiar institution. "It is said negroes are often treated inhumanly," she said, "but those are single cases." As far as von Rosenberg was concerned, oppressed Europeans suffered more than did the average American slave.[28]

Elise Willerich was not so sure. Her own experiences seemed to contradict those of von Rosenberg. Willerich desperately missed her farm hands but could not bring herself to keep the slaves she and her husband owned. They sold them, she wrote, because "they always ran away." In a letter to her father in 1848, Willerich reported that many Americans believed that "Germans don't know how to handle Negroes—are too good to them, and Willerich above all!" Their American neighbors had urged them to whip their slaves to ensure obedience, but neither she nor her husband could bear to do it. Their ambivalence paralleled that of other Germans. Many found themselves caught between pro- and antislavery forces and were uncertain how to negotiate the two. Frequently this resulted in little action that violated the status quo, as in the case of the Willeriches. Regardless of their views on slavery, Germans such as Emma Altgelt still struggled with racist tendencies. Altgelt had read *Uncle Tom's Cabin*, a sign of a mind open to antislavery possibilities, but she admitted that it did not change her perception of blacks themselves. When visiting one farmer's home, she met a woman holding her own child and that of her slave and rocking them in her chair. Regardless of having read Stowe, "I felt no desire to carry around the little woolly-headed child."[29]

To an extent, the same dilemma faced American whites, except that their numbers changed the nature of the argument. American arrivals came from several different regions, each with their own ideas about slavery and how it figured into Texan life. The majority of emigrants were from the South. They had been raised in a culture that accepted and supported slavery and therefore had far less difficulty with the institution than the four percent arriving from foreign countries. The seven percent that came from northern states, on the other hand, had little context from which to understand slavery. How these individuals dealt with the practice varied according to personal experience. Some came to accept the practice, even owning slaves themselves. Others retained staunch antislavery positions, insisting that liberty for only some was not true liberty, that for civilization to be achieved in Texas all inhabitants deserved to be free. (Of course, this idea rarely included Native Americans.)[30]

Southerners could not imagine life in Texas without slavery. Such assistance became even more important in this new territory and developed dimensions it had not had before. Because the land was so raw and desperately in need of cultivation, they took on every pair of hands they could find and afford. Frequently this did not amount to much. The majority of slaveholders—and women could own their own slaves—only owned one or two and frequently worked alongside them rather than leaving the slaves to do everything. Mistress and slave frequently faced the difficulties of frontier life side by side, each relying upon the other for assistance. Ella Fisher's grandmother, for instance, worked with all her slaves, teaching them how to do their various duties and helping them however she could.[31]

Admittedly, some of this bond between slave and mistress emerged in other parts of the South as well. As Catherine Clinton and Anne Firor Scott point out, white women frequently developed complicated emotional ties with their slaves because of their responsibility to them. Contrary to the idea of the frail southern flower living a reclusive life inside her mansion, plantation mistresses actively cared for their slaves, including demonstrating moral influence over those within their arena of responsibility. Fisher's grandmother demonstrated this interactive relationship, although her own work exceeded the bounds expected of most southern women. The rugged Texas landscape asked more from everyone for the ultimate goal of civilization. White women also faced the well-established pattern of obedience and submission, according to Scott, thanks to the well-worn tradition of master and slave. As slaveholders treated their slaves, they might also treat their wives and daughters, although admittedly to a lesser extent. This similarity of treatment purportedly created a feeling of pity for slaves that manifested itself in vaguely antislavery sentiments.[32]

Scott's theory of abolitionist mistresses finds little substance among slaveholding women in Texas. That some compassion existed is unmistakable, but slave owners needed their hands enough not to consider manumission very often. Instead, mistresses would usually try to make their slaves' lives as comfortable as possible. Emily Margaret B. Bryan Perry, for example, arrived in Texas from New York in 1831 and soon found herself the mistress of a plantation. Perry was the widowed sister of Stephen F. Austin, who wanted her to move to Texas along with their mother to be closer to his endeavors in the newly settled province. Her familiarity with plantation life was poor at best, yet she managed her property with common sense and savvy. She also showed her slaves as much consideration as she could to be certain she met their needs. Her story is not unusual in this respect. Although women felt concern for the well-being of their servants and others in their hire, they considered the slave system invaluable to the development of Texas. As they and their families had been called—indeed, destined—to move west with the country, so they had the responsibility to use whatever tools they had to accomplish their purpose of creating a garden out of the wilderness.[33]

Of course, Perry was not a southerner by birth, but by naturalization. Many northerners arrived in Texas in the same period, and most quickly acculturated to the southern way of life. Jane Cazneau, as always, provides a sterling example. She also came from New York and had little trouble adjusting to a mindset that allowed for slavery, although she did not own slaves herself. In her book *Eagle Pass*, Cazneau described the experiences of Mr. Grey, an Englishman with strong antislavery tendencies, as he traveled to Texas on a steamship with several nameless southern ladies. The discussion that followed paralleled typical southern apologetics of the time. One woman with whom he debated insisted that whites were divinely intended to be sovereign over other races, whereas blacks were designed for servitude. The women on board assured Grey that his ideas were better suited to a more temperate climate than Texas'. "Apples and anti-slavery are the natural growth of his latitude," Cazneau opined; "oranges and negro servitude demand a warmer climate." Grey would change his mind, she insisted, as soon as he experienced the climate for himself. Pages later she noted with some satisfaction that his ideas had indeed softened "in the warm rays of the southern sun." Experiences of some northerners and antislavery advocates in the state paralleled those of the befuddled Mr. Grey and Cazneau. Her own observations had drawn her to conclude that blacks, due to "their animal nature," could not without forcible assistance fully appreciate the opportunities civilization placed before them.[34]

Cazneau's last statement helps explain in part why northerners could assimilate to a culture founded on slavery. Regardless of their sentiments regarding the institution itself, many Americans held racial prejudices regarding blacks. As early as 1827, the Philadelphia-based *American Quarterly Review* called for an end to slavery but also insisted upon the "natural superiority of the whites over the blacks." Many northerners logically insisted on freedom for all as a necessary component of life in a republic but simultaneously rejected the concept of equality for all. Even the abolitionist classic *Uncle Tom's Cabin*, published in 1852, had its Ophelia St. Clare—the antislavery sister of plantation owner Augustine St. Clare—who held her own confused and racialist notions about blacks. Clearly such attitudes were common in the antebellum United States. With such a perspective already ingrained, it was easy to accept slavery as a natural extension of black inferiority. Geography, as it turned out, did little to shape racial attitudes.[35]

Like Ophelia, Lucadia Pease entertained beliefs regarding blacks that made it easier for her to accept slavery as viable. Pease came from Connecticut in 1850 after marrying her cousin Elisha, who would in a few years become governor of Texas. Along with her baggage came preconceived ideas of her own about how blacks should look and behave. (In fact, she maintained prejudices about most other "races" aside from her own; she once told a friend about the many Dutch—meaning German—and Irish inhabitants of Texas, describing them as "no very desirable society for the American population.") These ideas strengthened once she herself owned slaves. Her sister, Juliet Niles, soon absorbed similar notions upon arrival in Austin; in fact, her letters proved even harsher than those of Pease.[36]

The first difficulty Pease encountered was how to tell black from white. One of the servants in the house where she was staying was "whiter than any of the ladies, with light sandy hair," a fact that the recent arrival found difficult to absorb. She had concerned herself primarily with skin color; now that she had met a woman with mixed ancestry, Pease began to wonder how such a girl must feel, having to "associate with real black negroes." The idea appeared "awful" to her, but more complicated was "how seldom ones [*sic*] expectations are fully realized in the description of any person." Looks, she discovered, could not be conclusive. Of course, Pease soon replaced visual discrimination with that of personality. She had several run-ins with her slaves, whom she deemed lazy and thoroughly frustrating. In one letter to her husband, she wrote how she would not "allow myself to annoy you with any of my little domestic trials, even those relating to sable sons and daughters of the Afric [sic] race." Pease had not allowed her prejudices to hinder her from owning slaves, but that did not mean she had to enjoy the experience.[37]

Still, Pease's writings were circumspect compared to those of Niles. Rather than hinting at the "domestic trials" her sister's slaves created, Juliet accused them outright of allowing "waste & extravagance" so outrageous that their mother could not live in such squalor for a week. Pease's clothes had become moth-eaten rags, because her slaves "make it a rule never to do as they are told to do." This behavior hints at possible resistance, slaves' rejecting orders to make life more reasonable. Even with work going undone, however, Niles insisted along with other Texans that slavery proved "essential, or one thing needful to existence" to live comfortably. New arrivals could easily set aside "any little prejudices" to embrace slave ownership. Niles seemed to believe that prejudice only hindered slavery, whereas modern scholars would intimate that prejudice—the belief that blacks are inferior—supported an atmosphere in which whites could enslave blacks.[38]

But not all northerners harbored such views or allowed themselves the "benefit" of owning slaves, particularly by the late 1840s and early 1850s. By this point antislavery sentiment had grown so strong that its adherents refused to equivocate on the issue. As a staunchly Protestant New Englander, Helen Chapman wrote passionately of the evils of slavery and never changed her mind as she had regarding Texas' role in the ultimate destiny of the United States. For her, the debate maintained biblical proportions, separating northern sheep from southern goats; those retaining "Northern feelings and principles," for instance, pitied slaves caught trying to run away, while slaveholders obviously had no understanding of right and wrong or sympathy in their breasts for fellow suffering human beings. "The more I know of slavery," she wrote, "the more horrible it seems to me and darker and darker grow the clouds that hang over the future." Despite such strong words, the degenerative influence slavery had upon master and slave alike motivated Chapman to speak against it. The system itself dehumanized and led all involved onto a pathway to a hell on earth.[39]

Chapman's antislavery sensibilities carried over into her choice of literature as well. In 1852, she located a copy of *Uncle Tom's Cabin* to read— a rarity, because most southern bookstores had already decried the book and refused to carry it. "I believe this is the only copy in Texas," she wrote with some pride. Later she tried to explain its nuances to friends who had not followed her south and who could not grasp how accurately Stowe had portrayed slaves and slave life. Only those who had lived in the South understood how true the portrayals were, she noted. "You only know the African race as stupid, indolent, poor, pariahs among you as most of the free Negroes are," she wrote, "but I have seen enough to convince me that, in moral nobility, there may be many Uncle Toms in the lighter shades of the mulatto population." Of course, the term "Uncle Tom" did not at that time connote a racial sellout, pandering to white desires while rejecting black culture and interests. What struck her was the humanity of slaves, regardless of their treatment. Chapman's comparisons carried with them their own stereotyping (she also acknowledged having seen plenty of young black girls with a "most wonderful family resemblance to Topsey"), particularly given her comments regarding mulattos. Nevertheless she succeeded in freeing herself from some of the more negative characterizations that plagued others on both sides of the Mason-Dixon line and continued to hold slaves captive both literally and figuratively.[40]

Chapman focused not only on society or literary works. She also expressed interest in the political events of her day and the role of slavery in them. Slavery had been an issue between North and South since the days of the early republic, but by the 1840s the discussion had heated to the boiling point. The annexation of Texas and the Mexican War in 1846 presented a critical question: What to do with slavery in the newly acquired lands? Few northern legislators wanted to adhere to the agreement reached in the Missouri Compromise of 1820, concerned by the possibility of the extension of slavery; meanwhile, southern leaders feared imbalance in Congress and a loss of clout if territories south of the compromise line emerged as free territories. Such divisive topics flashed back and forth across Capitol Hill, but they also crowded the thoughts of average female citizens such as Chapman.

For example, Chapman regarded the Wilmot Proviso as an extraneous piece of legislation. As far as she was concerned, it could only hold sway over Texas, not the other territories the United States received during the war. She and other Americans probably recognized that places like New Mexico or Utah had little need for slaves, because the geography could not support plantation agriculture. Left to its own devices in such an arid location, slavery would die of attrition even without the help of abolitionists. Besides this, Chapman did not even believe that Texas required a slave population to keep things moving; Mexican labor was by far cheaper. "I fervently trust that Northern men will fight to the last moment against the introduction of slavery into the new territories," she wrote adamantly. Were she able to participate in politics as men did, she declared, "I would love to be carried dying to the Senate chamber to spend my last breath in this cause." Her imagination may have provided her with an overwhelming sense of melodrama, but the desperate times in which she lived required powerful statements to demonstrate the depth of the situation. "It *does* seem to me there are great dangers in the future," Chapman insisted. Everything she saw pointed to a coming disaster, one she readily recognized and expected.[41]

Understandably, much of the discord emerging from the slave question in antebellum America dealt with expansionist leanings in the South. Rather than focusing on the extension of the United States as a whole, however, southern expansionism by this point took on added characteristics of its own, championing the right of the South to pursue its interests west in accordance with the Missouri Compromise. Slavery had brought civilization to hundreds of thousands of blacks; to expand the institution could only benefit that many more. In this way, southerners could bring more people—of all races—into the sphere of Anglo American influence.

Therefore, when northern politicians sought to cut off southern interests in the West, southerners began to look elsewhere for satisfaction. Manifest destiny remained the prime directive; however, the direction of that goal changed. During the 1850s, southerners—as well as expansion-minded northerners and others who saw the possibilities to the west being fulfilled—began to encourage expressions of republican fervor abroad, specifically Latin America. Thwarted enthusiasts for manifest destiny looked even farther southward to share the American bounty with their neighbors. Some went even further than that, hoping for an American influence so pervasive that it swallowed up its neighbors in expansionistic glee. Such an interpretation was drastic and not always shared among expansionists in the United States. It was the last great gasp of manifest destiny before the Civil War temporarily extinguished its purpose, one that yet again called both men and women to its active service.

7

A Magnificent Empire

Near the end of her encomium on Texan expansion, *Following the Drum,* Teresa Vielé lauded the efforts of those who contributed to its annexation to the Union. Such a noble deed, she wrote, found its worth primarily "in the light of history." The absorption of Texas provided purpose in the Mexican War, allowed for the annexation of new territory into the United States, and made great strides for the cause of manifest destiny. Although it did not seem so to many at the time, Vielé insisted that only through an informed backward glance at history could Americans understand the "silent workings of a new and peculiar phase of civilization" that Texas had brought to fruition. Simply by insisting on their acceptance as part of the republic, she said, Texas had helped pave the way for even more expansion.

None of this meant that Anglo Texans relied completely on their mother country to maintain the state's greatness. Even without the assistance of the rest of America, the former Lone Star Republic could flourish on its own, expanding without anyone else's help. "There is no doubt," she said, "that were the rest of the Union to pass from existence, there would yet be left, within the limits of Texas, the element of a magnificent empire." Not only had Texas been the beneficiary of manifest destiny, it had also been its heir, learning the important lessons of expansion well enough to apply them without aid in the future should the need arise. Manifest destiny and Texas had become inseparable in Vielé's eyes.[1]

With such a legacy at their disposal, Texans maintained a sense of purpose regarding expansion. The dissolution of the United States seemed at the time unlikely, giving the state the opportunity to continue the cycle of regeneration and civilization. It had the means with which to promote the welfare of the nation, spreading civilization across the continent and abroad, wherever republicanism emerged. The process had worked for Texas, after all; its success assured westering Americans that they were representatives of a superior race who would quickly conquer all by sheer force of will and the benefit of its righteousness. As a result, these nascent republics (or, more preferably, future states in the Union) demonstrated both their value and that of the nation that influenced them by its own shining example. Texans' devotion to the cause of manifest destiny would prove invaluable, if the rest of the nation united in the push for further expansion.

Such was not to be the case. During the 1850s, North and South clashed on the questions of both slavery and expansionism. Northern antislavery advocates feared that southerners only desired increased opportunity to spread the peculiar institution. This complication made it almost impossible—aside from one or two brief and highly controversial incidents, such as the emergence of the Ostend Manifesto in 1854—to pursue manifest destiny by federal means. Thus, Texans took their enthusiasm for manifest destiny and applied it elsewhere, specifically to sectional interests. They believed that expansion would benefit the South; because of its ties to slavery, in this instance Texas allied itself with the region rather than the entire nation.

The push for manifest destiny still carried nationwide interest in the 1850s. The Young America movement, for instance, desired expansion into Latin America. Nevertheless, partisan disputes restricted enthusiasts from accomplishing their goals. Expansionists in Texas and elsewhere had to look to more unorthodox means to meet their goals. It was the decade of the filibusters, men who took the interests of state—or what they believed the state should be—into their own hands. Republicanism required Americans to act with force in those regions that had shown stirrings of liberalism. The López expedition in Cuba provides an example of this, as does the presence of the Liberty Party in Nicaragua before the arrival of

William Walker. These men then combined with this a considerable amount of personal interest. Not only power but wealth awaited those who agreed to take the reins.[2]

Of course, most Americans did not become filibusters, but they did participate indirectly by following the adventurers in their exploits, raising money for them, and cheering them on if they should happen to come to town. Audiences of women and men alike showed their support publicly, although in different ways. As the gentler species, unable to sign up for the next foray, women attended rallies and looked for other ways to realize expansionism in Latin America. Some found literary outlets to encourage Americans to devote themselves to expansionist causes. Jane Cazneau, who had always inadvertently stretched the boundaries of women's roles, soon made herself famous—or infamous, depending upon perspective—in the public arena with her bold involvement in diplomatic affairs. Overall, however, women tended to express themselves more reservedly, whether that meant presenting banners before an assembly or offering some other means of support.

Such enthusiasm for expansion permeated the region. As noted above, the bulk of political influence in Texas came from the Democrats after the Mexican War, primarily due to the influence of debates over slavery. By the mid-1840s to early 1850s a branch of the Democratic Party had emerged and taken hold of the vibrant energy that the recent victory over Mexico had created. In a short amount of time, the United States had added an incredible amount of territory. Where would the country go next? The answers to this question were myriad. Some endorsed the All Mexico movement, insisting that the United States take the Mexican War to its logical conclusion; others looked north, to Canada. Cultural similarities had tied the two nations since both were British colonies. The United States had offered Canada annexation (with more than a hint of force) as early as the American Revolution and had invaded its northern neighbor again during the War of 1812. Although these attempts at unification failed, many Americans still believed that it was only a matter of time until Canada would acquiesce and become part of the United States. Helen Chapman, who had once dreaded the idea of taking in the land annexed by the Treaty of Guadalupe Hidalgo, welcomed the idea of absorbing the northern Dominion in the same way. "As for me," she announced, "the more snow and ice they annex to the mammoth Republic the better." (One can only assume that Chapman, after years on the Rio Grande, missed her New England winters.) Unfortunately for those who endorsed this plan, no one could obtain Canada's permission to do so. Interest remained, even though expansionists never managed to achieve their goals.[3]

Those who pushed expansion in the 1850s included a group that called themselves the Young America movement. According to Edward Widmer, the label Young America had existed for some time before the 1850s; men such as New York journalist John O'Sullivan and Nathaniel Hawthorne had banded together to establish the movement in 1837. Under its aegis they created the *United States Magazine and Democratic Review,* which became one of the most popular journals in the country for the next twenty years. Prior to the Mexican War, Young America carried with it primarily a literary connotation, celebrating the energy of democracy in writing and, to a far lesser extent, in politics. After the war matters changed; the perpetuation of manifest destiny meant not only the promotion of American culture and philosophy, but its proliferation in areas never before available. For some this also meant the use of force, if necessary, to obtain these lands and sow republicanism upon their fertile soils. Widmer tends to focus on Young America I (as he calls it), separating it from the Young America II of the 1850s while negating the presence of O'Sullivan in both. Still, he astutely points out that these latter Young Americans focused heavily upon the absorption of territory by whatever means and whenever possible. The difficulty with Young America was its partisan affiliation. Because of increasingly inflammatory arguments in Congress regarding slavery, its interests rarely made headway.[4]

As a result, more Americans turned to the idea of filibustering to obtain land and spread the gospel of republicanism wherever they could. The term "filibuster" ultimately came from the Dutch *vrijbuiter,* or freebooter (pirate), and although the pirate label still applied (and many Americans used similar terms freely when referring to overly adventurous individuals in the nineteenth century), filibuster carried a more political connotation. Although filibusters did search for treasure in whatever form they could find it, they primarily sought power and influence over the area that they tried to conquer. American filibusters typically went abroad under the banner of nascent republicanism, fighting to bring the American political system to life in the country of their choice. In this way, they could gain the approval of their countrymen while disguising an egocentric thirst for attention, but it was difficult to discern individual motives in the thick of battle.[5]

The benefit of filibustering was that it did not depend on the fickle whims of Congress to act. In fact, although individual legislators and others often supported the actions of various men to some degree, filibusters typically emerged while the government opposed intervention altogether. In such cases filibusters often served as the corporeal will of the people, moving forward where the government, for whatever reason, feared to tread. This sort of unabashed political enthusiasm represented democracy in its purest form as it responded to supporters (and their money). Without popular support, the movements faded into obscurity, not only because they lacked funding but because they could not garner the men, supplies, and enthusiasm they required to sustain themselves. The political climate of the 1850s provided the perfect opportunity for filibusterism. Due to sectional pressures, cries of manifest destiny frequently failed in the face of governmental inaction, only to resurface in enthusiasm for some private individual planning to take the mantle of freedom abroad.[6]

And filibusterism was nothing new to Texans. James and Jane Long followed the filibuster pattern when they arrived in Texas in 1820. Without political sanction, they gathered troops and advanced against a foreign nation to bring about the triumph of republicanism in the region. As in other examples, the Long expedition relied on private support to subsist. In James Long's case, however, it was more the Mexican government than lack of support from other Americans that destroyed him. Filibusters faced capture and possible execution from the beginning, but often wanderlust, thirst for adventure and gain, and even bursts of patriotism overwhelmed such motivations. Even civilians fell prey to this enthusiasm due to their acceptance of the basic principles of manifest destiny. Filibusters appeared to take seriously the idea of expansion of republican beliefs and American ideals. With that in mind, it would be easy to extend one's support to their cause.[7]

The example of such enthusiasm with the closest proximity lay directly to the south in Mexico. Thanks to their long history of awkward relations, Texans regarded Mexico with suspicion as well as contempt. The nation had held Texas captive, at least as far as its denizens were concerned, until 1836 and had then tried sporadically to retake the nascent republic until the end of the Mexican War. This left Texans understandably wary of the country's intentions. Simultaneously, they felt superior to their former rulers; at last, the subjects had become the overlords. Although new to

Texas herself, Helen Chapman remained certain that the conflict between the two would never subside "so long as the imperfect civilization continues." Her words imply an aggressive move on Mexico, reworking the nation by working around its people. Despite these feelings, Texans thought it appropriate to support any stirrings of republicanism Mexico might indulge. (Mexico did not seem to be a republic to Americans, given its internal political discord in the early nineteenth century.) Even Chapman feared that intervention in Mexico might trample on the rights of its people, who were, after all, partially civilized.[8]

After the war with the United States, it appeared that Mexico might be ready to move toward republicanism. Many Americans noticed the shift in Mexico's political climate and commented on it. "The Mexicans look for a new republic," Chapman noted. For many, this new republic was not far distant. "When you hear of a revolution in Mexico," opined Jane Cazneau, "you may prepare to celebrate the birth of another nation." Cazneau recognized that Mexico had been a nation since 1821; what concerned her more was the birth of a republic looking to the United States for tutelage. Cazneau did not stop there; she became heavily involved in what became known as the All Mexico movement. Merely setting a good republican example for one's neighbor no longer made sense. Annexation became the only means to the appropriate end. Otherwise the country would collapse during the attempt. Vielé agreed. Although Mexico could offer the United States little in return for its favor, only annexation could save it from a grim fate.[9]

The focus of the All Mexico set concerned Mexicans and Americans alike. On a trip to Mexico City for her health in 1851, Chapman reported the country's political climate in a letter home. The Mexicans were greatly disturbed by the talk they had heard from the United States, she said. Any step they took had to be made carefully, as they feared they might "precipitate the progress of the United States" if they moved without concern for their more powerful northern neighbor. Still, Chapman's observations did not deter her from her support of an American Mexico. "I may seem visionary in saying that if I should live to an ordinary age," she wrote, "I believe I shall see the whole southern part of North America included within the United States."[10]

For a time, Chapman's prophecy appeared to have some validity. After the collapse of the All Mexico movement, filibusters turned their attention to their southern neighbor and attempted to make a republic out of it by force, if necessary. Vielé eagerly recorded the details of one such expedition into northern Mexico in *Following the Drum*. According to her information, the filibusters scattered the Mexicans and their allies, forcing many into a nearby river where they drowned. The Americans won the fight long after nightfall, depending on Indian reinforcements from the United States. Rather than considering the experience barbaric or bloody, as Chapman would have been prone to do, Vielé celebrated it. Such displays of gallantry, she determined, only added to the aura of respect and veneration granted them by the "simple and ignorant peasantry of our border." As the Mexicans along the Rio Grande watched, in other words, they learned to appreciate American ways.[11]

By 1858, when Vielé's book was published, Americans had become accustomed to the idea of filibusters working toward a Mexican republic. The best known of these was the quintessential filibuster William Walker, who entered Baja California in November, 1853, and soon declared himself president of the Republic of Lower California. Two months later he invaded Sonora, annexed it, and renamed the expanded region the Republic of Sonora. Walker held power only a few months longer, after tensions between him and his men resulted in mass desertions. More than likely, however, Vielé referred instead to the actions of later groups such as the Knights of the Golden Circle. Cincinnati resident George Bickley formed the Knights on July 4, 1854. The secret society emphasized expansion in Latin America. The "golden circle" had Havana at the epicenter and extended to encompass the southern United States, part of Kansas, Mexico, Central America, and the West Indies. (The establishment of slavery remained of central importance in the KGC platform.) Texans in particular flocked to the Knights due to their strong emphasis on Mexico; as noted earlier, any attempt to subjugate their former oppressors came as a golden opportunity. Although the group's secrecy makes it difficult to determine exact numbers, it appears that about thirty KGC "castles" operated in twenty-seven Texas counties. In 1859, the Knights launched a filibuster against northern Mexico as Bickley recruited men for the task. So many men traveled through Texas heading for Mexico that the army had to stop all parties posing as emigrants. Two expeditions reached the border in the spring and fall of 1860, but nothing came of either of them. The Knights abandoned their expansionist bent in 1860 with the election of Abraham Lincoln to the presidency, focusing instead on the merits of secession. By then, however, the society had already made its mark.[12]

The Knights of the Golden Circle might have hoped to be a secret organization, but they were not so secret that their neighbors did not know of their endeavors. The women of Henderson, for instance, managed to follow what their local branch had been up to for some time. In fact, to show their own support for unorthodox expansion, the ladies presented the Knights with a flag in March, 1860, not long before the group moved toward Mexico for the first time. By doing so, they became involved in the group's activities indirectly, endorsing the cause of manifest destiny with a banner, as they had done for decades in military and social struggles alike, for wars of state as well as wars of the spirit. Here they had both. Like Vielé, other women wanted to participate in the exciting events of the day; providing public, symbolic support brought both them and their cause to the forefront.[13]

Mexico remained important to Texans for obvious reasons. If nothing else, proximity made republicanism crucial. Their support for Cuba, on the other hand, requires more explanation. Local focus on Mexico had been ongoing since the 1820s; the movement within the United States to annex (or at least liberate, which nevertheless implied eventual annexation) the island emerged as an argument of any weight only after the Mexican War. Still, prior to this, the idea had its supporters. The *American Quarterly Review* had considered the potential of Cuban annexation as early as 1831 but had determined that it was currently "impracticable." Annexation would occur eventually, but the editors saw no reason to force the issue. Eleven years later, the *Southern Quarterly Review* mentioned Cuba, insisting that the island had seeds of greatness that only the United States could bring to full flower. Regardless of how it occurred, said the *Review,* Cuba would one day become a satellite within the American "constellation." How that would occur, and when, remained to be seen.[14]

Apparently the time was right in 1848, when it remained the only country in the Western Hemisphere still under Spanish control, a fact that rankled lovers of independence and liberty across the United States. Natives were "mercilessly fleeced" by the brutal Spaniards, their dreams of liberty checked by a tyrannical government that served only itself. By virtue of their superior character and abilities, it would take three to four thousand Americans at most to rout fourteen thousand Spanish and claim the island for liberty. Idealistically, the editors reasoned, democracy impelled Americans to spread its interests abroad, wherever liberty promised to bloom, as appeared the case in Cuba. Still other, more pragmatic, reasons made the possibility that much more appealing. The island offered "land and gold" for those bold enough to claim it. There were also trade benefits. The island made its fortune from sugar; although plantations in Louisiana also grew sugarcane, taking control of the fields in Cuba could provide a corner on the market. Economically it could offer its sugar and trade for American benefit. Slavery on the island also provided American southerners potential benefits. If the country were to be annexed as a state rather than a territory, it would add to the South's representation in Congress and buttress its defense against abolitionists and Northern aggressors. It would also contribute to the foundation of slavery in the United States, making it that much harder to uproot—if it ever came to that. In Cuba enthusiasts for manifest destiny had the ultimate prize: both the triumph of republicanism abroad and potential economic expansion. For many Americans, the two concepts did not conflict.[15]

Jane Cazneau, writing as Cora Montgomery to shield herself and her husband William from excessive attention, tried to win the cause of Cuba for her country several times. She had traveled to Cuba with Moses Y. Beach in 1847 en route to Mexico when he had been appointed special agent during the war. In June and July of that year, the New York *Sun* published reflections of her travels in "Letters from Cuba." From this point on she supported the Cuban independence movement, coupled with eventual annexation to the United States. She even helped to run a bilingual newspaper designed solely to promote the Cuban cause. *La Verdad* published between 1848 and 1853 from the *Sun*'s offices in New York with Cazneau as one of its columnists. The independence of Cuba meant so much to her that she even lobbied for American intervention on the island, pressing Secretary of State James Buchanan and Presidents Zachary Taylor and Franklin Pierce to act on the situation. Although her political efforts gained her little, Cazneau maintained her influence through her writing in the public arena.[16]

In 1850, Cazneau wrote *The Queen of Islands, and the King of Rivers*, a book on Cuba and the Mississippi River. *The Queen of Islands* served primarily as a propaganda piece for the independence movement, trying to persuade Americans that the absorption of Cuba into their country would be in the best interests of all involved. Like other writers of the day, Cazneau began her work with a plea for compassion from all those who loved freedom and desired it for everyone. "An oppressed nation stands in the gates of our confederation and pleads with God and man for liberty,"

she announced. The Cubans were at last rising up against their domina-
tors, even as Washington and Jefferson had done decades before. If our
Founding Fathers had acted appropriately, she reasoned, "Cuba cannot
be wrong in following their example."[17]

Cazneau did not stop with patriotism in her pamphlet for Cuban annexation. Carefully she outlined the material and political benefits of the
island's location, not only for security's sake (eliminating European presence in the Western Hemisphere) but as a gateway to one of several westward routes to California. Given the contemporary rush to that state
thanks to the discovery of gold, the timing of current American interest
in Cuba was fortuitous. Cazneau also addressed the value of Cuban trade.
What interested her most, however, was the question of slavery on the
island. She recognized that this caused the most controversy among
Americans. Here she stepped carefully, trying to reason out the condition of slaves in Cuba to justify American perpetuation of the system. Were
the United States to annex Cuba, she said, slaves on the island could relax
in the knowledge that Americans were far kinder taskmasters than were
the Spanish. Under the Spanish, all Cubans suffered, and slaves even more
so. In contrast, American slaves had benefited in their slavery, having been
blessed with "happiness and civilization." This was more than Cazneau
could say for blacks in Haiti and Jamaica, where they ruled themselves
and still suffered. For all Cubans, then—slave and "free"—the United
States had a duty to intervene.[18]

Attempts such as Cazneau's helped create sympathy for the Cuban
cause but spurred little action. Nevertheless, the first large-scale filibustering expeditions occurred in Cuba in 1850 and 1851. The attempts began not as American ventures, as was typically the case, but native ones.
Narciso López, a Venezuelan who had made Cuba his home for decades,
wanted to see his adopted country break from Spain. Because of his ideological ties to the United States, López identified Americans as kindred
spirits who might assist in his quest for Cuban freedom. He even offered
the possibility of eventual annexation—a goal after which expansionists
had lusted for decades—to sweeten the deal. However, the fear that Cuba
might strengthen the power of pro-slavery forces kept many northerners
from pledging themselves to López's cause. Undaunted, the Venezuelan
turned to the West and South instead. Soon his filibuster army swelled
with Americans in its ranks until he at last felt prepared to face the
enemy.[19]

During the first assault in May, 1850, the eager troops lasted little more than a day on the island before retreating to the United States. After time to reconsider and regroup, López returned to Cuba in August, 1851. He and his fellow liberators fared slightly better this time, fighting almost five days against the Spanish, but this time they could not escape. The Spanish executed the captured filibusters, many of whom were American. López himself was garroted on September 1, effectively ending the republican movement in Cuba for the time being. Americans who had supported López and his ideals protested vehemently his death and the deaths of the Americans involved, crying vengeance against Spain. Their words met a sympathetic audience, but one that was unwilling to move against the Spanish. Soon the movement dwindled to an undercurrent of proannexationist sentiment.[20]

The López expeditions captured the hearts and imaginations of the American people. The tale of the Cubans seemed to match their own. It behooved those who had already triumphed over tyranny to assist those who still hoped to. As Michael Hunt notes, Americans have felt an affinity for those fomenting revolutions since the beginnings of the republic. The caveat with this principle was that not all revolutions bore the marks of an orthodox rebellion, meaning the War for Independence. Without any control over events, Americans often became uncomfortable with the unexpected twists and turns. Cuba enthusiasts seldom dwelled on such concerns. By linking their own country with the struggling republic-to-be, expansionists could direct what transpired, molding Cuba into their own image and simultaneously preparing it for eventual annexation.[21]

One American captivated by López was Lucy Holcombe Pickens, who moved with her family to Marshall, Texas, in 1850, when she was eighteen. Much of her attraction to the Cuban cause was attached to her attraction for an anonymous soldier who was captured and executed by the Spanish in the second expedition of 1851. Some speculation exists that the soldier was Colonel William Logan Crittenden, one of the more famous recruits. Apparently she had met him while visiting New Orleans, the same time she met John A. Quitman, governor of Mississippi. Quitman was a leading figure in the López expeditions and an avowed expansionist who was in Louisiana recruiting volunteers. Pickens also met López himself and became transfixed. Although her father disapproved of his filibustering ways, she devoted herself wholeheartedly to his cause.[22]

After meeting Quitman and the others, Pickens believed strongly enough regarding a free Cuba that she ventured into the public sphere to write a novel on López's behalf (as well as that of her dead friend). Under the asexual pseudonym H. M. Hardiman, she published *The Free Flag of Cuba; or, The Martyrdom of López,* a study in contradictions. Defying clear definition, it was a part-romance, part-adventure apologetic for the cause of manifest destiny. The work emerged in typical, nineteenth-century sentimentalist fashion, not unlike *Uncle Tom's Cabin* or *Ten Nights in a Bar-Room* (although clearly it never obtained the audience of either), and similarly devoted itself to serious issues. Pickens even dedicated the work to Quitman. Still, her former beau had motivated Pickens to write; this book was not for fame, but for the release of the oppressed in Cuba in memory of those such as her "kindred blood" who had died for it.[23]

The tale revolves around two women, Genevieve Clifton and Mabel Royal, and their beaux. Royal comes to visit Clifton in Louisiana as the latter struggles against her lover's desire to fight for López in Cuba. While Clifton insists that the Cubans do not deserve freedom, everyone else in the novel disagrees with her, including her beau, Ralph Dudley. "Poor Cuba!" he cries. "She is burning, she is pining for the dear light of freedom. Her children send to us from every quarter, and shall the cry of the oppressed reach the American and find him cold and dumb? God forbid that freemen should scorn the wail of the weak!" Clifton mocks his idealism, calling his goal a dream, but soon her words are thrown back in her face. "You have called it a dream," Dudley replies, "but is it not a glorious one when a people dream of freedom and wake to liberty?" Against his love's wishes, Dudley leaves for Cuba. Soon Eugene de France, Dudley's friend, also wishes he had volunteered for the fight, but he needs more motivation to take the next step.[24]

That motivation comes from Mabel Royal. Royal has recently arrived from the North. Royal is a strong character, fiercely supportive of the López expedition and beloved of de France. Under her guidance, he decides to join Dudley in Cuba. She and Clifton soon fight over the legality of the situation, the latter insisting the filibuster is illegal, while Royal says it would be against the principle of the law not to go. Royal's forthright manner soon antagonizes others at a dinner party, where she finds herself in deep conversation with Captain Stuart Raymond over the propriety of a woman's supporting such matters in what appears to be an unladylike manner. With words like hers, Raymond says accusingly, Royal "would give woman the right to throw herself into the whirlpool of politics, and wrestle with the plebeian democracy." She quickly denies the accusation but notes that, "if man was truer to his duties, woman would not seek to assist him in his legitimate sphere." Such words win the argument for Royal, as well as for Pickens herself, who thereby justified her own intrusion into the "whirlpool of politics" in her work.[25]

The story then shifts to Cuba, where both Dudley and de France fight as patriots and liberators (López himself preferred the terms over "filibusters") for the glorious cause. De France is killed with one blow, and later López dies for his "*dear* Cuba!" and is buried in the United States. After this, somewhat incongruously, a double wedding occurs between all the surviving main characters: Dudley marries Clifton (having barely rescued her from her deathbed as she pined away for him in true sentimentalist fashion), and Raymond marries Royal, who has finished grieving for de France. Despite the joy of the occasion, Royal still looks sad, and the others ask her why. She replies that she will only be happy "*when Cuba is free!*" And with that tableau Pickens turned to her audience and interposed her own feelings regarding the needs of the struggling island. Fellow monarchs helped each other willingly in times of trouble, she noted—why not one republic for another? Although López was dead and buried, the cause remained to be fought.[26]

The Free Flag of Cuba revealed several things about women's interest in filibustering. First, it showed that women did have interest in political affairs, foreign affairs in this case. Pickens was only one of many women who supported López and his quest for liberty, although she was unusual in her public support of it. This also demonstrated a willingness to step beyond what many considered to be women's arena to promote such causes actively. Not every woman embraced public attention as willingly or as often as Jane Cazneau. Still, Pickens chose, like Cazneau, to use a pseudonym when writing her book. Like Mabel Royal, she flinched from ambition but nevertheless felt constrained to rally for the Cubans. Literature frequently offered a borderland for women to step into the limelight to entertain and, more importantly, inform. Pickens did the same. Above all, her work showed how women's prized moral influence helped to shape men's actions. As she wrote, "Woman has great power, if she would realize and accept it. . . . It is woman, after all, who crowns the hero." A woman of intelligence and understanding could make considerable difference in her world, which Pickens clearly attempted to do with her book.[27]

Of course, the fact that Pickens preferred to use a pen name seems to contradict her statements on the virtue of feminine influence in *The Free Flag of Cuba*. A contemporary reader might deduce the work of a female author due to the sentimental nature of the work and despite its political angle, but because Pickens used only initials, this was not a sure thing. "H. M. Hardiman" provided a convenient veil behind which a lady of decorum could work; no one would be able to target the individual and declare her in violation of gender boundaries. Such a convenience, given the nature of Pickens's work, is ironic.

Pickens never had the opportunity to visit Cuba and see for herself what was happening on that island. Teresa Vielé, on the other hand, stopped briefly at Havana on her way to Texas and recorded her observations in *Following the Drum*. Above all, her portrait of the country was one of race: Spanish and black alike. When Spanish authorities met their boat, she was repulsed by "their ugly, swarthy faces, that beamed with anything but benevolence or beauty." Their features appeared to match their government, which burdened the innocent Cubans with "taxation and oppression" and then watched them with a suspicious eye. Similarly, Vielé seemed shocked by the "brutal animal features" of slaves in Havana. As had Cazneau in *The Queen of Islands,* she asserted that blacks in the United States had clearly benefited from Anglo-Saxon slavery, at least in one respect; they, unlike the Cuban blacks, had been elevated to a state of civilization otherwise unavailable to them.[28]

After her brief stay in Cuba, Vielé insisted that the island desperately needed the help of the United States to free itself from the evils of Spain. The Cubans yearned for revolution, years after the López debacle, and yet nothing had changed since 1851. "It must be the impulse of every generous heart," she wrote, "to become a filibuster in feeling if not in principle." Not only did Americans have a responsibility to bring republicanism to Cuba, but also civilization to its blacks. Both ideals bore the mark of philanthropy for Vielé, not base "aggrandizement," but either motive would eventually lead to annexation. Even in 1858, years after the failed López expedition, the cry of filibusterism rang in the author's ears.[29]

But by this point Cuba no longer had the bulk of America's attention. After López's execution, the filibuster movement on the island disintegrated. It would not be until after the Civil War that the United States tried to move on Cuba again, and by 1898 they would be far more successful. However, the filibustering spirit did not fade after the Cuban fever subsided. What had occurred during the López expeditions was only a small part of the rush for manifest destiny in Latin America. Ever since the Latin American republics began to declare their independence from Spain in the early nineteenth century, the United States had borne an interest in their welfare. The Monroe Doctrine of 1823, although not followed as law, outlined Americans' desire for freedom in the hemisphere and remained a loose guideline for foreign policy into the next century. As secretary of state, Henry Clay had also promoted good relations with the young republics. Such a stance benefited not only the nation's southern neighbors as they struggled to create stable governments, but the United States as well. As Pickens had noted in *The Free Flag of Cuba*, monarchs helped each other; republics should do likewise. But this attitude carried with it some condescension—a superior nation assisting its lesser brethren—and as Latin American countries struggled, racialist beliefs helped convince many that these republics would succeed only in the American constellation.[30]

In the West Indies, for instance, Santo Domingo (today known as the Dominican Republic) faced the same stereotypes and expansionist rhetoric as had Cuba. Americans feared that, without outside help, the islands of "our American Mediterranean" would suffer decay. For the time being, the backward denizens of the West Indies only held onto their territory as tenants, not independent citizens; some American would undoubtedly intervene soon, rescuing the inhabitants from themselves. Such patterns had already emerged in past filibusters. "Suppose that Lopez [*sic*], Walker, or some other *Norman* or *Saxon-man* filibuster, should make a decent [*sic*] on St. Domingo, confiscate the island," *DeBow's* said, "the civilized world would be a gainer, and its present population probably not losers by the operation." How the journal managed to transform the Hispanic López into a Saxon remains a mystery. Nevertheless, its point was clear: the current residents did not have the ability to civilize their nations. The blacks in Santo Domingo were racially incapable of doing so. Only the United States could make that possibility a reality.[31]

Even the U.S. government tried to get involved in Santo Domingo. As had often been the case, the unstoppable Jane Cazneau positioned herself in the middle of the fray. In November, 1853, Franklin Pierce appointed Cazneau's husband, William, to be a special agent to the country. Primarily his mission was to survey the area and determine its potential value to the United States. Although William, not Jane, held the public position, the latter attracted far more attention thanks to her tireless writing in the *Sun* and other publications. Wags referred to the hapless agent as "Mr. Cora Montgomery," demonstrating that her pseudonym did not completely protect her or her family from publicity. Despite the negative attention, Cazneau arrived on the island in December, her husband following weeks afterward, and the two lived there sporadically for the next twenty years in service to the government.[32]

In fact, many believed that Jane had the upper position in Santo Domingo. She was the primary publicist for the venture as she continued to write. According to the New York *Evening Post*, Cazneau had told locals that the country would be American in six months. (Other sources report that William, not Jane, made this claim.) Robert May notes that it was she who had the necessary ties to officials—such as Secretary of State William L. Marcy—to obtain the position. She had also been in New York and her husband in Texas when the position was made known. The *Post* thus concluded that she was the actual agent.[33]

Regardless of who was involved and in what capacity, the Cazneaus spent their time in Santo Domingo hard at work. William Cazneau determined that Samaná Bay merited attention due to its ideal location for trade and American defense and recommended its purchase. Jane was not as conservative as her husband, urging annexation of the entire country. Santo Domingo could prove an ideal location for free blacks, she believed, as Cuba was ideal for slavery. Primarily, however, Cazneau appeared more interested in "economic penetration" of the island than political or military involvement, using trade as a means of suasion rather than force. Both ideas made some headway in political circles. Although the government seemed disinterested, the Cazneaus pushed the Samaná Bay idea in the mid-1850s and then again in 1859, to no avail. They then pushed for the absorption of Santo Domingo into the 1860s and 1870s until an annexation treaty failed in Congress in 1876.[34]

By that point filibustering had become a lost art, having disappeared from public view after the last and greatest of the expeditions in the mid- to late 1850s. However, where most efforts had proved unmitigated disasters almost from the beginning, William Walker's filibustering foray into Nicaragua nearly succeeded. Without the help of the U.S. government (in fact, frequently despite the government), the filibuster held the Central American country under his tight control for nearly two years— part of which he spent as Nicaragua's president—until a combined army of the other nations in the region and a U.S. naval vessel forced his resignation. Walker remained undeterred, returning to Central America three more times to try to retake his empire until the British captured him and turned him over to the Hondurans. They executed him on September 12, 1860.[35]

Nicaragua quickly captured the media's attention for both economic and racial reasons. Central America appeared to many to be the best way to travel from the East Coast to California, particularly after the 1849 gold rush created a surge in emigration. By 1850 the nation had signed a treaty with Great Britain that arranged for joint construction of a transisthmian canal across Nicaragua to ease transportation. The United States was in a prime position to take advantage of Nicaraguan geography. The *Democratic Review* declared Walker's attempts in Nicaragua to be proof that "in no part of the world nor in any age, are the traits of a conquering and a dominant people to be found in greater perfection than among ourselves." Although his own attempts seemed to be on the verge of failure, the *Democratic Review* insisted that he proved "that at no distant period Central America will become a part either of the territory of the U.S. or of a second system of American republics." Even the *American Whig Review,* the political opponent of the *Democratic Review,* lauded the value of involvement in Central America. The region had until recently "been in the possession of a sluggish race," the *Whig Review* said. For its own good, Central America required "the speedy rise of a great and powerful State, occupied by a population unsurpassed for its industry and enterprise, and ready to seize upon every advantage which the resources of that vast coast or its commercial facilities may afford." Whatever anyone thought about American involvement, *DeBow's* said, "it is not to be supposed that, having gained the foothold they have in Central America, they can be restrained by the weak and indolent people by which they are surrounded from extending their dominion." The superiority of "the Anglo-Saxon character" would emerge victorious in this cultural war. All this was to the Nicaraguans' benefit, as they were clearly unable to govern themselves under the "antiquated absurdities of Spanish law."[36]

While expansionists encouraged involvement in Central America because of potential economic benefits, they did not neglect another crucial aspect of the expansionist argument: republicanism. Walker arrived in Nicaragua in 1855 at the behest of the Nicaraguan Liberals, who were currently embroiled in a civil war against their more conservative brethren. The sight of one republican aiding others could not help but stir patriotism in American observers. Anna Ella Carroll published *The Star of the West* in 1857 to praise republicans such as Walker. "A light from heaven has now guided a son of our American republic," she sang, "to open the way for the beautiful flag of the free, to deliver that misguided people, and bring them out of the humiliating condition to which tyranny and priestcraft have subjected them." Nicaragua embodied all the benefits of manifest destiny. As a result, Walker's efforts found considerable support among men and women alike.[37]

Cazneau was again no exception. Although Edward Wallace states that her interests in Nicaragua were limited to writing, in reality she and her husband had both political and economic interests in Nicaragua. Cazneau owned part of the Chontales Silver Mining venture in Nicaragua. Walker's presence there, she apparently reasoned, would help her own investments significantly. Both Cazneaus also had some interest in the guano trade in that country. Jane also helped William and others to organize a rally in New York City on Walker's behalf on December 20, 1856. (William had signed a contract with Walker to provide settlers for Nicaragua in August, after he and Cazneau traveled to that country to visit with the new president. Under the terms of the contract, the Cazneaus would organize the immigration of one thousand colonists to the country. After one year, colonists would own eighty acres of Nicaragua free and clear.) Not only did they support Walker, they also lent whatever clout they could muster to aid Henry L. Kinney, a businessman from Corpus Christi who was working toward an empire of his own along the Mosquito Coast of Nicaragua.[38]

Cazneau felt confident enough in Walker's abilities to lobby officials in Washington on his behalf. His government was stable, she wrote from Nicaragua in July, 1856, and she persisted in this belief into the next year. Even as the filibuster's star was falling, she met with President James Buchanan's attorney general, Jeremiah Black, to plead his case. Later she wrote letters to Black and Buchanan to press for recognition or at least for expanded American rights to trade in Nicaragua. She asked the president—without success—to allow Walker to return to Nicaragua in November, 1857. Although she used her rhetorical skills fervently throughout the Walker affair, Cazneau's efforts availed her no better than in Cuba and the Dominican Republic.[39]

Cazneau's involvement in various expansionist ventures significantly tested the boundaries of women's accepted sphere. Writing was an acceptable pursuit for women, admittedly, but her work had little foundation in sentimental literature. She used some of the flowery rhetoric of the day but did so to bolster economic and political argument. Her republican fervor exceeded typical patriotic language and pressed for action, which was unusual for someone of a gender assumed to be largely passive. Such attempts may have succeeded in 1845 with the annexation of Texas, but not afterward. The nation had changed; now that expansionism had become a southern issue, Cazneau found herself part of a vocal but ultimately fruitless minority.

Stories such as Cazneau's in this period are rare but nevertheless telling. Although women's diaries and letters revealed little regarding what occurred south of the border, more public examples such as Cazneau's, Pickens's, and even to an extent Chapman's demonstrate the interest among Texas women. Attention to Mexico makes the most sense, given its proximity and the state's past history in foreign relations. Ties to slavery helped to link Texans and other islands in the Caribbean and Central America. Because slavery was part of their worldview, it would follow that any endeavor buttressing or building the institution would merit support. Still, these women's words were just that—words—and ultimately gained them and the United States as a whole nothing. Only their example remained for a later generation during the push for empire in the late nineteenth and early twentieth centuries. The time was not yet right for such involvement.

The actions of the ladies of Henderson as they donated a flag to the local castle of the Knights of the Golden Circle may provide a better example of how women in Texas dealt with the hemispheric turn that manifest destiny took in the 1850s. At the least, their example is more representative of the behavior of the "average" American woman. Typically they expressed expansionist sentiment through domesticity, sewing banners rather than carrying them into battle themselves. Their position, reinforced by the ideals of true womanhood, ultimately proved one of power through persuasion rather than by force, winning the hearts and minds of American men in their silence more often than by their words.

$\rightarrow$8$\leftarrow$

Of Politics and
True Womanhood

Women in Texas always had an active interest in the success of American expansion. As fellow citizens, the security of their country affected them as much as it did men, and additional territory translated into a buffer to achieve that security. It also meant for many the establishment of an Anglo American empire in the Western Hemisphere in which whites attained authority over less-civilized cultures. The Anglo-Saxon race in the United States could then assist these lesser peoples in reaching their potential. Safe from outside aggression and ensconced in their position of divinely mandated supremacy, Americans through manifest destiny would fulfill their ultimate calling as presaged by triumphs such as the American and Texas Revolutions.

The achievement of manifest destiny required all its proponents to play a role. Because of their position in politics and the public arena, men are more prominent in the record. For this reason their involvement in expansionism has received considerable attention. Still, as this work has demonstrated, women also contributed to make their hopes reality. They did this in two ways. One utilized the concept of separate spheres and the cult of true womanhood to achieve manifest destiny. As mothers and wives, women used domesticity to influence their neighbors and society by maintaining moral superiority. Their situation gave women both the right and the opportunity to persuade others of the rightness of their cause and encourage action. Their own behavior frequently remained low-key or hidden altogether, but it nevertheless had an impact on society. Similarly, domesticity had its own part in the drama of manifest destiny. Expansion relied not only on the manipulation of politics for its fruition, but of society as a whole. How people behaved also contributed to an expansionist mindset. Simply by keeping their houses and living out their lives in a frontier environment as they did in Texas, women helped to establish a beachhead for civilization.

At the same time, women participated in a second, less obvious, role apart from that of true womanhood. Some women, like Mary Austin Holley or Jane Cazneau, ventured into the public arena. Usually this entailed a foray into the literary world, that shadowy land between the spheres where men and women mingled together without the taint of "promiscuous" interaction. (After all, no author could control who read her book.) Even this bore some suspicion, however, as Lucy Pickens's use of a pseudonym demonstrates. Venturing into print involved some level of risk. But not all public women constrained themselves strictly to the written word, launching instead into politics with little concern for what others considered proper. Cazneau's efforts violated most Americans' ideas of appropriate female behavior, yet this did not stop her from pursuing what she considered a critical agenda. Expansion was far more important than remaining within the boundaries of strangers' expectations.

Women like Cazneau, of course, were rare at mid-century. The boundaries between male and female might have been blurry in spots, but they remained mostly distinct for the majority of the population. Nevertheless, women got involved in the political process to a greater extent than many expected. This was particularly the case where manifest destiny was concerned. That women created banners demonstrating their support of various efforts serves as a case in point. Not only did the words and symbols communicate the seamstresses' opinions for all to see, typically the women involved in the project presented their gift with a speech as well. Often newspapers captured the essence of these presentations in their pages, which meant that the ladies responsible had a male audience not once, but twice. Such women used their domestic skills and influence through this medium, yet their demonstration of enthusiasm was implicitly political.[1]

Particularly in the decade prior to the Civil War, politics became the primary venue for expansion. Most issues affecting the United States, in fact, hinged on the gap between Democrat and Whig or, after 1854, Republican. As Frederick Merk notes, most Democrats promoted expansion, while their opponents rejected it. When Washington debated the annexation of Texas and the necessity of the Mexican War, expansion figured heavily in the discussion and eventually helped divide Congress. This split between parties stemmed in part from the debate over slavery—as did most conflict in the 1850s—and for the most part also represented a sectional schism between North and South. At this point in history, then, manifest destiny, politics, and the changing role of women collided.[2]

The position of women in public politics in the 1840s and 1850s is open to much interpretation. Lydia Sigourney warned young ladies to remain free from "political convulsions" that might distract from domestic affairs. Others nevertheless noted and even tacitly approved women's interest in political matters. In 1842, the *Southern Quarterly Review* mentioned how "our intelligent females" recognized party differences and were familiar with crucial topics. Of course, southern women were not so forward that they became involved in debates or elections, but their interest in the public arena did find outward manifestations. "Their influence," said the *Review*, ". . . is not unfelt throughout the whole body politic."[3]

Women in this period influenced politics primarily through their participation in voluntary societies. Because of their involvement in social issues, women lent a "social drama" to government, calling for change in the way Americans dealt with those in need. This concept can be taken a step further. Women realized by the late 1840s that moral persuasion had not succeeded in establishing a righteous nation or purer Americans. From that point, activists leaned more toward electoral activity and away from more traditional means of influence. This was a difficult decision to make, as they feared the possible negative effects of public involvement. What if it overwhelmed the responsibilities of home and family? Despite such concerns, political involvement appeared more reasonable under the guise of true womanhood.[4]

Women's involvement in politics grew slowly and was even more slowly accepted. Women did not typically have symbolic importance in the public arena until mid-century at the earliest; anything beyond that proved too unusual and radical even to consider. Only with the 1840 election did women achieve this status. That year the Whig Party included women in their campaign, much to the surprise of the Democrats. Still, their inclusion proved merely symbolic, as they had no real (meaning electoral) impact upon the outcome of the election. Exceptions to the rule included the Whig Party's fusion of popular reformist sentiments and politics by allowing women to demonstrate their support. As the moral backbone of the family, Whig women took what information they had and used it to sway their families. Not only did women serve as symbols, demonstrating their dedication by their presence, but they also gave speeches, wrote pamphlets, and designed banners for public display. Such activities continued to tie true womanhood's calling to political activism.[5]

Southerners, Texans included, were less affected by the modernizing aspects of reform because of their ties to a more traditional agricultural base. They also tended to hold to Democratic ideas of what was appropriate for women politically. The *Democratic Review* elaborated on the appropriate course of action for women in 1852, which followed this line of thinking. The idea of presenting banners and other manners of "public display of personal animosities, and of unfeminine virulence" appalled the editors with its destructive capability. "Such aberration from the sacred domestic routine," they insisted, "cannot often be repeated without serious efforts upon the delicate harmonies of the family and social structure." Southern women, noted the *Review,* easily avoided such violations of femininity, as they had too much to do at home to busy themselves with topics not meriting their attention.[6]

The *Dallas Herald* issued similar statements during the 1856 election, when Republican candidate John Frémont's wife, Jessie (daughter of Thomas Hart Benton, Missouri senator), involved herself heavily in her husband's campaign for the presidency. Other Republican women rallied around Frémont as well, forming "Jessie Circles" in support. How fortunate that the paper's female readers did not immediately recognize the phrase, said the editors with relief. It appeared that only the radical "abolition females" carried on in such a fashion, while "the wives and daughters of the friends of Buchanan and Fillmore have the good taste and good sense to eschew politics." Such behavior proved far more sensible than rampaging around the country doing things beyond one's ken. "These demented females," said the *Herald* of the opposition, "would much better form sewing circles, bread, pudding, and knitting circles, spanking-bad-children-and-putting-them-to-bed circles, than to be

Jessying around the country." It was far better for southern women to remain "discreet" in their activities than draw unnecessary attention.[7]

Yet neither the *Democratic Review* nor the *Dallas Herald* seemed to know exactly what occurred among the women of Texas. While remaining fully feminine, they absorbed local politics with understanding and reflected upon it as separate political entities from their husbands. For example, Sarah Devereux's husband Julien recognized his wife's interest in national affairs. When he wrote her while apart from each other, he filled his letters with information on the Democrats, the rise of the Know-Nothings, and other issues in state and national politics. Apparently Julien thought her intelligent enough to understand what had occurred as well as being interested in events beyond the domestic arena. (Julien died in 1856, leaving Devereux a widow at twenty-nine and in charge of their plantation. The ease with which she handled the job demonstrates in another capacity her comfort in supposedly masculine areas of interest.)[8]

Henrietta Embree poured her own political opinions into her diary. Unlike most Texans in the 1850s, Embree supported the American, or Know-Nothing Party rather than the Democrats. The Know-Nothings had a small but significant following in the state, including Sam Houston, former Texas president. Typically the Democratic newspapers accused the nativist Know-Nothings of being racist and cruel because of their dislike of the countless German immigrants in Texas. Embree declared her devotion to the 1856 American Party candidate, Millard Fillmore, to her diary. "We will soon know who is to preside," she wrote; "how I hope it will be Fillmore." Ten days after the election, she tried to restrain her frustration with the jubilant local Democrats who insisted that Buchanan had won before the final vote had emerged. "It may be that he is elected [*sic*]," she said, "think it more than likely but I don't beleave [*sic*] they have had any news from the Election at least am in hopes so." The diary does not note if she shared her husband's political views, but her feelings on such issues were so clear that it is evident she had developed her own devotion to them.[9]

Even more unladylike than Devereux or Embree (for more conservative citizens, at least), other Texan women made their political views public. Despite the fact that the *Democratic Review* encouraged women to remain in the domestic background (except in times of crisis), female supporters of the Democratic Party stepped forward boldly in the late 1850s. As had been the case since 1820, when Jane Long created a flag for her husband's expedition, women spoke through the banners that they made. Although Ryan says that such symbols did not emerge and become popular until the 1870s, an article in the *Texas State Gazette* in 1857 proves that many women—worse, southern ladies—indulged in such things far earlier. In fact, given their prevalence in Texas history, the presentation of banners had become by the 1850s something of a tradition. In July of that year, the Democratic Ladies of the City of Austin declared they would give a flag to the county with the largest poll for the state convention. "Democrats worship no man," the banner read; "they pay their homage to principles—and to God." The purpose of this banner was twofold: not only would it encourage involvement in politics, but it would also reminded its observers of the ideal for all who indulged in politics. Rather than criticize the women for going where they were supposedly not wanted, the *Gazette* lauded them for their "deep and abiding interest . . . in the cause of a great party."[10]

The *Dallas Herald* did the same in 1860 when another group of women presented yet another banner to the Dallas County Company of Texas Rangers. Virginia Millier marked the occasion by dressing in white robes to portray the Goddess of Liberty. Millier even spoke before the mixed audience, extolling the rangers' success and expressing her hopes for their ultimate safety. R. W. Lunday then gave an oration of his own on the women's behalf, tying their efforts for the rangers to those of their revolutionary ancestors. The rangers' work in Texas' defense along the border and elsewhere was like that of the patriots' fighting for freedom; therefore, these women deserved to be honored for "the interest manifested . . . in the achievements of [Texas'] gallant sons." Even the *Herald* forgot its earlier criticism of women's interference in public affairs. "The ladies of Dallas have crowned themselves with laurels of grateful remembrance from the band of gallant Rangers," the editors crowed.[11]

The *Herald*'s ambivalence paralleled that of the rest of the nation in this period. After the Seneca Falls Convention of 1848, some uncertainty filtered into American culture regarding the place of gender in politics and society. Not every woman desired the vote—some considered it detrimental to their feminine influence—but often women took on more overt responsibilities in the public sphere without realizing the precedent they set by their behavior. Nevertheless, it is interesting that such confusion existed in Texas, given its heritage of active female involvement in public affairs. Earlier in the century, before Texas became a state, the territory existed primarily as a frontier environment, where (as Turner put it) savagery and civilization met and wrangled for supremacy. Because of the nature of the struggle in Texas, Anglo American expansion required everyone to contribute to the fight, whether male or female. As a result, women became more and more involved in the fulfillment of manifest destiny. Their continued involvement into the 1840s and 1850s represented the natural evolution of their earlier efforts.

Another possible explanation for antebellum Texans' lack of recognition of historical continuity was the differing responsibilities for each gender. Men and women worked in very different arenas, but every act proved critical to the ultimate goal: the civilizing of the territory. No one's duties were superior or inferior. Men used politics and commerce to bring the land under submission, along with the rifle and the plow. Women exercised the special ability to tame the land through education, domesticity, and particularly through childrearing. Like the republican mothers at the turn of the nineteenth century, their greatest worth lay in passing on their own accumulated knowledge, wisdom, and virtue to the next generation. To a nation that extolled the educated, virtuous citizen, there could be no higher calling, placing women in a highly honored position. Not until later did Americans assume that dealing with children and remaining at home somehow made women less worthy of respect. Nevertheless, despite the subjective evaluation of the masses, women remained crucial to the development, maturation, and perpetuation of civilization (and, in turn, manifest destiny) of Texas and the United States as a whole.

The golden era of manifest destiny died with the advent of the Civil War in April, 1861. Suddenly politicians and laymen alike turned to more immediate concerns than the absorption of additional territory, namely the preservation of what they already had. The interests of sectionalism-turned-nationalism dominated southern thinking; there would be time to expand their empire for slavery after they had defended their honor against northern aggressors. Besides that, the South needed every man for the fight. Filibustering quickly fell out of vogue as a result. Then southern hopes dissolved with Lee's surrender at Appomattox. After the Confederacy's defeat, expansion lost its appeal. The North, of course, had abandoned its enthusiasm for manifest destiny long before, when antislavery sentiment grew too strong to sustain it. Only after Reconstruction ended did the United States again begin to consider expansion in the hemisphere or beyond. By the end of the century, however, manifest destiny campaigned in a far more organized and effective guise—imperialism rather than mere expansion.[12]

Still, in a sense, the pursuit of manifest destiny continued in the society that gave it birth. While the war for the Union raged, women continued to hold fast to "traditional" folkways to maintain their sense of stability. These behavior patterns in turn perpetuated the notion of civilization holding out against the wilderness, whether it was a physical or spiritual reality. By doing so, women offered hope for a more secure future. Like the women in the poem printed in the *Telegraph and Texas Register* years before, their efforts remained anonymous but would bring honor for years to come by establishing a foundation for later generations. However else women in Texas distinguished themselves in the cause of manifest destiny, it was as adherents of the cult of true womanhood that they made the greatest impact.

Notes

1. Albert K. Weinberg, *Manifest Destiny: A Study of Nationalist Expansion in American History;* Frederick Merk: *Manifest Destiny and Mission in American History: A Reinterpretation;* Thomas R. Hietala, *Manifest Design: Anxious Aggrandizement in Late Jacksonian America;* and Reginald Horsman, *Race and Manifest Destiny: The Origins of American Racial Anglo-Saxonism.* Other titles are listed in the bibliography and cited throughout the course of this book. While not trying to create confusion, I use the terms "manifest destiny" and "expansionism" interchangeably in this work for the sake of variety, although I recognize that the former term has a more specific application historiographically.
2. See John Mack Faragher, "History from the Inside-Out: Writing the History of Women in Rural America," *American Quarterly* 33 (winter, 1981): 538, 556–57. One example of a historian breaking past what appears at first glance merely to be laundry lists of responsibilities to find a brilliant expression of one woman's world view emerges in Laurel Thatcher Ulrich, *A Midwife's Tale: The Life of Martha Ballard, Based on Her Diary, 1785–1812.*
3. *United States Magazine and Democratic Review* 17 (July, 1845): 5. Past historians typically attributed the article to editor John O'Sullivan. Recently, Linda S. Hudson has challenged this view, noting that the grammatical errors in the article match more closely the works of Texas émigré Jane Cazneau than O'Sullivan (*Mistress of Manifest Destiny: A Biography of Jane McManus Storm Cazneau, 1807–1878,* pp. 59–62, 209–10). Hudson's argument provides a provocative—and for purposes of this work, ironic—perspective to the discussion.

CHAPTER 1

1. San Felipe de Austin *Telegraph and Texas Register,* Jan. 27, 1837; and *Democratic Review* 9 (July, 1841): 33.
2. *Telegraph and Texas Register,* Feb. 14, 1837.
3. See Earl W. Fornell, "Texans and Filibusters in the 1850's," *Southwestern Historical Quarterly* 59 (Apr., 1956): 411, 427; Frederick Merk with the collaboration of Lois Bannister Merk, *Slavery and the Annexation of Texas,* pp. 38, 47; Gerald Douglas Saxon, "The Politics of Expansion: Texas as an Issue in National Politics, 1819–1885," (Ph.D. diss., North Texas State University, 1979), p. 252; and Robert E. May, *The Southern Dream of a Caribbean Empire, 1854–1861,* pp. 245–58.
4. Although Americans from all regions traveled to Texas, the vast majority came from the South, primarily due to the possibility of extending slavery to new land. This will be discussed in more detail later.

5. Lillian Schlissel, *Women's Diaries of the Overland Journey,* p. 28; John Mack Faragher, *Women and Men on the Overland Trail,* pp. 67, 163; and Julie Roy Jeffrey, *Frontier Women: The Trans-Mississippi West, 1840–1880,* pp. 30–31. Jeffrey notes that women had some sway over their husbands' decision-making processes; however, she recognizes that women's say was not typically the last word.

6. For discussion on early nineteenth century social structure, see Edward Pessen, *Jacksonian America: Society, Personality, and Politics,* pp. 77–100; John F. Kasson, *Rudeness and Civility: Manners in Nineteenth-Century Urban America,* pp. 34–37; Richard L. Bushman, *The Refinement of America: Persons, Houses, Cities,* pp. 25–29, 182–86, 420–25; and Stuart M. Blumin, *The Emergence of the Middle Class: Social Experience in the American City, 1760–1900,* pp. 285–90. Regarding women, see Pessen, *Jacksonian America,* pp. 46–52; Kasson, *Rudeness and Civility,* pp. 128–36; Bushman, *Refinement of America,* pp. 440–46; Karen Halttunen, *Confidence Men and Painted Women: A Study of Middle-Class Culture in America, 1830–1870,* pp. 57–59; and Christine Stansell, *City of Women: Sex and Class in New York 1789–1860,* pp. 22–23, 36–37.

7. Barbara Welter, "The Cult of True Womanhood: 1820–1860," *American Quarterly* 18 (summer, 1966): 151–74; and Stansell, *City of Women,* p. 11.

8. Welter, "Cult of True Womanhood," p. 151; Kathryn Kish Sklar, *Catharine Beecher: A Study in American Domesticity,* pp. 96–97, 137, 158–59.

9. Jeffrey, *Frontier Women,* pp. 128–30, 135–43; Sandra L. Myres, *Westering Women and the Frontier Experience, 1800–1915,* pp. 203–206; and Lori D. Ginzberg, *Women in Antebellum Reform,* pp. 90–117.

10. Mary Beth Norton, *Liberty's Daughters: The Revolutionary Experience of American Women, 1750–1800,* pp. 245, 248; and Linda K. Kerber, *Women of the Republic: Intellect and Ideology in Revolutionary America,* pp. 11, 36–37, 80, 199–200, 228, 269.

11. See Carol Lea Clark, *Imagining Texas: Pre-Revolutionary Texas Newspapers, 1829–1836,* p. 10.

12. See Kerber, *Women of the Republic,* p. 11.

13. Although primarily white American women contributed to expansionism, for the sake of brevity I often use "women" to refer to Anglos. Context should make clear where another meaning should be inferred to avoid confusion.

14. *A Visit to Texas: Being the Journal of a Traveller Through Those Parts Most Interesting to American Settlers,* pp. 22–27; and *DeBow's Review* 10 (June, 1851): 632. See also Weinberg, *Manifest Destiny,* pp. 190–91; and Patricia Nelson Limerick, *The Legacy of Conquest: The Unbroken Past of the American West,* pp. 40–41.

15. Henry Nash Smith, *Virgin Land: The American West as Symbol and Myth,* pp. 123–24, 128–29; Weinberg, *Manifest Destiny,* pp. 73–74, 85–86; and Clark, *Imagining Texas,* pp. 58–71.

16. *DeBow's* 10 (June, 1851): 630, 20 (Feb., 1856): 242, and 17 (July, 1854): 76; and Richard S. Hunt and Jesse Randel, *A New Guide to Texas: Consisting of a Brief Outline of the History of Its Settlement, and the Colonization and Land Laws; A General View of the Surface of the Country; Its Climate, Soil, Productions, &c. With a Particular Description of the Counties, Cities and Towns,* pp. 3–4.

17. Faragher, "History from the Inside-Out," pp. 541, 548.
18. *Democratic Review* 8 (July, 1840): 82–83.
19. See Ray Allen Billington, *The Far Western Frontier, 1830–1860*, pp. 37–38; Limerick, *Legacy of Conquest*, pp. 61, 284–85; and Perry Miller, *Errand into the Wilderness*, pp. 3–5, 11–12.
20. *American Quarterly Review* 9 (June, 1831): 399; Michael H. Hunt, *Ideology and U.S. Foreign Policy*, pp. 29–30; Merk, *Manifest Destiny and Mission*; and Horsman, *Race and Manifest Destiny*, pp. 82–85.
21. Quoted in *Telegraph and Texas Register*, Feb. 12, 1845.
22. Anna Ella Carroll, *The Star of the West; Or, National Men and National Measures*, pp. 346–47; and *DeBow's* 6 (July, 1848): 9 and 9 (Aug., 1850): 167. For more information on Anna Ella Carroll, see Janet Coryell, "Duty with Delicacy: Anna Ella Carroll of Maryland," in *Women and American Foreign Policy: Lobbyists, Critics, and Insiders*, ed. Edward P. Crapol.
23. *Democratic Review* 16 (May, 1845): 495. Scholars tend to reinforce this aspect of manifest destiny through the study of missionaries in the trans-Mississippi West, particularly in the Oregon Country. For information on this, see Limerick, *Legacy of Conquest*, pp. 36–41; and Billington, *Far Western Frontier*, pp. 79–85.
24. Gabriel Franchère, "Voyage to the Northwest Coast of America," in *Early Western Travels, 1748–1846*, ed. Reuben Gold Thwaites, vol. 6, p. 401; Alexander Ross, *Ross's Adventures of the First Settlers on the Oregon or Columbia River, 1810–1813*, in *Early Western Travels*, vol. 7, pp. 304, 310, 311–13; and *DeBow's* 25 (Dec., 1858): 620, and 26 (Mar., 1859): 266–67.
25. Welter, "Cult of True Womanhood," pp. 152–54; and *Telegraph and Texas Register*, Apr. 18, 1851.
26. Horsman, *Race and Manifest Destiny*, pp. 10–15, 103–104; Weinberg, *Manifest Destiny*, pp. 179–80; and Limerick, *Legacy of Conquest*, pp. 259–62, 290–91.
27. *Telegraph and Texas Register*, Dec. 16, 1847; [Austin] *Texas State Gazette*, Aug. 2, 1851; *DeBow's* 6 (July, 1848): 8, and 10 (June, 1851): 636; and *American Whig Review* 14 (Sept., 1851): 192.
28. For examples of race and class based behavior, see Stansell, *City of Women*, pp. 30–32, 61, 69–73; Ginzberg, *Women in Antebellum Reform*, pp. 66–70; and Pessen, *Jacksonian America*, 11, 42–46.
29. Jeffrey, *Frontier Women*, pp. 46–47, 59–60; and Sandra L. Myres, *Westering Women*, pp. 72–80, 160–65.

Scholarship on women in the trans-Mississippi West is still in development, the vast majority emerging after 1970. Much appears to be a response to ideas promulgated by works like Ray Allen Billington's *The Far Western Frontier*, which marginalized women's role in the West, or Dee Brown's *The Gentle Tamers: Women of the Old Wild West*, which reduced women to a few cookie-cutter stereotypes. In contrast, John Mack Faragher's *Women and Men on the Overland Trail* and Lillian Schlissel's *Women's Diaries of the Overland Journey* see women as distinct entities with a unique perception of their travels as well as far greater roles than earlier described. Julie Roy Jeffrey's *Frontier Women* and Patricia Limerick's

The Legacy of Conquest challenge the notion that western women were either noble homesteaders or "bad" women, broadening the scope of research as a result.

CHAPTER 2

1. *American Quarterly Review* 6 (Dec., 1829): 264, 282.
2. Roy Harvey Pearce, *Savagism and Civilization: A Study of the Indian and the American Mind*, pp. 48–49; Horsman, *Race and Manifest Destiny*, 104–108. Native Texans, at this point, could mean both Native Americans and Hispanics. However, I will focus on the former in this chapter and will save the majority of discussion concerning the latter in chapter 3.
3. Smith, *Virgin Land*, pp. 123–24, 152–53; Limerick, *Legacy of Conquest*, pp. 190–91; and Clark, *Imagining Texas*, pp. 60, 62.
4. Faragher, *Women and Men*, pp. 16–18, 20; and Schlissel, *Women's Diaries*, pp. 19–22.
5. David J. Weber, *The Spanish Frontier in North America*, pp. 191, 195. For examples of studies of the frontier community (in this case, the Illinois frontier), see Don Harrison Doyle, *The Social Order of a Frontier Community: Jacksonville, Illinois, 1825–70*, pp. 6–14; and John Mack Faragher, *Sugar Creek: Life on the Illinois Prairie*, pp. 130–31, 136–42, 144–45, 156–70.
6. Limerick, *Legacy of Conquest*, pp. 46, 92–93, 190, 191, 194–95; and Horsman, *Race and Manifest Destiny*, pp. 76–77, 156.
7. Frederick Jackson Turner, *Rereading Frederick Jackson Turner: "The Significance of the Frontier in American History" and Other Essays*, ed. John Mack Faragher, pp. 33–34.
8. Noah Smithwick, *The Evolution of a State, or Recollections of Old Texas Days*, p. 5; and *American Whig Review* 11 (May, 1850): 526.
9. Faragher, *Women and Men*, pp. 110–12, 120–28; Faragher, "History from the Inside-Out," p. 553; Schlissel, *Women's Diaries of the Overland Journey*, pp. 28–29, 67–68, 77–78; for further discussion of women's communal stance toward work, see Laurel Thatcher Ulrich, *A Midwife's Tale: The Life of Martha Ballard, Based on Her Diary, 1785-1812*, chapter 2.
10. Edward D. Jervey and James E. Moss, eds., "From Virginia to Missouri in 1846: The Journal of Elizabeth Ann Cooley," *Missouri Historical Review* 60 (Jan., 1966): 173, 183, 186–87. This is not to say that all women were alone. However, community as it was understood back east had yet to be developed in Texas.
11. Harriet Ames, *The History of Harriet A. Ames During the Early Days of Texas*, Texas State Library, Austin, pp. 24–25, 32, 34.
12. Mary Sherwood Helm, *Scraps of Early Texas History*, p. 30.
13. Ann Raney Coleman, *Victorian Lady on the Texas Frontier: The Journal of Ann Raney Coleman*, ed. C. Richard King, pp. 25, 27.
14. Faragher, *Women and Men*, pp. 97, 119–20; see also Welter, "Cult of True Womanhood," pp. 152–53; and Cott, *Bonds of Womanhood*, pp. 147–48. Chapter 4 contains more information regarding women's moral suasion.

15. Flora L. von Roeder, *These are the Generations: A Biography of the von Roeder Family and Its Role in Texas History,* p. xiii.
16. Mary Austin Holley, *Texas: Observations, Historical, Geographical and Descriptive,* p. 12; and Annette Kolodny, *The Land Before Her: Fantasy and Experience of the American Frontiers, 1630–1860,* pp. 93–111.
17. Mattie Austin Hatcher, *Letters of an Early American Traveller: Mary Austin Holley, Her Life and Her Works, 1784–1846,* pp. 28, 42; and Holley, *Texas,* pp. 5–7, 15. See also Kolodny, *Land Before Her,* p. 98.
18. Holley, *Texas,* pp. 31, 37–38, 39–40, 85–86.
19. Ibid., pp. 123–24; see Cott, *Bonds of Womanhood,* pp. 43–45, 50. Still, this did not mean that niceties were completely unavailable; upper-class Mexican women in San Antonio, for example, often dressed in the latest fashions from New Orleans. By the 1850s, matters had shifted. Lucadia Pease could comment on the fine dresses women wore in Galveston and Austin, odd as they seemed on "ladies issuing from log houses" (David J. Weber, *The Mexican Frontier, 1821–1846: The American Southwest Under Mexico,* p. 220; Katherine Hart and Elizabeth Kemp, eds., *Lucadia Pease and the Governor: Letters, 1850–1857,* pp. 19, 178).
20. Holley, *Texas,* pp. 14–15, 129–30; see also *DeBow's* 20 (Feb., 1856): 242.
21. Mary Austin Holley to Harriette Brand, Dec. 19, 1833, and Holley to Brand, Jan. 6, 1832, Mary Austin Holley Papers, Center for American History, University of Texas at Austin; Holley to Orville L. Holley, Dec. 24, 1831, in E. W. Winkler, ed., *Manuscript Letters and Documents of Early Texians 1821–1845.*
22. Holley, *Texas,* p. 84.
23. Mildred Richards Stone Gray, *The Diary of Millie Gray, 1832–1840,* pp. 78, 123, 152.
24. Coleman, *Victorian Lady on the Texas Frontier,* pp. 22–23.
25. Mary Crownover Rabb, *Travels and Adventures in Texas in the 1820s,* p. 3; quoted in Weber, *Mexican Frontier,* p. 283; Caleb Coker, ed., *The News from Brownsville: Helen Chapman's Letters from the Texas Military Frontier, 1848–1852,* pp. 9, 77–78; Dilue Rose Harris, "The Reminiscences of Mrs. Dilue Harris," *Quarterly of the Texas State Historical Association* 4 (Oct., 1900): 88.
26. Jane Cazneau [Cora Montgomery, pseud.], *Eagle Pass: Or Life on the Border,* p. 13; Ottilie Fuchs Goeth, *Memoirs of a Texas Pioneer Grandmother (Was Grossmutter Erzaehlt),* translated by Irma Goeth Guenther, p. 40; Teresa Griffin Vielé, *Following the Drum: A Glimpse of Frontier Life,* p. 79.
27. Jane Cazneau papers, Oct. 29, 1835, Center for American History, University of Texas at Austin; and Faragher, "History from the Inside-Out," p. 547.
28. Malone, *Women on the Texas Frontier,* pp. 3–4; Jean Louis Berlandier, *The Indians of Texas in 1830,* ed. John C. Ewers, pp. 33–37; and Weber, *Spanish Frontier,* p. 89.
29. Weber, *Spanish Frontier,* pp. 87, 89, 92; Robert F. Berkhofer, Jr., *The White Man's Indian: Images of the American Indian from Columbus to the Present,* pp. 13–14; Jeffrey, *Frontier Women,* pp. 54–55; Riley, *Women and Indians,* pp. 122, 152, 156–59, 167–69; Clark, *Imagining Texas,* pp. 90–91.
30. Richard Drinnon, *Facing West: The Metaphysics of Indian Hating and Empire Building,* p. 177.

31. Anne A. Brindley, "Jane Long," *Southwestern Historical Quarterly* 56 (Oct., 1952): 225. More details regarding the Long expedition are in chapter 3.

32. Brindley, "Jane Long," pp. 225–26; Martha Anne Turner, *The Life and Times of Jane Long*, pp. 70–76.

33. Julia Lee Sinks, *Chronicles of Fayette: The Reminiscences of Julia Lee Sinks*, ed. Walter P. Freytag, pp. 10–11, 22; see also Riley, *Women and Indians*, pp. 83–84.

34. Holley, *Texas*, pp. 88, 95, 97–98.

35. Cazneau, *Eagle Pass*, pp. 41–43, 169.

36. Berkhofer, *White Man's Indian*, pp. 30, 92; Pearce, *Savagism and Civilization*, pp. 48–49; Anthony F. C. Wallace, *Jefferson and the Indians: The Tragic Fate of the First Americans*, p. 276; and Cazneau, *Eagle Pass*, pp. 32–33.

37. Crystal Sasse Ragsdale, *The Golden Free Land: The Reminiscences and Letters of Women on an American Frontier*, pp. 3, 23; and Don H. Biggers, *German Pioneers in Texas*, pp. 74, 75.

38. Harris, "Reminiscences," 4 (Oct., 1900): 118–19; and Mary Crownover Rabb, *Travels and Adventures in Texas in the 1820's*, pp. 3–4, 8.

39. Helm, *Scraps of Early Texas History*, pp. 35–36, 42; Paula Mitchell Marks, *Turn Your Eyes Toward Texas: Pioneers Sam and Mary Maverick*, p. 77; and Mary A. Maverick, *Memoirs of Mary A. Maverick*, ed. Rena Maverick Green, pp. 12–14.

40. Sinks, *Chronicles of Fayette*, p. 39; *Texas State Gazette*, Dec. 29, 1849; and Maverick, *Memoirs*, pp. 25–30.

41. Maverick, *Memoirs*, p. 27.

42. Emma Murck Altgelt, "Emma Altgelt's Sketches of Life in Texas," *Southwestern Historical Quarterly* 63 (Jan., 1960): 378.

43. Maverick, *Memoirs*, pp. 38–40, 41.

44. Sarah Ann Horn, *A Narrative of the Captivity of Mrs. Horn, and Her Two Children, with Mrs. Harris, by the Comanche Indians*, pp. 16–19, 24, 33–35.

45. Clarissa Plummer, *Narrative of the Captivity and Extreme Sufferings of Mrs. Clarissa Plummer*, pp. 11–13; and Kathryn Zabelle Derounian-Stodola and James Arthur Levernier, *The Indian Captivity Narrative*, pp. 32–33. See also Ann Fabian, *The Unvarnished Truth: Personal Narratives in Nineteenth-Century America*, pp. 5–6.

46. Horn, *A Narrative of Captivity*, p. 60; see also Riley, *Women and Indians*, p. 227.

47. James W. Parker, *Narrative of the Perilous Adventures, Miraculous Escapes and Sufferings of the Rev. James W. Parker*, pp. 31–32; JoElla Powell Exley, *Frontier Blood: The Saga of the Parker Family*, pp. 56, 57, 62, 69, 71; and Grace Jackson, *Cynthia Ann Parker*, p. vii.

48. June Namias, *White Captives: Gender and Ethnicity on the American Frontier*, pp. 3–4; Jackson, *Cynthia Ann Parker*, pp. vii–viii, 58–59, 97–99; and Exley, *Frontier Blood*, pp. 177, 179. For a concise retelling of Parker's story, see Margaret Schmidt Hacker, *Cynthia Ann Parker: The Life and the Legend*.

49. Maverick, *Memoirs*, p. 41; and Riley, *Women and Indians*, pp. xiii–xiv, 122, 152, 156–59.

50. John Q. Anderson, ed., *Tales of Frontier Texas 1830–1860*, pp. 246–48; and *Dallas Herald*, June 28, 1856.

51. Riley, *Women and Indians,* p. 15; Horn, *A Narrative of Captivity,* p. 60.
52. Kolodny, *Land Before Her,* pp. 55–57.
53. Turner, "Significance of the Frontier," pp. 58–59.

CHAPTER 3

1. Crystal Sasse Ragsdale, *The Women and Children of the Alamo,* p. 43.
2. Maurice Elfer, *Madam Candelaria: Unsung Heroine of the Alamo,* pp. 8, 9, 17–18.
3. Elfer, *Madam Candelaria,* p. 19; Ragsdale, *Women and Children,* p. 100; *Petition from Alamo Monument Association for Relief of Madam Candelaria, February 12, 1891,* Texas State Library, Austin; and Randy Roberts and James S. Olson, *A Line in the Sand: The Alamo in Blood and Memory,* pp. 129, 154–55.
4. *Niles' Weekly Review,* Oct. 31 and Nov. 14, 1835; *Telegraph and Texas Register,* Feb. 27, 1836; and Merk, *Slavery and the Annexation of Texas,* p. 38.
5. Harris Gaylord Warren, *The Sword Was Their Passport: A History of American Filibustering in the Mexican Revolution,* pp. 236–37; Frank L. Owsley and Gene A. Smith, *Filibusters and Expansionists: Jeffersonian Manifest Destiny, 1800–1821,* pp. 32–60, 178–80; and Robert E. May, *Manifest Destiny's Underworld: Filibustering in Antebellum America,* p. 5. May defines filibusters as "American adventurers who raised or participated in private military forces that either invaded or planned to invade foreign countries with which the United States was formally at peace" (p. xi). However, Owsley and Smith note that, at times, the government tacitly approved of filibustering as a means to expand with little public effort.
6. Brindley, "Jane Long," pp. 215–16; and Turner, *Life and Times of Jane Long,* pp. 39–40.
7. Turner, *Life and Times of Jane Long,* pp. 53–54.
8. Ibid., pp. 70–72, 76, 80, 83.
9. Warren, *Their Sword Was Their Passport,* p. 258; Brindley, "Jane Long," pp. 231–34; Turner, *Life and Times of Jane Long,* pp. 88–89; Henderson Yoakum, *History of Texas from Its First Settlement in 1685 to Its Annexation to the United States in 1846,* vol. 1, pp. 207–208.
10. Smithwick, *Evolution of a State,* p. 48; Brindley, "Jane Long," p. 236; Turner, *Life and Times of Jane Long,* pp. 94–96, 113, 119.
11. Yoakum, *History of Texas,* vol. 1, pp. 281, 303; Ernest Wallace and David M. Vigness, eds., *Documents of Texas History,* pp. 98–99; Randolph B. Campbell, *An Empire for Slavery: The Peculiar Institution in Texas, 1821–1865,* pp. 15–24, 39–42; Gray, *Diary,* p. 78; *A Visit to Texas,* p. 28; and Clark, *Imagining Texas,* pp. 90–91.
12. *American Whig Review* 12 (Oct., 1850): 338; *American Quarterly Review* 4 (Sept., 1828): 111; and John J. Johnson, *A Hemisphere Apart: The Foundations of United States Policy Toward Latin America,* p. 47.
13. Helm, *Scraps of Early Texas History,* pp. 48, 52–53; Johnson, *A Hemisphere Apart,* 46; and Horsman, *Race and Manifest Destiny,* pp. 213–14.
14. Arnoldo DeLeón, *They Called Them Greasers: Anglo Attitudes Toward Mexicans in Texas, 1821–1900,* pp. 9, 25–26; and *Telegraph and Texas Register,* Feb. 27, 1836.

15. Johnson, *A Hemisphere Apart*, pp. 21–27; Ray Allen Billington, *The Protestant Crusade 1800–1860: A Study of the Origins of American Nativism*, pp. 41–43; *Visit to Texas*, pp. 53–54, 104; and Helm, *Scraps of Early Texas History*, pp. 30, 60.
16. Harris, "Reminiscences," 4 (Oct., 1900): 104, 114; and Billington, *Protestant Crusade*, pp. 118–19.
17. Johnson, *A Hemisphere Apart*, p. 24; *Visit to Texas*, p. 223; and *Texas in 1837*, pp. 102–103.
18. Yoakum, *History of Texas*, vol. 1, pp. 272, 294–95.
19. Coleman, *Victorian Lady*, pp. 30–32. For a comparison of women's roles in the American Revolution, see Kerber, *Women of the Republic*, pp. 99–105, 110; and Norton, *Liberty's Daughters*, pp. 157, 164–65, 178–88.
20. Coleman, *Victorian Lady*, pp. vii, viii, 186–87. She did not receive the pension she requested.
21. *Telegraph and Texas Register*, Mar. 5, 1836.
22. Welter, "Cult of True Womanhood," p. 159; *Telegraph and Texas Register*, Mar. 5, 1836.
23. Hatcher, *Letters of an Early American Traveler*, p. 60; Henry David Pope, *A Lady and a Lone Star Flag*, pp. 11, 12–13, 16, 28. Troutman's body was moved to the State Cemetery in Austin in 1913; her picture hangs in the Capitol, her flag draped across her lap.
24. Jane Cazneau to Joseph Speers(?), Oct. 29, 1835; and Cazneau to Samuel Williams, Jan. 3, 1836, Jane Cazneau papers, Center for American History, University of Texas.
25. Helm, *Scraps of Early Texas History*, p. 26.
26. Harris, "Reminiscences," 4 (Jan., 1901): 157.
27. Ames, *The History of Harriet A. Ames*, p. 8. Ultimately, Ames was freed of her husband, but by divorce rather than death.
28. *Niles' Weekly Register*, Apr. 30, 1836; Willard Griffith Nitschke, "Susanna Wilkerson Dickinson (1814–1883)," *Women in Early Texas*, ed. Evelyn M. Carrington, pp. 71, 74; *Hannig (Susannah) Testimony Re Battle of Alamo, Dated September 23, 1876*, Texas State Library; Yoakum, *History of Texas*, vol. 2, p. 81; Smithwick, *Evolution of a State*, p. 74; and Roberts and Olson, *Line in the Sand*, pp. 166–67, 173. The contradictions in Dickinson's stories may have stemmed from age rather than selective memory. In her second petition for compensation from the Texas Legislature, she swore that she had "never called on the Government for aid." No one called her on it, possibly out of respect for a victim of a state tragedy, out of respect for the elderly, or the desire to preserve the myth that had already arisen around her. (See *Petition and Vouchers for Susanna E. Dickinson for Relief, October 16, 1836; Petition for Susana Bellows, November 9, 1849*, Texas State Library.)
29. *Hannig Testimony; Petition of Juana Navarro Alsbury for Relief for Losses at Siege of Alamo, November 1, 1857*, Texas State Library; see also Ragsdale, *Women and Children*, pp. 99, 101.
30. Sinks, *Chronicles of Fayette*, p. 49; Rabb, *Travels and Adventures*, p. 10; and Harris, "Reminiscences," 4 (Jan., 1901): 162–63.

31. Coleman, *Victorian Lady*, pp. 83–85, 97, 149–51.

32. Helm, *Scraps of Early Texas History*, p. 16; Harris, "Reminiscences," 4 (Jan., 1901): 164; and Sinks, *Chronicles of Fayette*, p. 49.

33. Kleberg, "Some of My Early Experiences" 1 (Apr., 1898): 302; Caroline von Hinueber, "Life of German Pioneers in Early Texas," *Texas Historical Association Quarterly* 2 (Dec., 1898): 231; and Helm, *Scraps of Early Texas History*, p. 56.

34. Harris, "Reminiscences" 4 (Oct., 1900), 170.

35. Sherrie S. McLeRoy, *Mistress of Glen Eden: The Life and Times of Texas Pioneer Sophia Porter*, pp. 3, 14. Of course, there is always the story of Emily D. West, the "Yellow Rose of Texas," who was undoubtedly present. Her story is in chapter 6.

36. Welter, "Cult of True Womanhood," pp. 163–64; and *Telegraph and Texas Register*, Nov. 21, 1835.

37. Gloria Frye, "Eva Catherine Rosine Ruff Sterne (1809–1897)," *Women in Early Texas*, p. 236; Kleberg, "Some of My Early Experiences" 1 (Apr., 1898): 32; and *Telegraph and Texas Register*, Oct. 4 and 26, 1836.

38. *Telegraph and Texas Register*, Dec. 13, 1836.

39. Hatcher, *Letters of an Early American Traveler*, p. 87; see also *Telegraph and Texas Register*, Aug. 25, 1846.

40. Arnoldo DeLeón, *The Tejano Community, 1836–1900*, pp. 4, 13; and Glen Scott, "Anna Salazar de Esparza (circa 1806–1849)," *Women in Early Texas*, p. 219.

41. DeLeón, *Tejano Community*, pp. 130–32; *Texas in 1837*, p. 108; Jane Dysart, "Mexican Women in San Antonio, 1830–1860: The Assimilation Process," *Western Historical Quarterly* 7 (Oct., 1976): 366; and Weber, *The Mexican Frontier*, p. 215.

42. Scott, "Anna Salazar de Esparza," p. 219; Dysart, "Mexican Women," p. 370; Ragsdale, *Golden Free Land*, p. 26.

43. Weber, *The Mexican Frontier*, pp. 160, 177, 254; Smithwick, *Evolution of a State*, 18; DeLeón, *They Called Them Greasers*, pp. 39–42; Dysart, "Mexican Women," pp. 367, 372; and Mark E. Nackman, *A Nation within a Nation: The Rise of Texas Nationalism*, pp. 3, 13.

44. Dysart, "Mexican Women," pp. 365, 375; David E. Montejano, *Anglos and Mexicans in the Making of Texas, 1836–1986*, p. 26; DeLeón, *Tejano Community*, p. 14; and DeLeón, *They Called Them Greasers*, p. 14.

45. *Democratic Review* 14 (Feb., 1844): 171; and *Telegraph and Texas Register*, Mar. 5, 1836.

46. Sinks, *Chronicles of Fayette*, p. 1.

CHAPTER 4

1. Leonora Siddons, *The Female Warrior, an Interesting Narrative of the Sufferings, and Singular and Surprising Adventures of Miss Leonora Siddons*, pp. 6, 7.

2. Siddons, *Female Warrior*, pp. 9–11, 18–20, 23.

3. *Telegraph and Texas Register*, Jan. 29, 1845.

4. Ibid.

5. In her study of middle-class women in the early nineteenth century, Ann Douglas

states that women did not have "power" outright, as did men who functioned freely in the public sphere. Instead, feminine "influence" worked surreptitiously to mold society in a more passive fashion (*The Feminization of American Culture*, pp. 8–10).

6. Welter, "Cult of True Womanhood," pp. 151–52, 173–74; Carroll Smith-Rosenberg, "The Female World of Love and Ritual: Relations between Women in Nineteenth-Century America," *Disorderly Conduct: Visions of Gender in Victorian America*, p. 60; Cott, *The Bonds of Womanhood*, pp. 160–96. The concept of separate spheres fits in with the idea of a "market revolution" in early-nineteenth-century America, when the shift from a subsistence economy to a market economy took place. (See Charles Sellers, *The Market Revolution: Jacksonian America, 1815–1848*.)

7. William Alcott, *Letters to a Sister, or Woman's Mission*, pp. 25–26, 306–307; Catharine Beecher, *A Treatise on Domestic Economy*, p. 158; *DeBow's Review* 23 (Aug., 1857): 122; and *Telegraph and Texas Register*, Nov. 30, 1846. See also Cott, *Bonds of Womanhood*, 132; and Ryan, *Cradle of the Middle Class*, p. 81.

8. *Southern Quarterly Review* 2 (Oct., 1842): 292, 297, and 2 (Feb., 1857): 402–403; Alcott, *Letters to a Sister*, p. 84; and *Telegraph and Texas Register*, Mar. 12, 1845.

9. L. H. Sigourney, *Letters to Young Ladies*, p. 194; Beecher, *Treatise on Domestic Economy*, p. 13; *Telegraph and Texas Register*, May 10, 1849; and Norton, *Liberty's Daughters*, p. 257.

10. Elizabeth Jameson, "Women as Workers, Women as Civilizers: True Womanhood in the American West," *The Women's West*, ed. Susan Armitage and Elizabeth Jameson, p. 147.

11. Helm, *Scraps of Early Texas History*, p. 91.

12. See Douglas, *Feminization of American Culture;* and Mary P. Ryan, *Cradle of the Middle Class: The Family in Oneida County, New York, 1790–1865*, pp. 83–88.

13. *Telegraph and Texas Register*, Apr. 30, 1845, and May 6, 1846.

14. *Telegraph and Texas Register*, Oct. 19, 1842; William Seale, *Sam Houston's Wife: A Biography of Margaret Lea Houston*, pp. 94, 99–100, 135–36.

15. Chapman, *News from Brownsville*, pp. xi, xvi, 97.

16. Ibid., pp. 96, 98, 128, 131.

17. Ibid., pp. 111–12, 130, 143.

18. *Telegraph and Texas Register*, Apr. 18, 1851; Seale, *Sam Houston's Wife*, pp. 151, 168–71; and Jeffrey, *Frontier Women*, p. 79.

19. Ronald G. Walters, *American Reformers, 1815–1860*, 2nd ed., pp. 9, 15–17; and Ryan, *Cradle of the Middle Class*, pp. 116–27.

20. W. J. Rorabaugh, *The Alcoholic Republic: An American Tradition*, pp. 8, 35–36, 125, 174–75; and Thomas R. Pegram, *Battling Demon Rum: The Struggle for a Dry America, 1800–1933*, p. 19.

21. Pegram, *Battling Demon Rum*, pp. 30–31; Rorabaugh, *Alcoholic Republic*, p. 220; and Gray, *Diary*, p. 123.

22. *Telegraph and Texas Register*, Oct. 1, 1845; T. S. Arthur, *Ten Nights in a Bar-Room, and What I Saw There;* and Rorabaugh, *Alcoholic Republic*, pp. 198–200.

23. Chapman, *News from Brownsville*, pp. 65, 142, 143, 196.
24. Madge Thornall Roberts, *Star of Destiny: The Private Life of Sam and Margaret Houston*, p. 87; and *Texas State Gazette*, Mar. 28, 1857.
25. *Texas State Gazette*, Aug. 25, 1849, and May 4 and Aug. 17, 1850.
26. For a discussion of the merits and flaws of social control theory, see Paul Johnson, *A Shopkeeper's Millennium: Society and Revivals in Rochester, New York, 1815–1837*, pp. 102–15; and Lawrence F. Kohl, "The Concept of Social Control and the History of Jacksonian America," *Journal of the Early Republic* 5 (spring, 1985): 21–34.
27. *Texas State Gazette*, Mar. 31, 1855.
28. *Telegraph and Texas Register*, Nov. 4, 1847; Chapman, *News from Brownsville*, pp. 202–203.
29. Beecher, *Treatise on Domestic Economy*, p. 13. See also Cott, *Bonds of Womanhood*, pp. 104–109; and Norton, *Liberty's Daughters*, pp. 256–87.
30. Dan R. Manning, "Frances Trask: Early Texas Educator," *Southwestern Historical Quarterly* 103 (Apr., 2000): 483, 489; and *Telegraph and Texas Register*, Nov. 14, 1835, Dec. 13, 1836, and Apr. 29, 1846.
31. *Dallas Herald*, Aug. 10, 1859.
32. Katherine Hart and Elizabeth Kemp, eds., *Lucadia Pease and the Governor: Letters, 1850–1857*, p. 159; and Erika L. Murr, ed., *A Rebel Wife in Texas: The Diary and Letters of Elizabeth Scott Neblett, 1852–1864*, pp. 35, 40. See also Cott, *Bonds of Womanhood*, pp. 200–201.
33. Sigourney, *Letters to Young Ladies*, p. 244.
34. Siddons, *Female Warrior*, p. 6.
35. See Nackman, *Nation within a Nation*, p. 3.
36. Mexico was also purportedly a republic—Texans often called for a return to the standards of the Constitution of 1824—but by the late 1830s centralism had returned to power under Santa Anna. See Weber, *Mexican Frontier*, pp. 32, 244–45.
37. Lewis O. Saum, *The Popular Mood of Pre-Civil War America*, pp. xvi, 226; and Clifford Geertz, *The Interpretation of Cultures*, pp. 10, 17. See also David Waldstreicher, *In the Midst of Perpetual Fetes: The Making of American Nationalism, 1776–1820*, p. 8. Andrew Burstein pursues a similar question of nationalism in private writings in *America's Jubilee: How in 1826 a Generation Remembered Fifty Years of Independence.*
38. See Waldstreicher, *Perpetual Fetes;* Simon P. Newman, *Parades and the Politics of the Street: Festive Culture in the Early American Republic*, p. 85; and Len Travers, *Celebrating the Fourth: Independence Day and the Rites of Nationalism in the Early Republic*, pp. 152, 217, 225.
39. Mrs. J. W. (Henrietta) Embree, Apr. 21, 1859, *Diary*, Center for American History, University of Texas at Austin; DeLeón, *The Tejano Community*, p. 7; Harris, "Reminiscences" 4 (Oct., 1900): 110.
40. Mary A. Baylor, *Reminiscences*, Center for American History, University of Texas at Austin; Gray, *Diary*, p. 126; Harris, "Reminiscences" 4 (Jan., 1901): 184.
41. Embree, Jan. 1, 1861, *Diary*.

42. Mrs. Memucan Hunt, *Diary,* Texas State Library; see also Nackman, *Nation within a Nation,* p. 70.

43. Chester William Geue and Ether Hander Geue, eds., *A New Land Beckoned: German Immigration to Texas, 1844–1847,* pp. 2, 16; and Rudolph Leopold Biesele, *The History of the German Settlements in Texas, 1831–1861,* pp. 16, 20, 66.

44. Goeth, *Memoirs,* pp. 1, 36; and Von Roeder, *These are the Generations,* p. xiii. See also Altgelt, "Sketches," p. 364; Biesele, *History of German Settlements,* pp. 16, 20, 191; and Hagen Schulze, *The Course of German Nationalism: From Frederick the Great to Bismarck, 1763–1867,* translated by Sarah Hanbury-Tenison, pp. 62–63.

45. Goeth, *Memoirs,* p. 1.

46. James J. Sheehan, *German Liberalism in the Nineteenth Century,* p. 7; Schulze, *Course of German Nationalism,* pp. 62–63; Biesele, *History of German Settlements,* p. 16; Ray Allen Billington, *Land of Savagery, Land of Promise: The European Image of the American Frontier,* pp. 241–48, 255–56.

47. Vera Flach, *A Yankee in German-America: Texas Hill Country,* pp. 42–43; Viktor Bracht, *Texas in 1848,* translated by Charles Frank Schmidt, p. 59; Elisa Willerich, quoted in Crystal Sasse Ragsdale, ed., *The Golden Free Land: The Reminiscences and Letters of Women on an American Frontier,* p. 55; and Billington, *Land of Savagery,* p. 90. See also Goeth, *Memoirs,* p. 40.

48. Sheehan, *German Liberalism,* p. 1; Ragsdale, *Golden Free Land,* pp. 4, 32, 58; Biesele, *History of German Settlements,* pp. 191–92; and Geue and Geue, *New Land Beckoned,* p. 12. See also *Telegraph and Texas Register,* Jan. 22, 1845; and *Texas State Gazette,* Mar. 28, 1857.

49. Biesele, *History of German Settlements,* pp. 186–87; Ragsdale, *Golden Free Land,* pp. 6, 14, 23, 45–46; and Biggers, *German Pioneers,* p. 74. See also Altgelt, "Sketches," pp. 377–78.

50. Ragsdale, *Golden Free Land,* pp. 121, 126; and Goeth, *Memoirs,* p. 49.

51. Ragsdale, *Golden Free Land,* p. 25; Flach, *Yankee in German America,* p. 43; Altgelt, "Sketches," pp. 371–72; and Goeth, *Memoirs,* p. 41.

52. Schulze, *Course of German Nationalism,* p. 47; Sheehan, *German Liberalism,* p. 7; von Roeder, *These are the Generations,* p. xi; and Ragsdale, *Golden Free Land,* p. 73.

53. Billington, *Land of Savagery,* pp. 191, 193–94; Bracht, *Texas in 1848,* p. 68; Ragsdale, *Golden Free Land,* pp. 73, 129; and Altgelt, "Sketches," p. 370.

54. Bracht, *Texas in 1848,* pp. 70–71; Ragsdale, *Golden Free Land,* p. 89; Flach, *Yankee in German America,* p. 39; and Altgelt, "Sketches," p. 367.

55. Crystal Sasse Ragsdale, "The German Woman in Frontier Texas," *German Culture in Texas: A Free Earth; Essays from the 1978 Southwest Symposium,* ed. Glen E. Lich and Dona B. Reeves, p. 146; and Goeth, *Memoirs,* p. 237.

56. Goeth, *Memoirs,* p. 237; Altgelt, "Sketches," p. 365; Flach, *Yankee in German America,* p. 43; and Ragsdale, *Golden Free Land,* pp. 110, 142.

57. Ragsdale, *Golden Free Land,* p. 142; and Altgelt, "Sketches," pp. 365, 372.

58. Ragsdale, "German Woman," *German Culture,* pp. 146–48; Ragsdale, *Golden Free Land,* p. 45; Biesele, *History of German Settlements,* pp. 222–23; and Goeth, *Memoirs,* pp. 63–65.

59. Schulze, *Course of German Nationalism*, p. 67; and Biesele, *History of German Settlements*, pp. 222–23.

60. *Telegraph and Texas Register*, Feb. 11, 1846.

CHAPTER 5

1. Chapman, *News from Brownsville*, p. 134.

2. Ibid., p. 9.

3. Otis Singletary, *The Mexican War*, p. 5; Limerick, *Legacy of Conquest*, pp. 231–33; David Pletcher, *The Diplomacy of Annexation: Texas, Oregon, and the Mexican War*, pp. 598–611; Horsman, *Race and Manifest Destiny*, 166–67, 230–37; and Hunt, *Ideology and U.S. Foreign Policy*, pp. 32–35. See also Richard Bruce Winders, *Mr. Polk's Army: The American Military Experience in the Mexican War*, pp. 204–206.

4. See Merk, *Manifest Destiny and Mission;* Pletcher, *Diplomacy of Annexation;* Saxon, "The Politics of Expansion"; and Hunt, *Ideology and U.S. Foreign Policy.*

5. *Southern Quarterly Review* 2 (July, 1842): 110–11.

6. Yoakum, *History of Texas*, vol. 2, pp. 371–74; Sam W. Haynes, *Soldiers of Misfortune: The Somervell and Mier Expeditions*, pp. 66–79; and Joseph G. Dawson, III, ed., *The Texas Military Experience: From the Texas Revolution through World War II*, pp. 4, 156. For a firsthand account of the battle and what followed, see Thomas J. Green, *Journal of the Texian Expedition Against Mier, Subsequent Imprisonment of the Author, His Sufferings and Final Escape from the Castle of Perote with Reflections upon the Present Political and Probably Future Relations of Texas, Mexico, and the United States*, pp. 82–95.

7. Marks, *Turn Your Eyes toward Texas*, pp. 110, 116; and Samuel A. Maverick to Mary Maverick, San Antonio, Sept. 11, 1842, *Manuscript Letters and Documents of Early Texians 1821–1845*, ed. E. W. Winkler.

8. Haynes, *Soldiers of Misfortune*, pp. 21–22; Dawson, *Texas Military Experience*, p. 55; and Sinks, *Chronicles of Fayette*, p. 75.

9. Holley to Harriette Brand, Dec. 30, 1837, Mary Austin Holley Papers, Center for American History, University of Texas at Austin.

10. Green, *Journal of the Texian Expedition*, p. 411; and Merk, *Manifest Destiny and Mission*, pp. 46–47. See also *Southern Quarterly Review* 6 (Oct., 1844): 485–86; and *United States Magazine and Democratic Review* 14 (Apr., 1844): 426–28.

11. Saxon, *Politics of Expansion*, pp. 81, 97; Pletcher, *Diplomacy of Annexation*, p. 73; Merk, *Slavery and the Annexation of Texas*, p. 45.

12. *American Quarterly Review* 7 (Mar., 1830): 109; *Niles' Weekly Register*, Feb. 1, 1845; *Southern Quarterly Review* 6 (Oct., 1844): 500–502, 519; and [Washington-on-the-Brazos] *Texas National Register*, Dec. 28, 1844.

13. Merk, *Slavery and the Annexation of Texas*, p. 77; *Niles' Weekly Register*, Jan. 11, 1845; and *Democratic Review* 14 (Apr., 1844): 425.

14. *Texas National Register*, Feb. 22, 1845; and Green, *Journal of the Texian Expedition*, pp. 388, 407, 408–10.

15. Merk, *Slavery and the Annexation of Texas*, pp. 25–26, 38; Saxon, *Politics of Expansion*, pp. 81–82, 252; and Pletcher, *Diplomacy of Annexation*, p. 75.

16. *Telegraph and Texas Register,* Oct. 23, 1844.
17. Anna Kasten Nelson, "Jane Storms Cazneau: Disciple of Manifest Destiny," *Prologue* 18 (spring, 1986): 27; and Hudson, *Mistress of Manifest Destiny,* p. 45.
18. Robert E. May, "'Plenipotentiary in Petticoats': Jane M. Cazneau and American Foreign Policy in the Mid-Nineteenth Century," in *Women and Foreign Policy: Lobbyists, Critics, and Insiders,* ed. Edward P. Crapol, pp. 20–21; and Hudson, *Mistress of Manifest Destiny,* pp. 52, 63.
19. Maverick, *Memoirs,* p. 83.
20. Winders, *Mr. Polk's Army,* pp. 8–9; see also Pletcher, *Diplomacy of Annexation;* and Singletary, *Mexican War.*
21. Robert W. Johannsen, *To the Halls of the Montezumas: The Mexican War in the American Imagination,* pp. 136–41; Samuel C. Reid, Jr., *The Scouting Expeditions of McCulloch's Texas Rangers; or, the Summer and Fall Campaign of the Army of the United States in Mexico, 1846,* p. 38.
22. *Telegraph and Texas Register,* July 5, 1847.
23. Holley to Brand, May 10, 1846, Mary Austin Holley papers, Center for American History, University of Texas at Austin; and Maverick, *Memoirs,* pp. 85–86.
24. Vielé, *Following the Drum,* pp. 100–102, 241.
25. Martha Barbour, *Journals of the Late Brevet Major Philip Norbourne Barbour, Captain in the Third Regiment, United States Infantry, and His Wife Martha Isabella Hopkins Barbour, Written During the War with Mexico, 1846,* pp. xii, 108, 111, 115.
26. Merk, *Manifest Destiny and Mission.*
27. Ibid. For another perspective in this area, see Hunt, *Ideology and U.S. Foreign Policy,* 19–45.
28. Johannsen, *To the Halls of the Montezumas,* p. 299; May, "Plenipotentiary," p. 21; Pletcher, *Diplomacy of Annexation,* pp. 476–77, 491, 523–24; Hudson, *Mistress of Manifest Destiny,* pp. 71, 77ff.; Nelson, "Jane Storms Cazneau," p. 35; and Merk, *Manifest Destiny and Mission,* pp. 131–34. I have referred to Cazneau by her final surname throughout this paper for reasons of simplicity. Considering how many names Jane McManus Storm(s) Cazneau used throughout her lifetime, not to mention various pseudonyms, it makes more sense to refer to her by the name by which most people would recognize her.
29. *Scribner's Monthly* 18 (May, 1879): 137, 139, 140; Pletcher, *Diplomacy of Annexation,* pp. 492–93; and Hudson, *Mistress of Manifest Destiny,* pp. 80–82.
30. Chapman, *News from Brownsville,* p. xvi. For more exploration of pacifist movements in early-nineteenth-century America, see Walters, *America's Reformers,* pp. 112–21.
31. Chapman, *News from Brownsville,* pp. 55, 73.
32. Ibid., pp. 28, 109; Winders, *Mr. Polk's Army,* pp. 174–75; and Johannsen, *To the Halls of the Montezumas,* pp. 291–94.
33. Chapman, *News from Brownsville,* pp. 104–105, 134, 135. See also Vielé, *Following the Drum,* pp. 100–102.
34. Chapman, *News from Brownsville,* pp. 105, 109; Pletcher, *Diplomacy of Annexation,* pp. 551–52; Merk, *Manifest Destiny and Mission,* pp. 111, 116–18; *DeBow's* 6 (July,

1848): 9; see also Limerick, *Legacy of Conquest*, pp. 232–33; and Hudson, *Mistress of Manifest Destiny*, pp. 69–70.

35. James MacPherson, *Battle Cry of Freedom: The Civil War Era*, pp. 52–60, 65; and Pletcher, *Diplomacy of Annexation*, p. 460.

CHAPTER 6

1. Alwyn Barr, *Black Texans: A History of African Americans in Texas, 1528–1995*, p. 14; James F. Dobie, "Jane Long of Aloneness and Love," *Austin American Statesman*, Mar. 1, 1964, Jane Long Vertical File, Texas State Library; and Brindley, p. 227.

2. See Barr, *Black Texans*, p. 6.

3. Ruthe Winegarten, *Black Texas Women: 150 Years of Trial and Triumph*, p. 22; *Petition for Susana Bellows*, Texas State Library. In August, 1836, President Andrew Jackson's envoy Henry M. Morfit estimated the population of Texas to contain approximately 30,000 whites, 5,000 blacks, 3,470 Hispanics, and 14,500 Indians (Campbell, *Empire for Slavery*, p. 54).

4. "Emily D. West," *The New Handbook of Texas*, ed. Ron Tyler, et al., vol. 6, p. 887; and Frank X. Tolbert, *The Day of San Jacinto*, p. 147.

5. "Emily D. West," pp. 887, 888.

6. Campbell, *Empire for Slavery*, pp. 191, 256.

7. *DeBow's* 3 (Mar., 1847): 193, and 15 (July, 1853): 9–10; and *Southern Quarterly Review* 6 (Oct., 1844): 508–509.

8. Campbell, *Empire for Slavery*, pp. 2, 54, 91, 190; and Barr, *Black Texans*, p. 17.

9. Helm, *Scraps of Early Texas History*, pp. 52–53; Campbell, *Empire for Slavery*, pp. 15–17, 21, 27; Barr, *Black Texans*, p. 14. Campbell notes that the Imperial Colonization Law of 1823 disappeared only two months after it was enacted, but the government allowed it to apply to Austin's colony.

10. Henry Austin to Mary Austin Holley, Sept. 15, 1831, Henry Austin Papers, Center for American History, University of Texas at Austin.

11. Barr, *Black Texans*, p. 15; Harold Schoen, "The Free Negro in the Republic of Texas," *Southwestern Historical Quarterly* 40 (Oct., 1936): 87; and Campbell, *Empire for Slavery*, pp. 23–24.

12. Schoen, "The Free Negro," *Southwestern Historical Quarterly* 39 (Apr., 1936): 296–97; Helm, *Scraps of Early Texas History*, 17; and Barr, *Black Texans*, p. 29. For more on slave resistance, see Eugene D. Genovese, *Roll, Jordan, Roll: The World the Slaves Made*.

13. *Telegraph and Texas Register*, Nov. 23, 1842, and Mar. 23, 1848; and Deborah Gray White, *Ar'n't I a Woman: Female Slaves in the Plantation South*, pp. 76–80.

14. Kenneth W. Porter, "Negroes and Indians on the Texas Frontier, 1831–1876," *Journal of Negro History* 41 (July, 1956): 189–90, 208–209; Campbell, *Empire for Slavery*, pp. 59–60; Maverick, *Memoirs*, p. 27; George P. Rawick, ed., *The American Slave: A Composite Autobiography*, vol. 2, pp. 93, 97.

15. Wyatt F. Jeltz, "The Relations of Negroes and Choctaw and Chickasaw Indians," *Journal of Negro History* 33 (Jan., 1948): 25, 27, 30.

16. Rawick, *American Slave*, vol. 2, p. 181, and vol. 5, p. 1571.

17. Barr, *Black Texans*, p. 6; Weber, *Mexican Frontier*, p. 213; and Rawick, *American Slave*, vol. 2, p. 88, and vol. 5, pp. 1726–27.

18. Winegarten, *Black Texas Women*, p. 12; Barr, *Black Texans*, p. 3; Schoen, "The Free Negro" 40 (Apr., 1937): 295, 299; and "Tamar Morgan," *New Handbook of Texas*, vol. 4, p. 838.

19. Winegarten, *Black Texas Women*, p. 2; George Ruble Woolfolk, "Turner's Safety-Valve and Free Negro Westward Migration," *Journal of Negro History* 50 (July, 1965): 194–95, 196; George Ruble Woolfolk, *The Free Negro in Texas 1800–1860: A Study in Cultural Compromise*, pp. 20–23; and Schoen, "The Free Negro" 39 (Apr., 1936): 307–308.

20. Barr, *Black Texans*, p. 4; Schoen, "The Free Negro" 39 (Apr., 1936): 294–95, 301; Winegarten, *Black Texas Women*, p. 6; and Smithwick, *Evolution of a State*, pp. 163, 166.

21. Barr, *Black Texans*, p. 10; Schoen, "The Free Negro" 39 (Apr., 1936): 302, 33; and Winegarten, *Black Texas Women*, p. 6. For more concerning lower-class women and work in the nineteenth century, see Stansell, *City of Women*.

22. Winegarten, *Black Texas Women*, pp. 7–8; Schoen, "The Free Negro" 40 (Oct., 1936): 95–98; and "Tamar Morgan," *New Handbook of Texas*, vol. 4, p. 838.

23. DeLeón, *They Called Them Greasers*, p. 63; and Campbell, *Empire for Slavery*, p. 117.

24. DeLeón, *Tejano Community*, p. 15; Montejano, *Anglos and Mexicans*, p. 77; *Telegraph and Texas Register*, June 15, 1842; and Campbell, *Empire for Slavery*, pp. 217–18.

25. Vielé, *Following the Drum*, p. 158.

26. Terry G. Jordan, *German Seed in Texas Soil: Immigrant Farmers in Nineteenth-Century Texas*, pp. 107–109; Ragsdale, *Golden Free Land*, p. 109; Flach, *Yankee in German America*, pp. 43, 44.

27. Joe B. Frantz, "Ethnicity and Politics in Texas," *German Culture in Texas*, ed. Lich and Reeves, pp. 191–95; Jordan, *German Seed in Texas Soil*, p. 109; and Campbell, *Empire for Slavery*, pp. 215, 216.

28. Jordan, *German Seed in Texas Soil*, p. 109; von Roeder, *These are the Generations*, p. xi; and Ragsdale, *Golden Free Land*, pp. 121, 126.

29. Ragsdale, *Golden Free Land*, p. 55; and Altgelt, "Sketches," p. 371.

30. Campbell, *Empire for Slavery*, p. 191.

31. Ibid., pp. 191–92; Abigail Curlee, "The History of a Texas Slave Plantation 1831–63," *Southwestern Historical Quarterly* 26 (Oct., 1927): 88; Malone, *Women on the Texas Frontier*, p. 28; and Joseph W. McKnight, ed., *Girlhoods in Texas in the 1850s and '60s: Recollections of Cynthia Ann Willis Latham and Ella E. Scott Fisher*, p. 4.

32. Catherine Clinton, *The Plantation Mistress: Woman's World in the Old South*, pp. 89–91, 189; Anne Firor Scott, *The Southern Lady: From Pedestal to Politics, 1830–1930*, pp. 16–18, 46–50.

33. Curlee, "History of a Texas Slave Plantation," pp. 79, 113, 114. This concept comes close to the idea of paternalistic synergy put forward by Eugene Genovese in *Roll, Jordan, Roll*, although Genovese relies heavily on this notion to justify slavery.

34. Cazneau, *Eagle Pass*, pp. 17, 18–19, 20, 24.

35. *American Quarterly Review* 2 (Sept., 1827): 251, 256; Horsman, *Race and Manifest Destiny*, pp. 274–75; and Harriet Beecher Stowe, *Uncle Tom's Cabin*, pp. 162–63, 167–84.

36. Hart and Kemp, *Lucadia Pease*, pp. ix, 27.

37. Ibid., pp. 33, 112.

38. Ibid., pp. 87, 102. See also Winthrop Jordan, *White Over Black: American Attitudes Toward the Negro, 1550–1812*.

39. Chapman, *News from Brownsville*, pp. 106, 184.

40. Ibid., pp. 324, 325.

41. Ibid., pp. 72, 104.

CHAPTER 7

1. Vielé, *Following the Drum*, p. 241.

2. See Charles H. Brown, *Agents of Manifest Destiny: The Lives and Times of the Filibusters*, particularly pp. 17–18; Robert E. May, *The Southern Dream of a Caribbean Empire, 1854-1861*, and *Manifest Destiny's Underworld*, pp. 81–116; and Weinberg, *Manifest Destiny*, pp. 210–11.

3. Reginald Stuart, *United States Expansionism and British North America, 1775–1871*, pp. 87–96; and Chapman, *News from Brownsville*, p. 143.

4. Edward L. Widmer, *Young America: The Flowering of Democracy in New York City*, pp. 28, 39–41, 185–88; May, *Southern Dream*, pp. 20–21; and May, *Manifest Destiny's Underworld*, p. 112.

5. *Dallas Herald*, Sept. 12, 1856. For an example of the term "buccaneer" being used to refer to filibusters, see *American Whig Review* 11 (June, 1850): 567.

6. Robert F. May, "Manifest Destiny's Filibusters," *Manifest Destiny and Empire: American Antebellum Expansion*, ed. Sam W. Haynes and Christopher Morris, pp. 150, 160–61; and Brown, *Agents of Manifest Destiny*, p. 458.

7. May, *Manifest Destiny's Underworld*, p. 5.

8. Chapman, *News from Brownsville*, pp. 296, 331.

9. Ibid., p. 105; Cazneau, *Eagle Pass*, p. 188; May, "Plenipotentiary in Petticoats," p. 23; and Vielé, *Following the Drum*, p. 111.

10. Chapman, *News from Brownsville*, pp. 109, 206, 229.

11. Vielé, *Following the Drum*, pp. 191–98.

12. Edward S. Wallace, *Destiny and Glory*, pp. 107–108, 115, 118, 141, 148–54; May, *Southern Dream*, pp. 83–84, 149–51, 154; May, *Manifest Destiny's Underworld*, pp. 44–45; Brown, *Agents of Manifest Destiny*, pp. 191, 194–209, 446–47; C. A. Bridges, "The Knights of the Golden Circle: A Filibustering Fantasy," *Southwestern Historical Quarterly* 44 (Jan., 1941): 287, 288, 291–99, 301. Because the KGC was a secret orga-

nization, details of their venture into Mexico are sketchy. Bridges's article contains the best information available, but he admits that much of his evidence is "circumstantial" (p. 291).

13. *Dallas Herald,* Mar. 21, 1860.

14. *American Quarterly Review* 10 (Sept., 1831): 233, 242; and *Southern Quarterly Review* 1 (Apr., 1842): 395–96.

15. May, "Manifest Destiny's Filibusters," pp. 160–61, 162; Brown, *Agents of Manifest Destiny,* pp. 40–41; John J. Johnson, *A Hemisphere Apart: The Foundations of United States Policy Toward Latin America,* pp. 154–55; *Democratic Review* 25 (Sept., 1849): 194, 198–99, 200, 202–203; and *DeBow's* 9 (Aug., 1850): 173. See also *Southern Quarterly Review* 1 (Apr., 1842): 392, 396.

16. May, "Plenipotentiary in Petticoats," pp. 23–25; Hudson, *Mistress of Manifest Destiny,* pp. 96, 100; Brown, *Agents of Manifest Destiny,* p. 126; and Wallace, *Destiny and Glory,* pp. 257–58.

17. May, "Plenipotentiary in Petticoats," p. 25; Jane Cazneau [Cora Montgomery, pseud.], *The Queen of Islands, and the King of Rivers,* p. 3.

18. Cazneau, *Queen of Islands,* pp. 10, 22, 24–25.

19. Tom Chaffin, *Fatal Glory: Narciso López and the First Clandestine War Against Cuba,* pp. 50–53, 84; Wallace, *Destiny and Glory,* pp. 56–57, 59; *Democratic Review* 26 (Feb., 1850): 112; and May, *Southern Dream,* pp. 25–29.

20. Chaffin, *Fatal Glory,* pp. 104, 130, 136, 204–205, 213–16; Wallace, *Destiny and Glory,* pp. 60–100; and Brown, *Agents of Manifest Destiny,* pp. 41–91.

21. Hunt, *Ideology and U.S. Foreign Policy,* pp. 92–106. See also David Brion Davis, *Revolutions: Reflections on American Equality and Foreign Liberations.*

22. Sherrie S. McLeRoy, *Red River Women,* pp. 70, 71; Elizabeth Wittenmyer Lewis, *Queen of the Confederacy: The Innocent Deceits of Lucy Holcombe Pickens,* pp. 39–41, 43, 45–46.

23. Lucy Holcome Pickens [H. M. Hardiman, pseud.], *The Free Flag of Cuba; or, The Martyrdom of López: A Tale of the Liberating Expedition of 1851,* pp. 7–8; McLeRoy, *Red River Women,* p. 71. Lewis traces the pseudonym to Pickens's ancestor Henrietta Marie Hardeman (*Queen of the Confederacy,* p. 47).

24. Pickens, *Free Flag of Cuba,* pp. 21, 22, 28, 48.

25. Ibid., pp. 70, 73, 74.

26. Pickens, *Free Flag of Cuba,* pp. 117, 171, 178–80, 180–82, 198–99, 201, 205.

27. See Douglas, *Feminization of American Culture,* pp. 77, 78; Pickens, *Free Flag of Cuba,* pp. 70–71.

28. Vielé, *Following the Drum,* pp. 51–52, 56, 61.

29. Ibid., pp. 60–61.

30. Johnson, *A Hemisphere Apart,* pp. 38, 83; Lars Schoultz, *Beneath the United States: A History of U.S. Policy Toward Latin America,* pp. 1, 11–13.

31. *DeBow's* 22 (Apr., 1857): 418–19.

32. Wallace, *Destiny and Glory,* pp. 260–61; Nelson, "Jane Storms Cazneau" 18 (spring, 1986): 36; Hudson, *Mistress of Manifest Destiny,* 150–51; and May, "Plenipotentiary in Petticoats," p. 27.

33. Nelson, "Jane Storms Cazneau" 18 (spring, 1986): 36; Brown, *Agents of Manifest Destiny*, p. 351; and May, "Plenipotentiary in Petticoats," pp. 27–28.

34. May, *Southern Dream*, p. 88; Nelson, "Jane Storms Cazneau" 18 (spring, 1936): 36; May, "Plenipotentiary in Petticoats," p. 28; Hudson, *Mistress of Manifest Destiny*, p. 152; and Brown, *Agents of Manifest Destiny*, pp. 265–66, 268–74.

35. Brown, *Agents of Manifest Destiny*, pp. 273–82, 346, 454–55; Wallace, *Destiny and Glory*, pp. 164, 172–87, 196, 237–38; May, *Southern Dream*, pp. 77–110. For books relating specifically to Walker, see Frederick Rosengarten, Jr., *Freebooters Must Die! The Life and Death of William Walker, the Most Notorious Filibuster of the Nineteenth Century*; William O. Scroggs, *Filibusters and Financiers: The Story of William Walker and His Associates*.

36. Wallace, *Destiny and Glory*, pp. 159, 190–92; Brown, *Agents of Manifest Destiny*, pp. 222–27, 237–43; *Democratic Review* 39 (July, 1857): 10–11, 20; 40 (Oct., 1857): 329; *American Whig Review* 11 (Feb., 1850): 191; 13 (Feb., 1851): 123; *DeBow's* 20 (June, 1856): 686, 691–92; 21 (Aug., 1856): 126; see also *DeBow's* 24 (Feb., 1858): 151; 27 (Oct., 1860): 421, 429.

37. Wallace, *Destiny and Glory*, p. 164; and Carroll, *Star of the West*, p. 348.

38. Wallace, *Destiny and Glory*, pp. 200, 263, 385; Brown, *Agents of Manifest Destiny*, pp. 350–51, 385; Hudson, *Mistress of Manifest Destiny*, pp. 158–59, 160, 162; May, "Plenipotentiary in Petticoats," pp. 30, 32; and May, *Manifest Destiny's Underworld*, p. 199. For more on Henry Kinney, see Brown, *Agents of Manifest Destiny*, pp. 253, 256–60, 270–73.

39. May, "Plenipotentiary in Petticoats," pp. 31–32; and Hudson, *Mistress of Manifest Destiny*, p. 164.

CHAPTER 8

1. Elizabeth R. Varon, "Tippecanoe and the Ladies, Too: White Women and Party Politics in Antebellum Virginia," *Journal of American History* 82 (Sept., 1995): 498, 514.

2. Merk, *Manifest Destiny and Mission*, pp. 144–50, 153–56, 218.

3. Sigourney, *Letters to Young Ladies*, p. 212; and *Southern Quarterly Review* (Jan., 1842): 30.

4. Paula Baker, "The Domestication of Politics: Women and American Political Society, 1780–1920," *American Historical Review* 89 (June, 1984): 646–47; Lori Ginzberg, "'Moral Suasion is Moral Balderdash': Women, Politics, and Social Activism in the 1850s," *Journal of American History* 73 (Dec., 1986): 603, 609; also "Pernicious Heresies: Female Citizenship and Sexual Responsibility in the Nineteenth Century," *Women and the Unstable State in Nineteenth-Century America*, ed. Alison M. Parker and Stephanie Cole, p. 155.

5. Mary P. Ryan, *Women in Public: Between Banners and Ballots, 1825–1880*, pp. 135–37; Varon, "Tippecanoe and the Ladies Too," pp. 495, 498, 504, 514, 518–19.

6. *Democratic Review* 30 (Apr., 1852): 356, 357.

7. *Dallas Herald*, Sept. 6, 1856.

8. Joleene Maddox Snider, "Sarah Devereux: A Study in Southern Femininity," *Southwestern Historical Quarterly* 97 (Jan., 1994): 480, 492–93, 497–99.

9. Embree, Nov. 2 and 12, 1856, *Diary,* Center for American History, University of Texas at Austin.

10. *Texas State Gazette,* July 4 and Dec. 19, 1857.

11. *Dallas Herald,* Apr. 25, 1860.

12. May, *Southern Dream,* pp. 252–58. For more on the post–Civil War period, see Walter LaFeber, *The New Empire: An Interpretation of American Expansion, 1860–1898*

Bibliography

ARCHIVES AND MANUSCRIPT COLLECTIONS

Ames, Harriet. *The History of Harriet A. Ames during the Early Days of Texas.* Texas State Library, Austin.

Austin, Henry. *Papers.* Center for American History, University of Texas at Austin.

Baylor, Mary A. *Reminiscences.* Center for American History, University of Texas at Austin.

Cazneau, Jane. *Papers.* Center for American History, University of Texas at Austin.

Embree, Mrs. J. W. (Henrietta). *Diary.* Center for American History, University of Texas at Austin.

Holley, Mary Austin. *Papers.* Center for American History, University of Texas at Austin.

Hunt, Mrs. Memucan (Anna T.). *Diary.* Texas State Library.

Long, Jane. *Vertical File.* Texas State Library.

Memorials and Petitions. Texas State Library.

BOOKS AND ARTICLES

Alcott, William. *Letters to a Sister; Or Woman's Mission.* Buffalo: George H. Derby and Co., 1850.

Altgelt, Emma Murck. "Emma Altgelt's Sketches of Life in Texas." *Southwestern Historical Quarterly* 63 (January, 1960): 363–84.

Anderson, John Q., ed. *Tales of Frontier Texas 1830–1860.* Dallas: Southern Methodist University Press, 1966.

Armitage, Susan, and Elizabeth Jameson, eds. *The Women's West.* Norman: University of Oklahoma Press, 1987.

Arthur, T. S. *Advice to Young Ladies on their Duties and Conduct in Life.* Boston: Phillips, Sampson, and Co., 1850.

Baker, Paula. "The Domestication of Politics: Women and American Political Society, 1780–1920." *American Historical Review* 89 (June, 1984): 620–47.

Barbour, Martha. *Journals of the Late Brevet Major Philip Norbourne Barbour, Captain in the Third Regiment, US Infantry, and His Wife Martha Isabella Hopkins Barbour.* New York: G. P. Putnam's Sons, 1936.

Barr, Alwyn. *Black Texans: A History of African Americans in Texas, 1528–1995.* Norman: University of Oklahoma Press, 1996.

Beecher, Catharine. *A Treatise on Domestic Economy.* New York: Schocken Books, 1977.

Berkhofer, Robert F., Jr. *The White Man's Indian: Images of the American Indian from Columbus to the Present*. New York: Alfred A. Knopf, 1978.

Berlandier, Jean Louis. *The Indians of Texas in 1830*. Edited by John C. Evers. Washington, D.C.: Smithsonian Institute Press, 1969.

Biesele, Rudolph Leopold. *The History of the German Settlements in Texas, 1831–1861*. Austin: Von Boeckmann–Jones Co., 1930.

Biggers, Don H. *German Pioneers in Texas*. Fredericksburg, Tex.: *Fredericksburg Standard*, 1925.

Billington, Ray Allen. *The Far Western Frontier 1830–1860*. New York: Harper and Row, 1956.

———. *Land of Savagery, Land of Promise: The European Image of the American Frontier*. New York: W. W. Norton, 1981.

———. *The Protestant Crusade 1800–1860: A Study of the Origins of American Nativism*. New York: Rinehart and Company, 1952.

Blumin, Stuart M. *The Emergence of the Middle Class: Social Experience in the American City, 1760–1900*. New York: Cambridge University Press, 1994.

Bracht, Viktor. *Texas in 1848*. Translated by Charles Frank Schmidt. San Antonio: Naylor Printing Company, 1931.

Bridges, C. A. "The Knights of the Golden Circle: A Filibustering Fantasy." *Southwestern Historical Quarterly* 44 (January, 1941): 287–302.

Brindley, Anne A. "Jane Long." *Southwestern Historical Quarterly* 56 (October, 1952): 211–38.

Brown, Charles H. *Agents of Manifest Destiny: The Lives and Times of the Filibusters*. Chapel Hill: University of North Carolina Press, 1980.

Brown, Dee. *The Gentle Tamers: Women of the Old Wild West*. Lincoln: University of Nebraska Press, 1958.

Bryan, J. P., ed. *Mary Austin Holley: The Texas Diary, 1835–1838*. Austin: The University of Texas Press, 1965.

Burstein, Andrew. *America's Jubilee: How in 1826 a Generation Remembered Fifty Years of Independence*. New York: Alfred A. Knopf, 2001.

Bushman, Richard L. *The Refinement of America: Persons, Houses, Cities*. New York: Vantage Books, 1992.

Campbell, Randolph B. *An Empire for Slavery: The Peculiar Institution in Texas, 1821–1865*. Baton Rouge: Louisiana State University Press, 1989.

Carrington, Evelyn M., ed. *Women in Early Texas*. Austin: Texas State Historical Association, 1994.

Carroll, Anna Ella. *The Star of the West; Or, National Men and National Measures*. New York: Miller, Orton, and Company, 1857.

Cazneau, Jane [Montgomery, Cora, pseud.]. *Eagle Pass: Or, Life on the Border*. Austin: The Pemberton Press, 1966.

———. *The Queen of Islands and the King of Rivers*. New York: Charles Wood, 1850.

Chaffin, Tom. *Fatal Glory: Narciso López and the First Clandestine War against Cuba*. Chancellorsville: University Press of Virginia, 1996.

Clark, Carol Lea. *Imagining Texas: Pre-Revolutionary Texas Newspapers, 1829–1836*. El Paso: Texas Western Press, 2002.

Clinton, Catharine. *The Plantation Mistress: Women's World in the Old South.* New York: Pantheon Books, 1982.

Coker, Caleb, ed. *The News from Brownsville: Helen Chapman's Letters from the Texas Military Frontier, 1848–1852.* Austin: Texas State Historical Association, 1992.

Coleman, Ann Raney. *Victorian Lady on the Texas Frontier: The Journal of Ann Raney Coleman.* Edited by C. Richard King. Norman: University of Oklahoma Press, 1971.

Cott, Nancy F. *The Bonds of Womanhood: "Woman's Sphere" in New England, 1780–1835.* New Haven: Yale University Press, 1977.

———. "Marriage and Women's Citizenship in the United States, 1830–1934." *American Historical Review* 103 (December, 1998): 1440–74.

Crapol, Edward P., ed. *Women and Foreign Policy: Lobbyists, Critics, and Insiders.* Wilmington, Del.: Scholarly Resources, 1992.

Curlee, Abigail. "The History of a Texas Slave Plantation 1831–63." *Southwestern Historical Quarterly* 26 (October, 1922): 79–127.

Davis, David Brion. *Revolutions: Reflections on American Equality and Foreign Liberations.* Cambridge: Harvard University Press, 1990.

Dawson, Joseph G. III, ed. *The Texas Military Experience: From the Texas Revolution through World War II.* College Station: Texas A&M University Press, 1995.

DeLeón, Arnoldo. *The Tejano Community, 1836–1900.* Dallas: Southern Methodist University Press, 1982.

———. *They Called Them Greasers: Anglo Attitudes Toward Mexicans in Texas, 1821–1900.* Austin: University of Texas Press, 1983.

Derounian-Stodola, Kathryn Zabelle, and James Arthur Levernier. *The Indian Captivity Narrative.* New York: Twayne Publishers, 1993.

Douglas, Ann. *The Feminization of American Culture.* New York: Alfred A. Knopf, 1977.

Doyle, Don Harrison. *The Social Order of a Frontier Community: Jacksonville, Illinois, 1825–70.* Urbana: University of Illinois Press, 1978.

Drinnon, Richard. *Facing West: The Metaphysics of Indian Hating and Empire Building.* New York: Schocken Books, 1980.

Dysart, Jane. "Mexican Women in San Antonio, 1830–1860: The Assimilation Process." *Western Historical Quarterly* 7 (October, 1976): 365–75.

Elfer, Maurice. *Madam Candelaria: Unsung Heroine of the Alamo.* Houston: Rein Company, 1933.

Exley, JoElla Powell. *Frontier Blood: The Saga of the Parker Family.* College Station: Texas A&M University Press, 2001.

Fabian, Ann. *The Unvarnished Truth: Personal Narratives in Nineteenth-Century America.* Berkeley and Los Angeles: University of California Press, 2000.

Faragher, John Mack. "History from the Inside-Out: Writing the History of Women in Rural America." *American Quarterly* 33 (winter, 1981), 537–57.

———. *Sugar Creek: Life on the Illinois Prairie.* New Haven: Yale University Press, 1986.

———. *Women and Men on the Overland Trail.* New Haven: Yale University Press, 1979.

Flach, Vera. *A Yankee in German-America, Texas Hill Country.* San Antonio: Naylor Company, 1973.

Fornell, Earl W. "Texans and Filibusters in the 1850's." *Southwestern Historical Quarterly* 49 (April, 1956): 411–28.

Franchère, Gabriel. "Voyage to the Northwest Coast of America." In *Early Western Travels, 1748–1846.* Vol. 6. Edited by Reuben Gold Thwaites. Cleveland: Arthur H. Clark Company, 1904.

Geertz, Clifford. *The Interpretation of Cultures.* New York: Basic Books, 1973.

Genovese, Eugene D. *Roll, Jordan, Roll: The World the Slaves Made.* New York: Pantheon Books, 1974.

Geue, Chester William, and Ethel Hander Geue, eds. *A New Land Beckoned: German Immigration to Texas, 1844–1847.* Waco, Tex.: Texian Press, 1966.

Ginzberg, Lori. "'Moral Suasion is Moral Balderdash': Women, Politics, and Social Activism in the 1850s." *Journal of American History* 73 (December, 1986): 601–22.

Ginzberg, Lori D. *Women in Antebellum Reform.* Wheeling, Ill.: Harlan Davidson, 2000.

Goeth, Ottilie Fuchs. *Memoirs of a Texas Pioneer Grandmother (Was Grossmutter Erzaehlt).* Translated by Irma Goeth Guenther. Burnet, Tex.: Eakin Press, 1982.

Gray, Mildred Richards Stone. *The Diary of Millie Gray, 1832–1840.* Houston: Fletcher Young Publishing Company, 1967.

Green, Thomas J. *Journal of the Texian Expedition Against Mier, Subsequent Imprisonment of the Author, His Sufferings and Final Escape from the Castle of Perote with Reflections upon the Present Political and Probably Future Relations of Texas, Mexico, and the United States.* Austin: Steck Company, 1935.

Hacker, Margaret Schmidt. *Cynthia Ann Parker: The Life and the Legend.* El Paso: University of Texas at El Paso Press, 1990.

Halttunen, Karen. *Confidence Men and Painted Women: A Study of Middle-Class Culture in America, 1830–1870.* New Haven: Yale University Press, 1982.

Harris, Dilue Rose. "The Reminiscences of Mrs. Dilue Harris." *The Quarterly of the Texas State Historical Association* 4 (October, 1900): 85–127; 4 (January, 1901): 155–89; and 7 (January, 1904): 214–22.

Hart, Katherine, and Elizabeth Kemp, eds. *Lucadia Pease and the Governor: Letters, 1850–1857.* Austin: Encino Press, 1974.

Hatcher, Mattie Austin. *Letters of an Early American Traveller: Mary Austin Holley, Her Life and Her Works 1784–1846.* Dallas: Southwest Press, 1933.

Haynes, Sam W., and Christopher Morris, eds. *Manifest Destiny and Empire: American Antebellum Expansionism.* College Station: Texas A&M University Press, 1997.

Helm, Mary S. *Scraps of Early Texas History.* Austin: B. R. Warner and Co., 1884.

Hietala, Thomas R. *Manifest Design: Anxious Aggrandizement in Late Jacksonian America.* Ithaca, N.Y.: Cornell University Press, 1985.

Holley, Mary Austin. *Texas: Observations, Historical, Geographical and Descriptive.* Baltimore: Armstrong and Plaskett, 1833.

Horn, Sarah Ann. *A Narrative of the Captivity of Mrs. Horn, and Her Two Children, With Mrs. Harris, by the Comanche Indians.* St. Louis: C. Keemle, 1839.

Horsman, Reginald. *Race and Manifest Destiny: The Origins of American Racial Anglo-Saxonism.* Cambridge: Harvard University Press, 1981.

Hudson, Linda S. *Mistress of Manifest Destiny: A Biography of Jane McManus Storm Cazneau, 1807–1878.* Austin: Texas State Historical Association, 2001.

Hunt, Michael H. *Ideology and U.S. Foreign Policy*. New Haven: Yale University Press, 1987.

Hunt, Richard S., and Jesse F. Randel. *A New Guide to Texas: Consisting of a Brief Outline of the History of its Settlement, and the Colonization and Land Laws; A General View of the Surface of the Country; Its Climate, Soil, Productions, &c. with a Particular Description of the Counties, Cities and Towns*. New York: Sherman and Smith, 1845.

Jackson, Grace. *Cynthia Ann Parker*. San Antonio: Naylor Company, 1959.

Jackson, Jack, ed. *Texas by Terán: The Diary Kept by General Manuel de Mier y Terán on his 1828 Inspection of Texas*. Translated by John Wheat. Austin: University of Texas Press, 2000.

Jeffrey, Julie Roy. *Frontier Women: The Trans-Mississippi West, 1840–1880*. New York: Hill and Wang, 1979.

Jeltz, Wyatt F. "The Relations of Negroes and Choctaw and Chickasaw Indians." *Journal of Negro History* 3 (January, 1948): 24–37.

Jervey, Edward D., and James E. Moss, eds. "From Virginia to Missouri in 1846: The Journal of Elizabeth Ann Cooley." *Missouri Historical Review* 60 (January, 1966): 162–206.

Johannsen, Robert W. *To the Halls of the Montezumas: The Mexican War in the American Imagination*. New York: Oxford University Press, 1985.

Johnson, John J. *A Hemisphere Apart: The Foundations of United States Policy Toward Latin America*. Baltimore: Johns Hopkins University Press, 1990.

Johnson, Paul. *A Shopkeeper's Millennium: Society and Revivals in Rochester, NY, 1815–1837*. New York: Hill and Wang, 1978.

Jordan, Terry G. *German Seed in Texas Soil: Immigrant Farmers in Nineteenth-Century Texas*. Austin: University of Texas Press, 1966.

Jordan, Winthrop. *White Over Black: American Attitudes Toward the Negro, 1550–1812*. Chapel Hill: University of North Carolina Press, 1968.

Kasson, John F. *Rudeness and Civility: Manners in Nineteenth-Century Urban America*. New York: Hill and Wang, 1990.

Kerber, Linda K. *Women of the Republic: Intellect and Ideology in Revolutionary America*. Chapel Hill: University of North Carolina Press, 1980.

Kleberg, Rosa. "Some of My Early Experiences in Texas." *Texas Historical Association Quarterly* 1 (April, 1898): 297–302.

———. "Some of my Early Experiences in Texas II." *Texas Historical Association Quarterly* 2 (October, 1898): 170–73.

Kohl, Lawrence F. "The Concept of Social Control and the History of Jacksonian America." *Journal of the Early Republic* 5 (spring, 1985): 21–34.

Kolodny, Annette. *The Land Before Her: Fantasy and Experience of the American Frontiers, 1630–1860*. Chapel Hill: University of North Carolina Press, 1984.

LaFeber, Walter. *The New Empire: An Interpretation of American Expansion, 1860–1898*. Ithaca, N.Y.: Cornell University Press, 1963.

Lamar, Mirabeau Bonaparte. *Papers of Mirabeau Bonaparte Lamar*. Edited by Charles Adams Gulick and Katherine Elliott. Austin: Von Boeckmann–Jones Company, 1914.

Lewis, Elizabeth Wittenmyer. *Queen of the Confederacy: The Innocent Deceits of Lucy Holcombe Pickens*. Denton: University of North Texas Press, 2002.

Lich, Glen E., and Dona B. Reeves, eds. *German Culture in Texas: A Free Earth; Essays from the 1978 Southwest Symposium*. Boston: Twayne Publishers, 1980.

Limerick, Patricia Nelson. *The Legacy of Conquest: The Unbroken Past of the American West*. New York: W. W. Norton and Company, 1987.

MacPherson, James M. *Battle Cry of Freedom: The Civil War Era*. New York: Oxford University Press, 1988.

Malone, Ann Patton. *Women on the Texas Frontier: A Cross-Cultural Perspective*. El Paso: Texas Western Press, 1983.

Manning, Dan R. "Frances Trask: Early Texas Educator." *Southwestern Historical Quarterly* 103 (April, 2000): 481–92.

Marks, Paula Mitchell. *Turn Your Eyes Toward Texas: Pioneers Sam and Mary Maverick*. College Station: Texas A&M University Press, 1989.

Maverick, Mary A. *Memoirs of Mary A. Maverick*. Edited by Rene Maverick Green. Lincoln: University of Nebraska Press, 1989.

May, Robert E. *John A. Quitman: Old South Crusader*. Baton Rouge: Louisiana State University Press, 1985.

———. *Manifest Destiny's Underworld: Filibustering in Antebellum America*. Charlotte: University of North Carolina Press, 2002.

———. *The Southern Dream of a Caribbean Empire, 1854–1861*. Gainesville: University Press of Florida, 2002.

McGerr, Michael. "Political Styles and Women's Power, 1830–1920." *Journal of American History* 77 (December, 1990): 864–85.

McKnight, Joseph W., ed. *Girlhoods in Texas in the 1850s and '60s: Recollections of Cynthia Ann Willis Latham and Ella E. Scott Fisher*. Dallas: published by the author, 1982.

McLeRoy, Sherrie S. *Mistress of Glen Eden: The Life and Times of Texas Pioneer Sophia Porter*. Sherman, Tex.: White Stone Publishing Group, 1990.

———. *Red River Women*. Plano, Tex.: Republic of Texas Press, 1996.

Merk, Frederick. *Manifest Destiny and Mission in American History: A Reinterpretation*. New York: Alfred A. Knopf, 1963.

———, with the collaboration of Lois Bannister Merk. *Slavery and the Annexation of Texas*. New York: Alfred A. Knopf, 1972.

Miller, Perry. *Errand into the Wilderness*. Cambridge: Belknap Press of Harvard University Press, 1956.

Montejano, David. *Anglos and Mexicans in the Making of Texas*. Austin: University of Texas Press, 1980.

Muir, Andrew Forest, ed. *Texas in 1837: An Anonymous, Contemporary Narrative*. Austin: University of Texas Press, 1958.

Murr, Erika L., ed. *A Rebel Wife in Texas: The Diary and Letters of Elizabeth Scott Neblett, 1852–1864*. Baton Rouge: Louisiana State University Press, 2001.

Myres, Sandra L. *Westering Women and the Frontier Experience, 1800–1915*. Albuquerque: University of New Mexico Press, 1982.

Nackman, Mark E. *A Nation within a Nation: The Rise of Texas Nationalism*. Port Washington, N.Y.: Kennikat Press, 1975.

Namias, June. *White Captives: Gender and Ethnicity on the American Frontier*. Chapel Hill: University of North Carolina Press, 1993.

Nelson, Anna Kasten. "Jane Storms Cazneau: Disciple of Manifest Destiny." *Prologue* 18 (spring, 1986): 25–40.

The New Handbook of Texas. Edited by Ron Tyler, et al. 6 vols. Austin: Texas State Historical Association, 1996.

Newman, Simon P. *Parades and the Politics of the Street: Festive Culture in the Early American Republic*. Philadelphia: University of Pennsylvania Press, 1997.

Norton, Mary Beth. *Liberty's Daughters: The Revolutionary Experience of American Women 1750–1800*. Ithaca, N.Y.: Cornell University Press, 1980.

Owsley, Frank L., Jr., and Gene A. Smith. *Filibusters and Expansionists: Jeffersonian Manifest Destiny, 1800–1821*. Tuscaloosa: University of Alabama Press, 1997.

Parker, Alison M. and Stephanie Cole, eds. *Women and the Unstable State in Nineteenth-Century America*. College Station: Texas A&M University Press, 2000.

Parker, James W. *Narrative of the Perilous Adventures, Miraculous Escapes and Sufferings of Rev. James W. Parker*. Louisville, Ky.: *Morning Courier*, 1844.

Pearce, Roy Harvey. *Savagism and Civilization: A Study of the Indian and the American Mind*. Berkeley and Los Angeles: University of California Press, 1988.

Pegram, Thomas R. *Battling Demon Rum: The Struggle for a Dry America, 1800–1933*. Chicago: Ivan R. Dee, 1998.

Pessen, Edward. *Jacksonian America: Society, Personality, and Politics*. Homewood, Ill.: Dorsey Press, 1978.

Pickens, Lucy Holcombe [H. M. Hardiman, pseud.]. *The Free Flag of Cuba: Or, The Martyrdom of Lopez*. New York: DeWitt and Davenport, n.d.

Pletcher, David M. *The Diplomacy of Annexation: Texas, Oregon, and the Mexican War*. Columbia: University of Missouri Press, 1973.

Plummer, Clarissa. *Narrative of the Captivity and Extreme Sufferings of Mrs. Clarissa Plummer*. New York: Perry and Cooke, 1838.

Pope, Henry David. *A Lady and a Lone Star Flag*. San Antonio: Naylor Company, 1936.

Porter, Kenneth W. "Negroes and Indians on the Texas Frontier 1831–1876." *Journal of Negro History* 41 (July, 1956): 185–214.

Rabb, Mary Crownover. *Travels and Adventures in Texas in the 1820s*. Waco, Tex.: W. M. Morrison, 1962.

Ragsdale, Crystal Sasse. *The Golden Free Land: The Reminiscences and Letters of Women on an American Frontier*. Austin: Landmark Press, 1976.

———. *Women and Children of the Alamo*. Austin: State House Press, 1994.

Rawick, George P., ed. *The American Slave: A Composite Autobiography*. 41 vols. Westport, Conn.: Greenwood Press, 1979.

Reid, Samuel C., Jr. *The Scouting Expeditions of McCulloch's Texas Rangers; or, the Summer and Fall Campaign of the Army of the United States in Mexico, 1846*. Philadelphia: G. B. Zuber and Company, 1847.

Riley, Glenda. *Women and Indians on the Frontier, 1825–1915*. Albuquerque: University of New Mexico Press, 1984.

Roberts, Madge Thornall. *Star of Destiny: The Private Life of Sam and Margaret Houston*. Denton: University of North Texas Press, 1993.

Roberts, Randy, and James S. Olson. *A Line in the Sand: The Alamo in Blood and Memory*. New York: Free Press, 2001.

Rorabaugh, W. J. *The Alcoholic Republic: An American Tradition.* New York: Oxford University Press, 1979.

Rosengarten, Frederick, Jr. *Freebooters Must Die! The Life and Death of William Walker, the Most Notorious Filibuster of the Nineteenth Century.* Wayne, Penn.: Haverford House, 1976.

Ross, Alexander. "Ross's Adventures of the First Settlers on the Oregon or Columbia River, 1810–1813." In *Early Western Travels, 1748–1846.* Vol. 7. Edited by Reuben Gold Thwaites. Cleveland: Arthur H. Clark Company, 1904.

Ryan, Mary P. *Cradle of the Middle Class: The Family in Oneida County, New York, 1790–1865.* New York: Cambridge University Press, 1981.

———. *Women in Public: Between Banners and Ballots, 1825–1880.* Baltimore: Johns Hopkins University Press, 1990.

Saum, Lewis O. *The Popular Mood of Pre–Civil War America.* Westport, Conn.: Greenwood Press, 1980.

Saxon, Gerald Douglas. "The Politics of Expansion: Texas as an Issue in National Relations, 1819–1845." Ph.D. diss., North Texas State University, Denton, 1979.

Schlissel, Lillian. *Women's Diaries of the Overland Journey.* New York: Schocken Books, 1982.

Schoen, Harold. "The Free Negro in the Republic of Texas." *Southwestern Historical Quarterly* 39 (April, 1936): 292–308; 40 (July, 1936): 26–33; 40 (October, 1936): 85–113; 40 (January, 1937): 169–99; and 40 (April, 1937): 267–89.

Schoultz, Lars. *Beneath the United States: A History of U.S. Policy Toward Latin America.* Cambridge: Harvard University Press, 1998.

Schulze, Hagen. *The Course of German Nationalism: From Frederick the Great to Bismarck.* Translated by Sarah Hanbury-Tenison. Cambridge: Cambridge University Press, 1991.

Scott, Anne Firor. *The Southern Lady: From Pedestal to Politics, 1830–1920.* Charlottesville: University Press of Virginia, 1970.

Scroggs, William O. *Filibusters and Financiers: The Story of William Walker and His Associates.* New York: Russell and Russell, 1916.

Seale, William. *Sam Houston's Wife: A Biography of Margaret Lea Houston.* Norman: University of Oklahoma Press, 1970.

Sellers, Charles. *The Market Revolution: Jacksonian America, 1815–1846.* New York: Oxford University Press, 1991.

Sheehan, James J. *German Liberalism in the Nineteenth Century.* Chicago: University of Chicago Press, 1973.

Siddons, Leonora. *The Female Warrior: An Interesting Narrative of the Sufferings, and Singular and Surprising Adventures of Miss Leonora Siddons.* New York: E. E. Barclay, 1843.

Sigourney, L. H. *Letters to Young Ladies.* New York: Harper and Brothers, 1839.

Singletary, Otis. *The Mexican War.* Chicago: University of Chicago Press, 1960.

Sinks, Julia Lee. *Chronicles of Fayette: The Reminiscences of Julia Lee Sinks.* Edited by Walter P. Freytag. N.p.: Whitehead and Whitehead, 1975.

Sklar, Kathryn Kish. *Catharine Beecher: A Study in American Domesticity.* New York: W. W. Norton and Company, 1976.

Smith, Henry Nash. *Virgin Land: The American West as Symbol and Myth.* Cambridge: Harvard University Press, 1950.

Smith-Rosenberg, Carroll. *Disorderly Conduct: Visions of Gender in Victorian America.* New York: Alfred P. Knopf, 1985.

Smithwick, Noah. *The Evolution of a State, or Recollections of Old Texas Days.* Austin: University of Texas Press, 1983.

Snider, Joleene Maddox. "Sarah Devereux: A Study in Southern Femininity." *Southwestern Historical Quarterly* 97 (January, 1994): 479–508.

Stansell, Christine. *City of Women: Sex and Class in New York, 1789–1860.* Urbana: University of Illinois Press, 1987.

Stowe, Harriet Beecher. *Uncle Tom's Cabin.* New York: Bantam Books, 1981.

Stuart, Reginald. *United States Expansionism and British North America, 1775–1871.* Chapel Hill: University of North Carolina Press, 1988.

Tolbert, Frank X. *The Day of San Jacinto.* New York: McGraw-Hill, 1959.

Travers, Len. *Celebrating the Fourth: Independence Day and the Rites of Nationalism in the Early Republic.* Amherst: University of Massachusetts Press, 1997.

Turner, Frederick Jackson. *Rereading Frederick Jackson Turner: "The Significance of the Frontier in American History" and Other Essays.* Edited by John Mack Faragher. New York: Henry Holt and Company, 1994.

Turner, Martha Anne. *The Life and Times of Jane Long.* Waco, Tex.: Texian Press, 1969.

Ulrich, Laurel Thatcher. *A Midwife's Tale: The Life of Martha Ballard, Based on her Diary, 1785–1812.* New York: Vintage Books, 1990.

Varon, Elizabeth R. "Tippecanoe and the Ladies, Too: White Women and Party Politics in Antebellum Virginia." *Journal of American History* 82 (September, 1995): 494–521.

Vielé, Teresa Griffin. *Following the Drum: A Glimpse of Frontier Life.* New York: Rudd and Carleton, 1858.

A Visit to Texas: Being the Journal of a Traveller through those Parts Most Interesting American Settlers. Ann Arbor, Mich.: University Microfilms Inc., 1966.

Von Hinueber, Caroline. "Life of German Pioneers in Early Texas." *Texas Historical Association Quarterly* 2 (January, 1899): 227–32.

Von Roeder, Flora L. *These Are the Generations: A Biography of the von Roeder Family and Its Role in Texas History.* Houston: Baylor College of Medicine, 1978.

Waldstreicher, David. *In the Midst of Perpetual Fetes: The Making of American Nationalism.* Chapel Hill: University of North Carolina Press, 1997.

Wallace, Anthony F. C. *Jefferson and the Indians: The Tragic Fate of the First Americans.* Cambridge: Belknap Press of Harvard University Press, 1999.

Wallace, Edward S. *Destiny and Glory.* New York: Coward-McCann, Inc., 1957.

Wallace, Ernest, and David M. Vigness, eds. *Documents of Texas History.* Austin: Steck Company, 1963.

Walters, Ronald G. *American Reformers, 1815–1860.* New York: Hill and Wang, 1978.

Warren, Harris Gaylord. *The Sword Was Their Passport: A History of American Filibustering in the Mexican Revolution.* Port Washington, N.Y.: Kennikat Press, 1943.

Weber, David J. *The Mexican Frontier, 1821–1846: The American Southwest Under Mexico.* Albuquerque: University of New Mexico Press, 1982.

———. *The Spanish Frontier in North America.* New Haven: Yale University Press, 1992.

Weinberg, Albert K. *Manifest Destiny: A Study of Nationalist Expansionism in American History.* New York: Quadrangle Paperbacks, 1963.

Welter, Barbara. "The Cult of True Womanhood." *American Quarterly* 18 (summer, 1966): 151–74.

White, Deborah Gray. *Ar'n't I a Woman? Female Slaves in the Plantation South.* New York: W. W. Norton and Company, 1999.

Widmer, Edward L. *Young America: The Flowering of Democracy in New York City.* New York: Oxford University Press, 1999.

Winders, Richard Bruce. *Mr. Polk's Army: The American Military Experience in the Mexican War.* College Station: Texas A&M University Press, 1997.

Winegarten, Ruthe. *Black Texas Women: 150 Years of Trial and Triumph.* Austin: University of Texas Press, 1995.

———. *Black Texas Women: A Sourcebook.* Austin: University of Texas Press, 1996.

Winkler, E. W., ed. *Manuscript Letters and Documents of Early Texians 1821–1845.* Austin: Steck Company, 1937.

Woolfolk, George R. *The Free Negro in Texas 1800–1860: A Study in Cultural Compromise.* Ann Arbor, Mich.: University Microfilms International, 1976.

———. "Turner's Safety Valve and Free Negro Westward Migration." *Journal of Negro History* 50 (July, 1965): 185–97.

Yoakum, Henderson. *History of Texas from Its First Settlement in 1685 to Its Annexation to the United States in 1846.* 2 vols. New York: Redfield, 1855.

Index

ISBN 1-58544-409-X